The
THEORY
OF YOU

A guide to awakening personal
spiritual enlightenment

JEREMIAH SCOTT

Dedicated to the Reader:

Every conscious moment this Universe offers you is another opportunity to paint the life of your dreams.

May this book offer a fresh colour palette to aid in the creation of your own masterpiece.

Contents

Preface To The Second Edition

NEARLY A YEAR HAS passed since the day I sat down to begin writing the first edition of 'The Theory of You'. At that time, I was certainly unprepared for just how amazing this journey was going to be.

To all those wonderful people who supported me on this path and read that first book, I am eternally grateful. I was definitely unprepared for the influence my words would have on people's lives. There is a great sense of satisfaction in knowing that my years of dedication to pursuing an alternative path has resulted in a positive benefit for others.

Over the last six months, I have had the opportunity to discuss many of the topics addressed in this book with numerous different people: The result is that I started to see clear patterns of the areas that invoked the greatest amount of interest and curiosity. Many of those discussions shared common themes, so naturally, I decided to address these in a second edition.

Therefore, this updated version of The Theory of You contains a number of expanded descriptions relating to the various techniques I have written about. I have come to learn that many people also have a keen interest in the higher *self,* and in the way I interpret this important part of our beings.

To address this, I have included an entirely new chapter named Panoptic Mapping. The aim of this chapter is twofold; firstly, to explain the structure and purpose of the higher self from my own perspective. And secondly, to provide you – the reader – with a clear and easy method that will allow you to enjoy increased interaction and control working with this powerful guiding energy.

I have also taken some time to develop a website with a number of useful resources relating to the ideas within this book. These are all free to download on www.TheTheory-OfYou.com/Assets and will help you along your individual path of awakening personal spiritual enlightenment.

It is my hope that by continuing to explore the nonphysical aspects of this Universe, there will be future opportunities to discuss new findings in other books. From time-to-time, I will update the resource section of this website with any information I believe will benefit your path ahead.

I wish you an insightful read.

Welcome

Dear Reader,

It is with great gratitude that I bring you this book. Without meeting the most wonderful strangers over the last ten years, this guide would have perhaps remained a collection of thoughts and ideas within my mind. Each and every personality I have encountered – from the curious to the skeptical – have all left their unique impression on me. It is through these interactions that the idea for The Theory of You was born. We all lead unique lives, but strangers from opposite sides of the globe can still find common ground in the attempt to answer some of life's biggest mysteries.

As you read this book you will notice that although it is aimed at answering some of the deepest questions we all have regarding ourselves, our lives and our place within this Universe, I will often take an autobiographical approach to the subject matter. The reason for this is simple, to share the roots of my knowledge with you in the same way that this knowledge has been revealed to me. I hope that by writing from the heart, and by sharing with you, some of my most personal moments in this world, you will find *the knowledge* to be sincere and interesting.

Everything written herein comes from a collaboration of many years of hard work, determination, dedication and sacrifice. My journey of development has taken me to places I would never have previously expected and I have made friendships with people I would not have crossed paths with if it was not for embracing the path that was offered to me.

I believe if you follow the steps and guidance I have provided within this book there is every reason why you will be able to awaken your own enlightenment and enjoy all of the unexpected joy it will eventually offer.

Finally, after reading this book, if you would like to learn more about how I work and what I services I offer, please feel free to contact me via my website: www.TheTheoryofYou.com

Best wishes
Jeremiah Scott

CHAPTER 1

No Experience Required

I EXPECT YOU HAVE been searching for answers to persistent and inexplicable questions for a long time. Maybe you are driven by a fear of not being in control, or perhaps you over analyse every small thing so that you don't embarrass yourself in front of others. Does the voice that exists within your mind tell you whatever you do will go wrong, and that the world will know that you are a failure? Is the worry of leaving the people you love behind sitting in the back of your mind as a constant reminder that those you care about might one day have to live without you?

The path you have found yourself on in life has no doubt been difficult and almost unbearable at times. If only people could see inside of your mind. Maybe if they could see what you have been subjected to experiencing and the turbulent waters you have survived, there would be no need to explain yourself ever again. Perhaps if people knew the real *you*, the weight you – carry born from keeping it *all* to yourself – would be lifted.

Most of you who read this book will not know me personally, and will have no idea about the journey that brought me to write this guide. Therefore, I will take a moment to explain a little bit about who I am and where I have come from. (I have deliberately kept to the milestones here, as some parts of my experience will need further detail later on.)

It is my intention in this opening chapter to inspire you and demonstrate that anyone can take steps to change their path at any stage of life, no matter what has come before. I believe anyone can lift the mental and spiritual blocks that hold them back from awakening the personal enlightenment many people seek.

You already possess all the tools required to release the weight that has been holding you back and at times keeping you down too. The aim of this book is to demonstrate this in a way you have perhaps not considered before now, while offering actionable solutions to overcome the common blocks preventing the personal development that deep down you know is possible. I believe there is no experience required to become whatever it is you desire to become. With the correct shift in perception and a healthy appetite to act, anything is possible.

My story starts in a town called Chelmsford, Essex – which is around a forty-minute car journey east of London. I was the firstborn child to seventeen-year-old parents and my three sisters had all arrived by the time I was four-years-old. Naturally, being so young and experiencing the tough economic conditions of the late 1980s, with little support; the odds were stacked against my family from the start.

We moved frequently to various locations within the county while I was young, and I struggled with grades at school until my teenage years. It was tough being the new kid and each time I settled, it was usually shortly time to move on again. This pattern continued until I was fourteen. I vividly remember the Summer holidays before I was due to start a new school and after some reflection I decided I was not happy with my direction in life.

I decided to use the opportunity of starting a new school – in an unknown area – as a platform to try and change my path. The previous year I had failed exams, and to-be-honest, up until that point I had only ever really been interested in sport. But after giving it some thought I realised that if I continued with this view I would end up wasting eleven years of my life to an education system that would give me nothing back. In the grand scheme of events, school did not care if I failed or indeed if I succeeded. With this realization, I began understanding the responsibility of making something of my time there fell solely upon myself.

Looking back, this was probably the first time I began to experiment with tapping into the power I now know we all hold to transform ourselves. Over the following eighteen months I fully committed to my education. I listened to all of my teachers and started politely asking them to "please explain" when I did not fully understand something.

There were people who told me that wasn't enough; it was not possible to make such big changes in such a short amount of time! Yes, there were doubts in my mind too, and I worried those people were right. Perhaps I would not amount to anything after all, but I knew one way to ensure my failure was not to try.

I began to read books after school, stopped leaving my homework until the night before it was due to be handed in and committed time to make sure it was not rushed. Instead of speeding through everything, I developed a routine of completing these tasks to a standard I felt satisfied with. The repetition of these new habits over those final two years of school resulted in me achieving eleven GCSEs all between A* and C grades.

In eighteen months, I had gone from failing all but one of my classes to passing each of them with grades that I could feel proud of. The warm Summer's day I walked up to school and opened the results taught me two lessons that have remained with me until this day. Lesson one; never underestimate what is possible to achieve in the face of little expectation. Lesson two; I should not listen to other people's doubts about my abilities. In summary, at sixteen, I learned the importance of not taking criticism to heart from people I would not go to for advice.

I left home within a year of leaving school and found employment in a newly built local cinema. It was exciting to be out in the world, and I quickly worked up through the ranks and ended up being promoted to manager of the projection booth shortly after my eighteenth birthday. By the time I was nineteen, I was offered the chance to be part of the opening team for a brand-new cinema around forty-five miles away. This was a great opportunity and I duly accepted. I relocated and enjoyed my time there, but I was beginning to have the sense that I was not on the right path and wanted to try something new.

So, aged twenty, I decided to listen to this inner voice and made the decision to quit this cinema job. I had previously worked a Saturday position in a clothes' shop while still at school. It was good fun and I thought I would quite like to open my own store. I was interested in jeans so I set to work teaching myself how to make them. Once I reached a point I was happy with, I sent my design off to be manufactured ordering one-hundred-and-fifty pairs of my own designed jeans. The response from friends and family was good and it wasn't long before they were all sold.

Roughly a year later – still designing, manufacturing and selling more of my own jeans – I was visiting a local shopping centre one weekend and spotted a tiny little shop closed-up with paper covering the windows. Time seemed to slow down when I saw the empty building and after peering through an uncovered spot on the window I knew it was going to be mine. It was only about three-metres squared and to say the interior was a mess, is putting it politely. But I could not ignore the feeling that I was supposed to be there and so I immediately contacted the letting agent in charge to arrange a viewing.

At the time, I had no idea how to make it work but after some careful planning and a little bit of support from close friends, I was able make it happen and opened my very first shop. A period of hard work followed and I was extremely fortunate to open shop two and three around three years' later. Unfortunately, the challenges brought on by global recession during the early 2000s eventually put a stop to that business. I was thankful to have had an absolutely wonderful few years meeting fascinating people from all walks of life and I will always have fond memories of that time.

Each day was a chance to meet new people either in the shops or via the associated business. Little did I know then, but that time of my life and the interactions I had with some of the total strangers I had crossed paths with helped guide me to find my true passion in life. Through those random interactions of meeting people and the discussions that arose,

I began to realise that my words could have a profound impact on the course of other people's lives.

Many of the discussions I had with people during those years, not only clearly helped to alter how they felt about themselves for the better, but I began to learn that I was also influencing how they perceived the wider world. I recognise now that this was the early phase of my spiritual work and I took more satisfaction and happiness from the experiences with those people than anything else that had come in my life before.

So, as a direct result of the recession at age twenty-six, I went from managing twenty people, working eighty hour weeks across three separate shops – always having somewhere to be and something to do – to suddenly having an abundance of time on my hands. It was a difficult transition at first but as time passed I began to see the positive side of this abrupt upheaval. It was good to be able to slow down for a while. Eventually, I decided that in the future I would not pursue such a fast-paced way of life.

Intuitively, I understood from that point on that I wanted to find a way to create the time I would need to develop spiritually. Although I should mention I did not 'call in' spirituality at that time, instead I felt I wanted to learn how to create the space to make better decisions. I had often recalled that the moments in life in which time seemed to slow would precede big changes of direction for me and I wanted to explore whatever the cause of that was.

But I also knew it was essential that before working on myself I should try and build something to sustain a life that would keep those nearest to me emotionally happy and financially secure. To achieve this, I chose again to learn something new.

After fitting out three clothing shops myself and having to continuously create new window displays each month in an attempt to keep the stores appealing for customers, I had developed an interest in restoring furniture. Originally, it was purely for creating intriguing visual merchandising to attract people into my stores.

With that necessity well and truly in the past, after some more development, I was able to found and grow a small furniture business. It was a much more relaxed pace of work compared to the fashion industry, which created the space to propel me forwards towards the next stage of my journey.

By the age of twenty-seven, I was blissfully unaware (even though I was experiencing a pull towards spirituality), the stage had been set for the biggest transition of my life. A spiritual awakening was on the way that would kickstart the journey that has ultimately brought me to the writing of this book.

I could go into extreme detail about every step of this experience, but that is not the purpose of this guide. Each person who experiences a spiritual awakening will face their own set of challenges and realisations. I understand a number of people would like to hear exactly what happened with my experience and I plan to cover this in another book, but it is not my intention for this guide to become a complete autobiography.

For now, I will explain that as this personal spiritual development began to take shape, fate aligned my path with some fascinating and particularly gifted individuals. The result of these meetings meant that by the time I approached my thirtieth birthday, I had been invited to become a student of both a renowned Peruvian healer and a European spiritual expert.

Since 2015, I have been fortunate enough to find myself in the position to commit full-time to spiritual work. I spend roughly one month of each year continuing my study in the Amazon. While at home in the UK, I have been privileged enough to develop a busy routine that includes private, public and charitable work. This allows me to continue a path of unique development and the next phase of this journey will see me begin study in a Nepalese monastery.

From 2019, I have been able to regularly appear on TV in the UK, where I can continue to reach new audiences and share my insights into the nonphysical aspects of this Universe. I am driven by a desire to connect and study with various spiritual cultures around the world; from European spiritualists to Amazonian shamans and the monks of Nepal.

I do this in the search to uncover and share ancient knowledge that I believe we are today disconnected from in the

West. It is my belief that through the sharing of this powerful information we can together find solutions to certain forms of suffering that the modern world brings into our lives.

How does all of this affect you?

Many of you will no doubt be asking 'why I am going into detail about myself when the title of this book refers to you?' Well, it is simple, as you will shortly learn: I came from a disadvantaged background. I was not expected to do or achieve anything of significance. Yet, I have dramatically changed the course of my life a number of times... Starting as an under-performer to top grade student; cleaning the screens at a cinema to managing a team of projectionists; managing a projection booth to becoming a fashion designer with a chain of my own shops; fashion designer to furniture restorer, and then leaving it all behind to embrace a calling in life that has nothing in common with any of the above.

Throughout all of this, the good times and the bad, a simple set of beliefs have remained constant in my mind. I truly feel that if *I* can do it in life, then there is no reason anyone else can't. I also believe I shouldn't allow myself to be restricted by what others think I can or cannot achieve. At the end of my time here I do not want to look back and realise I worried too much about things that didn't really matter.

Over the years, when working with various people from a variety of backgrounds in a number of different countries, one shining factor has become completely apparent to me. When it comes to a person who is happy or sad, someone who is successful or miserable – the pattern I see is unmistakable. It isn't circumstance stopping someone from becoming what they want to become, neither is it luck or a certain level of support from friends, families or colleagues… What I have come to learn, is that the single biggest obstacle any individual person can face is their perception of this world. A happy person can slide into depression and a lucky person is not immune from losing all they have. Today's homeless have the potential to become tomorrow's rich, and the wealthiest business owners can face unexpected ruin. In my experience; current or past circumstance is not an indicator of future success and happiness in this world, perception is.

I have tasted absolute poverty, enjoyed comfort and excess, I have been surrounded by friends and spent long periods of time in isolation. My biggest losses helped set the stage for some of my proudest achievements. I have suffered abuse but also experienced love. I have felt the depths of despair – at points, wishing I was not *here*, to eventually overcoming it all, and finding a path to enjoying moments of total happiness.

Over the course of this book, it is my hope that you will learn exactly how and why I truly believe that every single one of us can release the burdens that hold us back in this world, and then use the knowledge to become whatever you choose. Sometimes all we need is a few small, but powerful alterations of our perception – while at other points, maybe radical shifts are in order. Whatever stage of your journey you are currently at, I hope you will find this guide to be an indispensable tool on the path to achieving your desires.

I believe that I think like a relatively 'normal' person and therefore, if I can change my life when it suits me, then you can as well. In my mind, we have all come from a similar place and there is common ground in many of our experiences. If you grew up in the UK at a similar time to when I grew up, we could easily share nostalgic memories of the TV shows, films, music, and games we played from childhood.

Remembering that on some level we are all in the same boat can help motivate us to accept that if one person can do something you can as well. The information within this book has already helped many people change the course of their lives for the better. There is no reason why it shouldn't pave the way for you to bring in the positive and lasting changes you seek, no matter what they may be.

You might be familiar with some of my ideas and others could be new to you. I take the approach of comparing the strategies within this guide to ingredients in a cocktail. We might have heard of them all individually, but combining these in the way described throughout this book will create something that has a new and unique flavour that you have not previously experienced.

PART 1

The Mind

CHAPTER 2

The Orgin of You

WHAT EXACTLY ARE YOU? Jane? John? Michael? Michelle? Man? Woman? Human? Citizen of Earth? You most likely know the name you were given at birth and at the very least you identify with this when people ask 'who are you?' Some of us identify ourselves with additional virtues such as gender, our career or a special title we hold. Maybe it's your status as a parent, or the particular friendship groups you belong to which most defines you. Perhaps it is even a word denoting what stage of life you are currently at; "I'm Susan and I am a student," or "I am Mark and I'm retired".

There are so many adjectives that can be used to describe who we are, what we have achieved and where we are in life; it is unsurprising that most of us do not feel the need to try and discover who and what we truly are. That is fine for the most part, until – in my opinion – we face one of the various personal crises that seem to come along every so often.

If our way of life is disrupted and those indicators of what we chose to identify ourselves with are challenged or broken, a crises or tragedy – which should perhaps have been manageable – over a long enough period of time can escalate. It can then be given the fuel to transform into a full blown downwards spiral of self-doubt and persistent long-term misery.

We have all seen and heard of this unfold around people our entire lives even if we don't realise it. A husband whose wife left him after twenty-five years and he knows no other way of living and cannot move forward. The employee who was made redundant after thirty-five years of working the same job and has no idea what to do next. The widow who remains alone for the rest of her days after losing the love of her life.

These are broad and typical examples, but to my mind, they raise a number of questions. One of which is: *Why are some people able to adapt to the most challenging of situations yet others are not?* Different people can experience the near exact same losses and disruptions to their lives but have totally different ways of reacting to and dealing with them.

Some people are quick to move on while others need years to heal; certain people never recover at all, becoming trapped for life in the same position they found themselves in at start of their difficulties. Why then, is there such a massive variation in the way each of us adapt?

Many years ago I met a woman who had been alone for eighteen years after the breakdown of her marriage that ended in divorce. This chance crossing of paths and the discussion we had resulted in me asking myself: *Why do people become stuck in these cycles of loneliness and self-imposed suffering? Haven't we all been told life is for living? Surely eighteen years alone is more than anyone should have to endure?*

We are also told throughout life that we all have a right to happiness. I will concede that some people will believe they feel (and perhaps are) happier alone, but this was not the case for the aforementioned. *Was she trying to play it safe and reduce the chance or future hurt?* If that *was the case how did she become stuck in that cycle for so long?* After a time of trying to understand why someone could end up suspended in a situation of long-term loneliness some interesting answers began to reveal themselves to me...

I believe one part of the answer is the strength of our sense of identity and how strongly we are attached to what we identify ourselves *as*. As we explore each of these questions the importance of holding onto personally identifying labels will be revealed. Once we understand that incorrectly assuming certain traits are what define us, and that holding onto such traits can wreak havoc with our long-term happiness, we can then begin to fully appreciate the stability and freedom a deeper understanding of ourselves through analysing this topic offers.

Throughout this book you will come to learn a lot of my realisations have arisen from sitting in meditation. This powerful tool offers knowledge to me in a particular style and I will always attempt to explain what has been learnt in the way it was revealed to me.

Many people use meditation to improve their sense of calm and relaxation. But as I will explain in later chapters it is also possible to access powerful knowledge when certain meditative states are achieved. If my explanations seem to wander from time to time please bear in mind everything threads together at the end to paint a picture that would not have been previously available.

I once read an analogy of how we view our Universe as being akin to cutting the Mona Lisa into twenty pieces and then sending each section to different art galleries across the world. Each piece is still a painting of the Mona Lisa, but we cannot appreciate its beauty until all the parts are put together. The form of meditation I have developed over many years allows me to take the time to study the importance of each small piece of the puzzle so I am better able to fully enjoy the grace when the complete picture is presented.

In this instance, as a result of asking myself the reasons behind why this person had been alone for so long, I began to see the power that people can offer towards their various identifying traits and labels. This lady seemed to accept her title of being 'single' – it defined who she was – and seeing this started teaching me the varying levels of disruptive potential that names, roles, positions in life etc. can have on us.

Naturally, I then began to wonder, 'what identifies me?' This was an interesting thought experiment that initially did not provide many answers. The question remained, until eventually I decided to delve a little deeper. I decided to meditate on what many might call a simple question: *What am I?* More precisely: *What is it that makes me the individual I am?*

As I made myself comfortable, went through my pre-meditative routine and settled into pondering this very question, it quickly became obvious that finding the answer was not going to be a quick or easy task. Every time I thought I had discovered a solution, I swiftly realised the points I came up with did not actually indicate *who I am*.

It started with my name. I asked myself; Am I Jeremiah? Well, it's probable I share my name with millions of people alive today and countless more throughout history. So what trait should I examine next? I pondered. I share my gender with billions of other people, so I couldn't use that. Hair colour (or the lack of), my eye colour, my blood type? No, none of these were unique to me. Even my unique combination of these traits is probable to be shared by another. Neither is my career unique, my relationship choices, the location I grew up in or where I live today.

So what am I?

Eventually, as I travelled deeper into this question I began to unravel every aspect of my being. After some time I realised that at the core of it all there are at least three distinctly separate parts of all of us; the body, the mind and the consciousness.

Big deal! You have probably heard it all before: Mind, Body, Soul. Nothing special here, it's not a new concept so let's move along! ...Not so fast, because although I feel many people have come to realise these separate systems are important parts of us as individuals, I would like to share with you the depths they have been revealed to me.

More importantly, I want to share what I came to realise about how to care for each of these individual parts of our beings and ultimately how this matters to you. Over the course of this book, I will take you through the same process of discovery that I experienced in the same way it unfolded within my life. I believe through doing this, a door will open to a deeper understanding of yourself, your place within this world and the Universe.

Once we are finished I am certain that you will never interpret the question of 'who am I?' the same way ever again. I believe that a direct consequence of answering and understanding this simple question is that you can begin to view yourself in a way that will inevitably bring about a personal enlightenment; therefore allowing you to live in a manner that had not been previously possible.

It might seem intuitive to start this journey together with explaining the physical body. Your body is what you and what everyone in this world can see; perhaps you feel your health levels and strength influence what you can do in this life. Maybe you think life would have been different if you looked differently or had different physical attributes?

Although the physical system is important to all of us it is possibly not the most important part of how you experience and perceive your life, or where you take navigational instructions from on your personal journey. The physical body is certainly responsible for a lot and we shall cover this in depth. It is, my opinion, that the mind has much deeper power over our daily existence and therefore I would like to start there…

So let us go back to the start of your time here, examining what likely shaped your mind before working upwards and outwards from there.

Childhood – let's face it – the way you are today more than likely has roots that extend to your early years. Much of the mind is shaped during these early years by circumstances of the life you are thrown into. Maybe, for you, what you saw or suffered in those early days no child should have to experience.

Perhaps you vowed early on, to never replicate the environment you grew up in or force it on any future children you may have. Your formative years might have been so traumatic that you decided you would not even have your own children. Do you feel guilty because you think others had it worse and you shouldn't bring your experiences up? Still, you cannot escape the troubling memories, no matter how good your upbringing was compared to those of others?

Maybe you reached an uneasy acceptance or even a place of peace with the past and now wish to leave it there. Do you feel that you found a path forwards and that is all that matters? Whatever your story is, many of us would agree that there are negative experiences from these early years that will never leave us. If these memories are based around things inflicted upon us by those who should have loved us most, the resulting damage can leave persistent scars within our minds that might even influence the consciousness itself.

Maybe you experienced abuse, a lack of love, little support or relentless bullying. Were you in the middle of a traumatic separation while your parents parted ways? Did you have to grow up watching a parent try and navigate life while dealing with an addiction? Maybe you didn't even get to meet your mother, father or other relatives? Were you lied to and now find it difficult to trust people?

You might not have been given the same opportunities as your peers, and as a result this created personal losses and suffering while others around you gained. Are you holding onto guilt because you felt powerless to help a sibling or loved one who themselves experienced a trauma? Did you witness others tragically suffering and it never left you? If only it had just been a little different or someone had recognised what you were going through and stopped it, then perhaps today you would be a happier, more successful person.

The repercussions of this time in our lives hold the potential to reach far into adulthood, and the power these memories can wield are able to spawn various types of restrictive behaviour that limit our future potential. I am not unique and did not escape the suffering that childhood can bring.

It is my hope that by sharing some personal experiences from my journey, we can together create the framework for expanding our consciousness. Through the insights I have discovered to the reasons *why* certain things can occur in life, I will reveal a powerful strategy for resetting the mind and bringing calm to your being. Therefore, opening the door to a level of empowerment that was previously hidden.

This chapter will contain some of the most personal things I have ever written. I did not take the decision to share these memories lightly. Ultimately, I feel it is important to highlight my perceptions of how it is possible to overcome the negative circumstances many of us have to endure. There is a path available in life free of dwelling on these experiences, difficulties, and disappointments; including the negative energy that can influence through experiencing such things.

During 2018 the UK NHS issued 70.9 million prescriptions for antidepressants. To my mind, this is a shocking figure but that number becomes even worse when we consider in that same year, the UK total population was 67 million people.

While researching these figures I found another study that claimed the UK is ranked forth out of thirty surveyed countries for the consumption rate of antidepressants. I was saddened by the situation in my home country, but learning about the true depths of global antidepressant consumption rates was a clear sign something within society is not working.

If we factor in the widely reported suicide epidemic within the UK, it is absolutely clear to me that our approach to restoring happiness in people's lives, who are deeply suffering, is currently flawed. Obviously, due to the sheer vastness of this situation it is going to take time to correct, but it is said that, 'even a journey of one-thousand miles starts with a single step'.

There is a growing idea that people should not feel scared to talk about their problems or how they are feeling, and I hope that by sharing some of my own experiences in this world I can show people that they are not alone in their suffering. Nobody is weird, damaged or broken beyond repair. Those of us struggling with life in a country that issues more antidepressant prescriptions in a single year than the total number of people living there are not the odd ones out.

I hope to inspire people through demonstrating that it is possible to experience a challenging start in life and still succeed. By doing this I hope you will learn, that even with little to no support right through into adult life, you can still shape life into whatever you desire. When we understand, embrace and accept our origins by viewing them from a universal standpoint as opposed to the deeply personal view as a current norm, then the power these experiences once held over us begins to weaken.

This in turn can then help us to release behaviours that prevent us achieving what we want. I liken this process to when a butterfly emerges from its cocoon. While the metamorphosis is occurring, the outside world cannot see the slow beauty that is developing inside the cocoon. But once the transformation is completed, the butterfly emerges into a world in which it not only enjoys a level of freedom that did not exist before, but also discovers it is now in a place where others can plainly see it for all its beauty.

By taking the necessary time to develop, the caterpillar is transformed into something entirely different and is therefore able to experience the world from a totally different viewpoint as the butterfly. The caterpillar needs to create the right conditions for itself before the transformation can occur.

I believe that if we create the right conditions for the mind and take the time to let the work unfold within, we can all see the world from a new perspective and enjoy an increased amount of freedom, calmness, inner peace and happiness. The confidence this energy can deliver us is plainly obvious for the world to see. Which is comparable to how eye catching a butterfly taking flight is.

I do not think by any means I was an easy child to bring up. The energy I brought forward to this lifetime serves me well as an adult, but I would not envy the job of looking after *me* as a child. There are many examples to support this and I will take a moment to share a few of my favourites.

At around three-years-old I was brought some red powder paint as a treat – the type you mixed water with – I was told I could play with it after my afternoon nap and that if I agreed to go to sleep then it would be left at the end of my bed for me when I woke up. I agreed to these terms knowing full well I was too excited to sleep. The moment the door closed I was up and looking at the paint. It was in a metal tin with one of those recessed lids that usually require a flat head screwdriver or butter knife to open…

That minor obstacle wasn't going to stand in my way though, and after some pinching and squeezing, I somehow managed to get the lid off. *What's next?* A determined three-year-old me thought. Obviously, I decided I needed to see the dust in the air, so I proceeded to shake the tin over my bedroom. Watching the afternoon light catch the paint particles as they filled the air and softly floated down towards the floor, was to me, a thing of absolute beauty. However, the subsequent shock of watching the vacuum cleaner break and spray the dust out of the back was not as enjoyable.

At four-years-old I was taken for a taster session at a Christian Sunday school about a mile from where I lived at that time. After the first session, it was decided I should attend each Sunday. I remember having a few problems with this in my mind. Firstly, I did not feel this was appropriate, as my sisters did not have to go. Secondly, I was also aware that I did not agree with the religious philosophy that was being taught. You might ask, how a child could be opposed to Christianity? I would answer that by explaining this, I would require a dedicated chapter; one that would digress from the concept of this book, therefore I have chosen to leave it out.

Back to the topic, after realising the concerns of a 4-year-old did not matter to the grownups, I decided I would have to accept this situation for the time being. On the positive side, I had some tough times at home and it was refreshing to be away from the house for a few hours. This attitude to the situation went on for a short while, until one Sunday our teacher had us put on the little cardboard hats we had spent the morning making and walk into the main Church and up to the stage where the priest was speaking. We had to stand in front of the congregation while hymns were sang, and it was in this moment I decided Sunday school was not acceptable to me anymore. I was determined this would be my last time attending, I did not wish to learn these hymns or have to listen to them again. So the next Sunday I sat quietly in class until the teachers were distracted. I proceeded to let myself out of the side door and ran the mile or so home. The look of shock I encountered when I let myself through the backdoor half an hour or so after I was dropped off is still with me today. That was the last time I went to Sunday school and perhaps

I could even have been considered for the title of the town's youngest atheist.

Fast forward a year; now five, and starting infants' school. I remember all too well the pleading from adults that I would need to wear the uniform like the other children. To my mind, the uniform did not fit with my sense of self and I did not want to dress the same as children going to school because I had no interest in being there.

Naturally I refused, there was no way I would willingly or peacefully leave the house unless I was allowed to wear what I deemed appropriate. The adults at home and school had to negotiate between themselves. A compromise was met and this allowed me not to wear the school uniform until eighteen months later.

These are a few examples of the determination and resourcefulness that I possessed from a very early age. In a time that children were expected to do as the adults said without question, I imagine my behaviour would be very frustrating and difficult for those responsible to comprehend. Therefore, it was absolutely inevitable my attitude was always going to provoke conflict.

Many of the people I speak with about their own childhoods have patchy, broken memories and lots of the time that they cannot account for. Other people are able to clearly remember many events from each year starting at a very young age. I am one of the latter and have vivid memories from around the age of three-years-old; I could give you detailed descriptions of where I was and the highlights of every year of my life since.

Although the above memories are somewhat entertaining I have decided I will not use any names or other personally identifying information when detailing the next set of memories. I will explain my reasoning towards the end of this chapter.

As you will learn there was a far more sinister side to my early years. The memories I have detailed above are for you to see that I accept my role as an agitator in some of the situations I experienced. These following experiences however, involve extreme violence and mental abuse and I apologise for any discomfort you might feel when reading the next few pages.

Certain adults I was surrounded with as a child thought nothing about dispensing violence at a moment's notice. If I think hard enough I can still feel the deep bruises that would make it difficult to walk or sit comfortably for a few days. The memories I have already spoken of have a much darker side to them as none of my behaviours were ever excused or forgiven.

Even the smallest 'wrong' I committed was met with severe pain. If I was too noisy or didn't respond quick enough to a question the outcome was guaranteed. Between the ages of three and five-years-old, at the time my earliest memories were forming, I can perfectly recall that there was a steady escalation in the frequency and intensity of this form of punishment. It would always be worse when one of the adults was out of the house.

A typical response to any wrong I had done would be that I was told first to fetch a shoe, next I would be told to pull down my trousers and underwear and then bend over. I would have to stand there in that position with hands touching toes until it was decided I would receive the inevitable whack on the back of my legs or buttocks. Many times I would develop a deep blue blister in the area that would eventually pop in the bath turning the water a pinky red colour.

Sometimes I would get a swift slap to the face that would send a ringing through my ears. A number of times this would result in split lips with the metallic taste of blood filling my mouth. I have a memory at around four-years-old of throwing up blood as I had swallowed too much after receiving a split lip. In later life I would learn that the human digestive system cannot process blood very well so if a person swallows enough its response is to make them vomit. By the age of five, things had begun to ramp up and there is one particular day that still stands out…

It was one of my sisters' birthdays and a party was being prepared. I was sent outside the back of the house to play, and found some older boys I knew. They were generally misbehaving, swearing and making a nuisance of themselves. Unfortunately for me just as the shouting and swearing escalated one of the adults who'd sent me outside appeared.

I was caught with the boys in the act and therefore I must have been 'guilty by association'. First I was marched to the

doctors under the pretense of being told that I must be mentally ill for my behaviour. Upon arrival I had to wait outside
while discussions about whether or not I should be taken to
live in a social care home for my involvement were had.

Later I discovered the adult was on the way to their own
appointment and happened to pass what was happening at the
exact perfect moment. To me this opens an interesting debate
about how much of life is predetermined as things would have
perhaps been very different if it was not for that day.

Next I was marched home and sent to my room. As I sat
there awaiting my fate, eventually one of the adults walked
into my room silently. This was unusual, no shouting or telling
me how evil I was. There were no instructions to remove my
trousers and no shoe in hand. I was confused as this was out
of character.

As I sat there on my bed trying to work out what was
coming next they reached over my right shoulder and closed
the curtains. This was new and a little confusing, I turned my
head to look at the window. In my mind, as it was daytime
I asked myself the question: 'It is light outside, why shut the
curtains?'

When I turned back from the window to look at the adult
and work out what was happening I caught the glimpse of
a fist. Then, just like you see in the movies, everything went
black. Strangely, when I woke up, the first thing I noticed was
no daylight shining through the thin fabric curtains. 'It was

daytime only a moment ago, now it was dark outside, how was this possible?'

I later understood this is my first memory of being knocked unconscious. My confusion began to grow as I realised that I was now laying down and tucked under my bed covers. I recall asking myself *how is this possible? I was just sitting up? How did I get into bed?* This was all quickly forgotten when the very next thing to arrive a few seconds later was a warm tingly stinging soreness sensation in my mouth.

I was familiar with these uncomfortable feelings but the intensity was much higher than usual. As I gently pressed my tongue onto the roof of my mouth I had to stop almost immediately because the pain was too strong. Next I tried to use my fingers to feel inside my mouth and work out why this hurt so much. To my confusion I felt only softness and fell back to sleep. Later that evening I found two teeth on my mattress and over the days that followed I found that I had lost four front teeth that afternoon. I must have swallowed the other two because they were never found.

In the aftermath of this my situation of receiving this most extreme punishment subsided for a while. The adults possibly had some guilt or maybe they realised it was getting to the point my constant injuries could not be simply explained away, as the self-inflicted actions of a boisterous child. I was ready to start school, and injuries – particularly ones as visible as that – would surely have been noticed. Either way, there was some change and the violence became less frequent from that point onwards.

Roughly a year later (approximately in the year I had turned 6), a new adult become involved in my life. I was subjected to a few notable extremes at their hands as well. The most memorable was when I was aged seven, and *this adult*, decided I would be punished with a dressing gown cord for a trivial misbehaviour. The cord was wrapped around my neck and both ends pulled tighter and tighter in opposite directions. I remember it clear as yesterday; the look in this adults eyes while the cord was pulled increasingly harder.

Perhaps I was conditioned to violence or maybe it was a fight or flight reaction, but I just stood there calmly not breaking eye contact. Upon reflection in later years I think the fact I did not show fear created an odd stalemate between us. Eventually, I felt like I was going to sleep and then finally I lost consciousness.

It's possible if I had panicked and acted scared that maybe the punishment would not have gone that far. Looking back, it felt like the idea was to continue until I had learnt my lesson so if I would not give in or show I was fearful, passing out was the only way to break the deadlock.

In addition to the violence, was the constant mental pressure of fearing various other terrible consequences to minor infractions. The result was that for the majority of my childhood, I grew up with a sense that I had no say over my own future and that I could lose everything I felt was dear to me without a moment's notice.

These memories are a very small sample of the almost endless situations I can recall detailing the suffering of my childhood. I have chosen to stop at this point because I do not want this to be a book of misery or boredom, this is The Theory of You, not the theory of me. There are enough details described to demonstrate that the experiences our pasts hold, do not have to cloud the present or ruin our futures. Whatever or wherever you come from, should not hold you back or prevent you from becoming anything or from going anywhere you want in this world.

I have forgiven each and every one of the people who played their roles; and this, in part, is why I have only referred to these people as them/they/adults. My childhood was complex and I have no ill will towards any of the people who were present. I do not dwell on what happened, neither do I feel trapped, defined, or that I cannot move on.

The truth is much simpler, I do not wish for the people there to suffer or be judged for what happened. No amount of judgement or punishment can undo what happened. I am in contact with some of them, but not others . I can honestly say I truly care for the wellbeing of each and every one of them.

Since the first edition of this book was published there has been a lot of interest in these early experiences and I have been asked some interesting questions on the topic. It seems a common theme is regarding the blame of 'who did what' and so on, therefore I have decided to share a little more insight about my views on those early years.

While planning and writing this book *balance* has always been a top priority. I have tried to make The Theory of You a functional guide that is both accessible and understandable for the majority of readers. All of the topics I have covered are structured in a way that is designed to stimulate a certain form of thought, which I believe, if implemented correctly, will open the path to personal enlightenment. That said, I could go into much deeper detail about every subject covered and I will perhaps expand on certain points as future editions are published.

For now, I would like to touch upon the line of time: and introduce to you how some of my understanding relating to this universal force influences my feelings regarding the past. I believe that the passage of time can be compared to a river: The source of a river is connected to the delta in a continuous flow, and without all parts of the river, it could not be called a 'river' at all. If we think about time in this fashion, we might feel that what happens *now*, and what will happen in the future, is always a result of what has happened in the past.

However, I believe that the present creates the past and the future simultaneously. To try and distinguish them as separate things or to ring-fence certain events as individual, is pointless. In fact, in my opinion the only purpose separating the past from the present is if you wish to be determined by it. If you choose to do this, that is your right, but I believe explaining things by the past just excuses you from action in the present.

If I was in a dingy, halfway down the river, and had left my oars at the start, or perhaps had them stolen – then, would fixating on this make them suddenly appear? Would imagining where they might be today, or how my journey would be easier with them help? All this type of thinking offers is a distraction that I am able to exert some influence on the water around me at that moment.

Each event we try to use to determine our arrival at a situation, required another prior event to have happened. I might have lost the oars or had them taken, but I had to have decided to go to the river to begin with. Without one event, no subsequent events could have unfolded.

When we correctly understand this concept, it reveals *blame* is a futile exercise. Recalling and writing about my early challenges should not be seen as a chance to ask where responsibility might fall. There is an old idea that to try and find blame for human mistakes will take us all the way back to the garden of Eden.

If I asked a person, *why did they do something bad?* They might argue that they knew of no other way, because people did worse to them. Perhaps if I then found those people and asked why they did that bad thing to the first person, it's possible they would say their parents did worse to them and they also knew no better. The great grandparents no doubt did worse to them and following this same path of questioning, a previous generation's impact on the next will lead us all the way back to the dawn of 'man' itself.

I feel it is pointless to think events are caused by previous events. In my mind, there are no events; everything is connected in the same way the source of a river is connected to delta. My oars were lost before the tree they were made from even sprouted its first branch.

It all starts here, and what I do today creates both, my past and my future. This does not mean I should ignore what has happened, but as you will learn in later chapters, there is purpose in places people overlook while in a state of trying to allocate blame.

I would also like to quickly point out that some of my eagle eyed followers have spotted that I have a front tooth missing today. This is not related to my childhood, at the point of the memory I detailed earlier I only had milk teeth. The reason for my missing adult tooth is related to an incident that occurred around my eighteenth birthday. This is an entirely different story, but it would certainly seem that my teeth didn't have much chance right from the get go!

Each person who had a part in the formation of my memories has experienced their own set of traumatic circumstances that they struggle with. Many of them feel that the world has treated them wrong, and that they themselves have suffered hard and difficult lives. This does not excuse their actions, but I am powerless to change the past. I understand that I live in the present and those early difficult circumstances are done and gone. *Why let any of it ruin my future?*

How could I help others in this world if I am secretly harbouring negative emotions towards a group of people I felt wronged by! People are remarkably good at picking up on the ulterior motives and insincere actions of others. Many people would most likely see straight through me if I were pretending to be full of joy while secretly holding discontent and anger in my heart.

So why share this with you? Well there are a few reasons, in addition to the reasoning at the start of this chapter, I cannot deny that others are personal. I have noticed over the years that many people assume I've had an easy life, and that I must have been given lots of support to achieve the things I have. This is great, I do not want to come across as a sorry case and it suits me fine that people assume I have had a good and happy life. Those people would also be partly correct, I have, and do enjoy my life.

To me, this is all evidence that I have not been limited by my previous situations. I personally believe if you, the reader, understand some of the challenges I have faced, it will help you along your own path. The techniques I explain within this book have helped me to truly overcome any negative impressions that lingered from those early experiences. Sharing what happened, and what is possible, feels to me, like a natural approach.

I have discovered a path to effectively supporting myself and creating the opportunities I desire. There is no need to begrudge anything that I might not have received in life. I feel the world owes me nothing; as thorough consciousness, it gave me everything. Life is full of abundance and countless new opportunities, we just need to learn how to grab ahold of them.

The powerful changes in perspective that will become available to you – when using the methods I will soon discuss – can teach you to truly set yourself free. The Theory of You offers a chance to learn how it is possible to redefine yourself and liberate your mind from the negative energy associated with the harshest memories you may have.

I also believe that my childhood experiences are far from unique. In addition to the figures I quoted regarding antidepressant prescription rates, I discovered another study worth a mention. The 2019 Crime Survey for England and Wales estimates that one in five children experience or witness some form of abuse before the age of 16. Within this report it states that many cases of abuse remain hidden; hinting the number is perhaps even higher.

From my work over the last ten years, I have developed a belief that many of the people I have encountered, are not able to come to terms with these types of experiences. It certainly appears a damaging culture, of keeping these things silent, exists. Perhaps for reasons relating to a fear of shame, embarrassment, or maybe self-blame. Some people even worry that they will be accused of making things up by those who were responsible. After all, there is often little evidence available today of what happened in the past.

I understand these fears, some people are expert manipulators who are also ruthless in their attempts to convince people of what they want them to believe. Certain other personalities prefer gossip and rumour, instead of balanced discussion or allowing themselves to hear more than one side of a story. Whatever the driving force behind this silence is – in my opinion – only compounding the long-term suffering of some people who, through no fault of their own, have experienced these things.

This book is a guide to awakening personal enlightenment and part of that journey is going to involve releasing yourself from any negative energy created in the past. Experiences that are weighing you down – while preventing the development, happiness and success you equally seek and deserve – will all have to be truly overcome. I plan to share with you how it is possible to weed out and transcend this type of deep and intensely personal negative energy that can persist through our entire lives if ignored and left unchecked.

While on this topic I would like to touch upon one more sobering truth. The 2019 Crime Survey talks about the one in five people who receive some form of abuse – But *what about the individuals who commit these actions? What do we learn about the perpetrators?* Well, to begin with, a person who has arrived at the place of hurting or abusing others is highly likely to have lost the battle of accepting their own suffering.

Considering this, even for a moment does not justify their behaviours. But, it reveals that the number of people suffering is at least double what is quoted in the survey. This means based on this single study alone, it would not be unwarranted to draw a conclusion that at least 40 percent of the population is living under a cloud of suffering. Perhaps in learning this, we are getting closer to understanding some of the drivers behind the antidepressant prescription rates I quoted earlier.

Finally, I believe there is a common misconception within society that an easy way to deal with our problems is to prove someone wrong or change their mind. We will go into greater detail about this later on. For now, I would like to touch upon the idea that I think it is far more important to try and change how a person feels. Preferably to change someone's feelings for the better.

As this book develops, I hope it becomes clear that I have chosen to share my personal experiences as a precursor to help initiate change for the better. How you might be feeling about your own suffering today is entirely possible to be reframed for the better.

I believe the origin of *you* should not be the end of you, it should not limit what you can do with your time here, in this life. There is absolutely no reason I know of that states you cannot experience the harshest of beginnings and still achieve whatever it is you desire. When we accept where we have come from, and what role the mind plays in processing these early experiences, we can begin to choose where we go to next. This new path can be free from the burdens that perhaps once restricted us. I firmly believe that if I can do it, there is no reason why others can't as well.

The mind is the bridge between the seen (the body) and the unseen (the consciousness). Your body can be broken or damaged in many ways and the mind has an important role (among many other things), in preventing this through learning to identify threats. We quickly learn not to touch the hot stove as a child or jump down the stairs. People are great at learning how to prevent physical pain, and they easily learn to avoid many of the dangerous things, places and situations that threaten their physical safety.

This instinctive protective process works brilliantly, but to my mind, it is very interesting that the physically painful memories that come hand-in-hand with learning our boundaries in this world, are usually of little concern to us as adults. In many cases, the opposite is true and we are able to laugh about the silly self-inflicted painful moments that taught us the limitations of what the physical body can tolerate. I clearly remember that the first time I tried to catch a bee with bare hands was also my last, but recalling this painful memory is not stressful, it just makes me smile at my naivety.

Our amazing hardwired protective response to physical pain prevention, unfortunately, applies to mental anguish as well. What serves us perfectly for teaching and warning about potentially dangerous physical situations can begin to turn on us when complex and emotionally painful scenarios unfold. We all learn to stay away from stinging insects easily, but how did we learn to deal with being left out of social situations as a child?

The moment we realised our first friend didn't want to play anymore, or when the school bully decided they would make fun of our clothes and hairstyle were not as easy to interpret. When the mind cannot easily identify, or reason with the source of these painful mental threats, a common result is that it will begin working overtime in the search for answers. In many cases, as we become adults, this type of response can become the default setting to our emotional difficulties. As the complexity of our grownup problems increase, so does the amount of time our minds can spend trying to work it all out.

What do we do if the perfect partner suddenly becomes unfaithful and leaves? How do we adapt if we lose our job for no apparent reason? A close relative suddenly passes away, or perhaps we find ourselves powerless to care for someone we love, as they are diagnosed with a life-limiting condition. In these situations, and when struggling to find answers, it is natural to ask: *How did this happen? Why did it happen?*

Perhaps everything was great and peaceful one moment, then in the next instance it flipped and reserved. These situations and others like them don't threaten us physically, but instead can potentially deliver immense emotional pain. If you feel the deepest parts of your identity have been built around relationships with certain people or the roles you have within the World, the negative effects on your life when experiencing disruption to those things will be magnified.

As a response to this type of upheaval, the mind can naturally begin to replay and loop these painful emotional experiences while searching for answers. Your mind wants to learn how to protect you from feeling this way again. Therefore, replaying the situations over and over in your head is an attempt to work out what went wrong and what could have gone differently. The simple reason for this is to help you learn how to recognise what any future warning signs might be. Therefore, and quite obviously, the deeper you personally identify with the loss or disruption, the longer and more difficult getting back on track can be.

Our deepest and most enduring emotionally painful memories are far more difficult to accept compared to the various physical pains that occasionally occur. For example, it is very straightforward learning not to touch the hot iron if we don't wish to burn our hand. In comparison, understanding why a loved one lashed out, a partner packed their bags and left, or we suddenly lost a job can be a much more complex task.

As a result, in the face of this complexity, it can be a common response for the mind to encourage emotional withdrawal or suppression to cope with the hurt. If we put on mental armour and develop a tough exterior then maybe we can avoid experiencing similar suffering again. However, the consequence of this closing down can be that many people will instinctively step back and limit their interactions with others. It is natural to think that in doing this a level of balance and control can be restored.

It is certainly true that both social and emotional withdrawal can prevent and protect us from new emotional pain occurring. We all understand that walls are built for protection. Your partner left, so you decided it is better to be single for the time being. No relationship surely equates to no new heartbreak? You lost the job that made you happy, so decided to seek employment in another industry. It does not matter you do not really like the work because the company is bigger with more security in a much more reliable sector.

Yet, when we think about it, we also know an obvious downside to this approach exists. Behaving in this way makes it easy to slip down the slope of choosing stability over emotional happiness. It is certainly a reasonable response to try and quieten the mind's defensive search for answers, while reducing future threats to happiness by shrinking our personal world.

Believing a smaller world, a smaller circle of close friends and allies, equates to less chance of unexpected disruption or negativity, is completely understandable.

This strategy can be very effective for the short-term, but eventually the feelings of loneliness or being unfulfilled, and that sense something is missing in life can creep in. *What next?* Well in my experience, the original unresolved problems will eventually catch up with us, at which point we have to face the big questions that were put off in order to find this temporary relief from the pain and confusion.

I believe that a failure to recognise and understand the protective function our minds deploy in the attempt to prevent future emotional pain is creating chronic and toxic misery within society. When I work with those people trying to overcome depressive feelings, I will explain that often depression is rooted in recalling painful past memories.

We can have little control over the onset and progression of depressive episodes and so it can sometimes help to explain that mixing these feelings with the natural response to pull away from what we don't understand is likely to only compound the problem. The World today is full of an ever-increasing amount of distractions and it is common to see people using the endless forms of entertainment on offer to distract themselves from dealing with their deepest concerns.

Have any of you ever heard of the phrase, 'divided we are stronger?' I very much doubt so, because it is not true! The actual phrase is 'divide and conquer'. You shouldn't forget the truth of the fact that you are not stronger alone. Do not divide yourself to partition and compartmentalise the negative experiences of this World, as doing so only defers the difficulties until a later date.

Keep in mind you will not overcome your emotional suffering by suppressing it. If you withdraw from both society and yourself you will certainly prevent situations that you might not like from happening, but it is highly likely that you will not experience as much of the joy and happiness that is also waiting to be discovered.

Therefore, this strategy just swaps the suffering from one form to another. Much in the same way that balance swapping one credit card for another does not reduce the overall debt. At best it only buys you a repayment holiday, perhaps you think the lower interest rate is better, but then you realise in the small print you will be paying more back over a longer period of time.

I believe understanding those instinctive methods the mind employs to protect us can open a path to reframing disappointments with an expanded outlook. This knowledge can empower you to become your own saviour and effectively heal your own wounds.

From the moment you were born to the moment you depart this life, nobody has to spend more time with you than yourself. In order to realise your purpose and truly flourish, self-acceptance must be obtained from self-examination.

CHAPTER 3

What? Will? Why?

IF, OR WHEN, WE decide to try and tackle our most painful memories, it is inevitable that some of us are going to face a flood of questions: Why did it happen to me? Why do good people suffer? Why is there so much evil in the World? Will my life ever get easier? What is the point? What did I do to deserve this? What am I here for?

No doubt you have either asked some of these questions or heard someone else ask them at some point in life. These are some of the most natural things the human consciousness can ask in response to emotional pain, but the answers can seem much more elusive.

Once we begin to understand the ways in which the mind wants to protect us, it is possible to see the failure to find answers to the questions about our most complex suffering could play a part in why so many antidepressants are being prescribed. The emotional suppression we spoke of in the previous chapter can perhaps prevent future difficulties from occurring, but it also creates blocks in healing past negativities.

Many of us will try to console people if we hear them ask any of the outlined questions, because many of us possess an inherently caring nature and do not want others to suffer. Unfortunately – as is often the case in these circumstances – we are usually unsure of what exactly is the correct thing to say because we have in fact asked the same questions at some point, possibly with little success in answering them.

This creates a paradox; we want to help others but we also want to help ourselves. It is unsettling to see people become visibly upset at certain points in their lives as a result of asking questions you yourself want answers for. Therefore if we can't truly answer ourselves we might end up reaching into our minds and come up with some sort of nicety to try and calm the other person down.

Typically, we will tell a person it wasn't their fault or that they are loved, etc. The listener is usually thankful for your efforts and understand you have good intentions, but more often than not, both parties eventually have to settle on the fact that neither person really knows the answer and therefore, maybe a distraction is in order! *Wine anyone? Cigarette?*

Before we work on these complex issues, let us refer back to your origin and the beginning of *you* in this lifetime. I assure you, we shall get around to dealing with each and every one of these persistent questions outlined. They are important topics that will have to be overcome if we are ever going to awaken the personal enlightenment we seek. I will explain some of the insights that brought me an acceptance with these common obstacles and how that matters to you. Before that, let us talk about the importance of understanding how the mind deals with emotional stress and trauma at different stages of life.

It occurred to me many years ago that as we grow from a child into an adult and face more and more responsibilities, we begin a slow separation from the carefree way of living that was normal in our early years. On the face of it, this sounds like a fairly simple and logical observation. But I believe it is important to take a step back and really analyse this natural transition and what it means to us as adults.

The adaptive and happy attitude often displayed in childhood is slowly replaced with a progressively more intense and seemingly serious race to acquire certain things and hit particular milestones as we grow up. A good job, more money, your own home, holidays, cars, clothes, jewellery, the perfect partner, the event tickets, a perfect weekend away, climbing mountains, parties with friends at the best venues… you get the picture.

With all of this another unfortunate truth that further complicates matters is that this transition often brings with it a sense that we must compete; competition with friends, siblings, coworkers, neighbours and even ourselves. In more recent years the rise of the Internet has created a whole new class of competition as we now have to be reminded daily of how every celebrity, model or influencer is living a better life than us.

In a nutshell, as we slowly grow up and move away from a simplistic way of living and viewing the World from a place of accepting each day for what it offers, we instead replace this outlook with building more and more complex lives. The innocence we enjoyed in childhood is eventually lost as we grow, and we can become distracted by replacing this simplicity with a competitive pursuit of goals and various forms of material gain that we are told will validate our happiness.

The rising tide of tension that this onslaught of expectation and constant self-judgement can often bring is such a distraction, it is no wonder we often forget some of the most simple truths the World has to offer. I would invite you to ask yourself the following questions.

When did you realise that the negative experiences in your early years were in fact negative? Was it the day these memories formed? How did you feel in the moments immediately after you experienced something bad? Can you remember what you felt in the days after? What did you do? What did you want to do?

I remember very well what went through my mind when I was experiencing what I would later call 'trauma and abuse'. It was simple, the vast majority of the time I thought, 'OK that thing that I don't like much is happening right now but it will be over in a moment. Then I can get back to playing, watching TV or riding my bike'.

At the time, I accepted the majority of those negative situations as a minor inconvenience that were neither long-lasting or permanent in the schedule of my day. It was just life! It was just how things were. I didn't like eating peas and gravy either but I knew that it was not the only meal I would ever eat, so I accepted it as a small road bump along the journey of me getting back to doing the things I most enjoyed.

It is true that as children we may have liked to blow up some problems for the attention factor and it is also true that we may not have been able to get past some of the hardest things we had to face during that time as soon as they occurred – But if we think hard enough, I expect many of us will remember having a surprising level of acceptance, as well as an ability to easily let go of the majority of our early problems.

Sometimes in adulthood we still do this naturally; for example, when you visit the dentist and you worry beforehand, but then afterwards you think, 'OK, I'm alive it's over,' and then you start thinking about what you have to do for the rest of the day. A trip to the dentist can be physically draining but we rarely feel the need to sit around and recount the trauma over and over again in the days, months and years afterwards.

Evidence of children living with this resilience is easily apparent if we take a moment to think about it. Children who are suffering terrible illnesses but just want to play. Hospital wards for children are usually colourful and full of toys. The doctors, nurses and parents will speak of the resolve and strength of character that child-patients often possess, and say things like, "Gosh, I can't believe how strong that child is. It is amazing they are so happy with all that is going on".

But how often is the child sad for his or her situation? Do we hear them ask, *Why me?* What did I do to deserve this? Rarely that happens; instead they are looking to fight and overcome whatever obstacle is holding them back from pursuing what makes them happy. This is not a new phenomenon; children have been this way throughout history.

Unfortunately, there often comes a point in our lives when we wake-up one morning and the memories we once accepted as a minor inconvenience suddenly begin to grow into this torturous beast that eventually spills out into the way we approach our lives. That moment we begin to realise those difficult memories actually represent something negative is different for all of us, and therefore there is no clear guidance on how to prepare for when or where that transformation could occur.

Once this seed of realisation takes hold within the mind, it often begins to grow and develop into an unwelcome and stressful burden that has the potential to disrupt the way we feel and behave. Maybe you are lucky and experience a low-level of influence from these types of memories and they just express themselves as an overly cautious temperament towards some particular situations.

You begin to think along the lines of, '-well I best be careful what I do and allow in my life from here on out because years ago I thought something was OK, and then eventually I discovered that it in-fact wasn't. Learning this left me with unexpected pain and so it would be best I do whatever I can to prevent any similar future suffering'. It is a very natural response to think, '-if I limit my choices and limit the occurrence of new unfamiliar experiences, I will surely prevent that type of misery repeating'.

Or maybe you have been more unfortunate and reached somewhere close to the other end of the scale. Relationships begin to suffer, your moods are affected, you start to wonder if justice needs to be retrospectively served, or ask yourself: Should someone else be told? Should you confront the perpetrator, or share the pain with a close friend? Then finally if you remain on that path, it can all become too much and you begin to spiral. Perhaps even beginning to engage in self-destructive behaviours in an attempt to escape, forget and suppress the pain.

This is surely one of adult life's first big challenges; how do we navigate this change in perception? We are thrown into situations beyond our control and understanding as a child, which then have the potential to rob us of our future productivity, success and most importantly our happiness.

The acceptance of adversity and carefree approach to living that was often the normality in childhood is now turned against us. As a result, we can begin to feel cheated that we were previously so naïve – and eventually, as a response, we vow never to be so silly or trustworthy of others again. Life also teaches us that if something doesn't work anymore we must simply throw it away. But, when we throw out the perceived stupidity of childhood, we also throwaway one of the best and most natural coping mechanisms we have ever learnt.

Today versions of this technique have lots of well-known names and many spiritual teachers will offer us the chance to learn these amazing and life transformational skills. You have probably heard people talk about mindfulness. This technique is potentially the most well-known in the category I speak of, so let us a take a moment to explore it.

Mindfulness in a nutshell teaches us that maintaining a moment-by-moment awareness of our thoughts, feelings, sensations of the body and our external environment, without believing that there is a right or wrong way to think or feel in any given moment. When we tune into the present moment instead of replaying the past in our mind or imagining the future we can remove expectation and judgement. Mastering this will help us develop a sense of peace and acceptance in our lives.

Is this not a very well worded version of the way children commonly view life? So why does this matter? It is simple, I believe reconnecting ourselves with this system of thought can begin to lift some of the mechanisms that prevent us from realising our individual potentials. When we are overly burdened with any fears or anxieties rooted in past events, we are giving precious time and energy up to situations that cannot be undone.

Acting overly cautious towards the future as a response to the past suffering therefore, only delays us going forward in life at the speed we wish for. Behaving in this way also continues to offer a power that allows the past to hold us back. In the worst cases, this cycle can create a vicious feedback loop where we try and get on in life but suffer more than necessary when having to face the inevitable knock-backs that are part of the journey. Then, when those typical natural disruptions occur we can experience the similar feelings and emotions that remind us of all the things we didn't like, so we pull away to stop 'bad' happening again.

The thoughts and experiences of the past are then triggered, and instead of looking forward and accepting the temporary nature of disruption we remember what we didn't like from before and spend time looking backwards focusing on all the bad stuff that came from the past that results in the inevitable, 'why does this always happen to me? When will it end?' questions being pondered upon. Understanding this reveals that we allow ourselves a dual disappointment, possibly without even realising it. We stopped something new from happening while reliving old pain.

Now, it is important for you to understand that in my opinion, there is not a one-stop solution to overcoming these common problems. Buying a book on exercise and diet is no good for losing weight if part of the reason you became overweight to start with was down to emotional and mental pain. If you stick to the methods of the book and lose the weight but the root cause of the problem is not also addressed it will not be long until the pounds pile up again.

I feel this is the reason why people try so many different forms of self-help and why new self-help systems can get so much traction only to then burn out. How many of us have also heard the term 'fad diet'? How often have we heard someone say, "-so and so tried that diet but it's just a fad, they lost a lot but then put all the weight back on two months later!"?

I believe the answers to overcoming deep-rooted emotional pain are very much like cooking a recipe from scratch. If the consciousness is the chef, the mind and body are the ingredients. We need to learn the flavours of the ingredients and then master which quantities should be added at which point to create the dish we desire. This mastery as with all skills comes from time, repetition and understanding. We must learn the delicate balance between how ingredients react with each other, what to add in which order and when.

Once we have learnt the recipes and practised repetitively, it is likely that a new and unforeseen result will show itself; the gift of adaptation. There comes a point when say for example, the chef is faced with ingredients that are not as fresh as he would like. What does he do? Should he complain, demand new supplies or stop making the dish altogether, and spend the evening remembering how good that dish tastes while he and his customers' bellies are empty? No! That is not the answer. Instead a skilled chef will instantly and effortlessly adapt the recipe and still produce a fine dish. There will be no complaints from anyone who samples the food, only praise and thanks that such a talented chef was able to put a twist on the meal.

So, the very first ingredient to overcoming the common questions alluded to in the title of this chapter is a lot simpler than anyone has perhaps told you before. **Reconnecting with the forgotten lessons of childhood.** I am not asking you to learn any new skills here, what is right for me is not right for everyone else, which is in my opinion, why so many self-help philosophies are short-lived.

The way you handled the difficulties of your early years are no doubt very different to mine. I cannot teach you to be me or anyone else. The best thing me or anyone can do for you here is to remind you of yourself. Aiming to attempt to reduce unnecessary emotional complexity in your life through accepting the unknown and trusting your ability to adapt, will allow you to focus on *who you are* and what you wish to be in this World without talking yourself out of it through fear of being hurt if it goes wrong.

Mindfulness is a powerful skill but why should we have to learn it as something new? It is not new to any of us, we just need to create the space in our own minds that will allow us to reconnect with this part of ourselves. Sure you can leave the naivety of childhood behind; the lack of control and power over your life that made you feel insecure when looking back, can also be left in the past. You are stronger and wiser now and can hold on to this fact.

I believe no matter how difficult that time of your life was, there was a day at least that you woke up as soon as the first light came through the window and you did not care about what had come before. You were full of enthusiasm for the day ahead, no one was going to break you down that day. Nothing was going to stand in the way of what you wanted to achieve.

Remaining present in the moment is an extremely powerful energy that is so natural to all of us we can easily forget it even exists. I liken this to when we put a perfume or aftershave on in the morning and by lunch time we think it has worn off, only to be complimented later in the day that we smell 'good', and then asked 'what are we wearing?' We just become so accustom to the feel of this energy within us, we forget it is even there.

The mind has a tendency to wander into the past or speculate on future scenarios. After a lifetime of engaging in this behaviour it is possible a person has forgotten the importance of paying attention to the *now*. This can mean that we miss some of the most precious moments life has to offer.

A well-trained mind is anchored in the moment, understanding that the only place true peace and happiness exists is in the *now*. Rediscovering this truth offers a level of empowerment that I feel is frequently underestimated. It is only in the now that we can change things, the past is done and the future is yet to occur and so spending too much time focusing on those places means we have less time available to make the changes we want.

There is no time like the present. The process of retraining your mind can begin right here and now. Together we can take a few moments to locate and reconnect with that dormant energy that exists within.

If you are reading this book you have the time to pause for a moment to follow the **Energetic Reconnection** exercise on the following page: It does not matter if you are on the train, in a park, some other public place or at home. This will only take a minute or two and all you need is somewhere to sit. I imagine the only exception is if you are driving or operating heavy machinery while listening via audiobook. If that is the case then come back to this later. If not simply read the method below, take a moment for yourself and repeat the instructions!

Energetic Reconnection:

To begin by closing your eyes, make sure you are sitting comfortably with as straight back as you can manage that does not feel uncomfortable. Place your hands on your thighs and relax.

Next, slowly take the deepest breath you have drawn all day. Once your lungs are full, pause for a moment and then slowly exhale. This should in turn be the most complete exhale you have taken all day. As you are breathing out, imagine you are releasing any stale air that needs to be cleared from your lungs. When you breathe in next it will only be fresh and clean air.

You should take a further two cycles of breath in this same fashion. Visualise breathing-in vibrant and clean air full of molecules that are excited and fully charged all the way to their most atomic scale. Allow this most basic and natural energy to revitalise the oxygen that is running through you entire body.

On the second exhale, check in with any thoughts that are bothering you. Anything on your mind you don't like or any jobs you have left for the day. Visualise that each and every one of those are now riding on the stream of used breath and exiting your system. You can reconnect with them later, but right now this a moment for only yourself.

With the third exhale you should visualise all physical tension beginning to quieten. Use your internal voice to give thanks to your body for showing you these areas of tension or discomfort.

Find your own words to say: *'Thank you for showing me the areas of myself I need to care for. I will not forget about them and will give them attention soon but for the moment I would like those feelings and sensations of pain and tension to quieten down to the lowest level that is possible for this moment.'*

Continue by letting your shoulders relax to the lowest and softest level they have been all day and then let any tension that can exit, leave the body through this third and final deep exhale. Next you can allow your breath to return back to its natural rhythm.

At this point, ask yourself the following question with your internal voice: 'Please show me my favourite memory of growing up. I would like to feel that energy again'.

As this memory begins to reveal itself, take note of the sensations you have in the middle of the chest. If this sensation is a positive one then allow it to grow.

It is possible that in rare circumstances a person will not be able to identify a clear positive memory from childhood. In this instance, you could ask for a sensation or colour to be revealed in the place of memory. What was it like the first time you enjoyed an ice-cream or watched your very first firework display?

This I believe, is where the adaptive energy lays within us. You can finish this exercise by allowing the memory to grow, then letting this energy to fill the chest outwards, and upwards rising into the neck.

Take as long as you wish in this moment, when you are ready you can open your eyes and return back to the tasks at hand.

Although mindfulness surrounds us remaining present in the here and now, I believe that if we are out of practice in doing so, a good place to start relearning this powerful tool is to recall the conditions in-which it was a normal thing for us to do. As the Japanese Zen Buddhist Koan says; *'The fearless hero is a loving child'.* Once you have spent some time reflecting upon this, you will be able to begin switching your perception to focusing on the current moment more often.

As you begin to do this it can be beneficial to start keeping a journal and recording the feelings that you experience when your mind is in the present. In doing this, it will not be long before you see the difference in this compared to when recalling the past or focusing on the future.

Eventually, it will be possible to see that recalling your difficulties of the past can be associated with heavy energy and potentially depressive feelings. While worrying about the future too much can spawn sensations of anxiety. I believe the biggest source of peace and calm comes from focusing on *the now.*

I expect if you took a moment to try the simple energetic reconnection technique described, there has been at the very least a slight improvement in your sense of wellbeing. So let us do something positive with this energy.

I would now like to explain some of the shifts in perception that have made sure I have never been held back in life. We spoke at the end of the second chapter about the way the mind can offer us social and personal withdrawal as a solution to dealing with and preventing future emotional pain. To my mind, this is like placing a plaster on a cut that requires stitches. The simple dressing will hold it together but it is unlikely to heal correctly.

Have you ever heard the saying, 'It is better to have loved and lost than to have never loved at all?' It offers an insight to a way of thinking I have found to be extremely powerful in my life when dealing with painful experiences. As a younger man, I crossed paths with an amazing woman. Time seemed to slow down when I saw her for the first time and after plucking up the courage and a lot of bravery I took the next time we bumped into each other as an opportunity to speak with her properly.

After some small talk, I realised there was a connection with her that prior to that moment I had never felt. As these things go all I could think about until I saw her again was obviously her. Incredibly she felt something towards me and after a few months of dating we became a couple. Now, over the next few years we spent together I experienced many feelings and emotions on levels that I previously had no idea even existed.

It was the first time in my life I felt truly happy and I wanted it to last forever. I had planned a long and happy future together in my mind and I often felt like I was the luckiest man alive; I had met my soulmate. However after some wonderful years together she unfortunately felt it was time to move on in a different direction and we separated.

Initially, after it was over, I experienced the deepest sorrow and misery I had ever felt. I didn't want to eat or go out, I did not want to see my friends or family. I thought my future was over. The partner of my dreams had left, what was the point of going on? I would never be happy again! Once the immediate pain lifted, I was left with this persistent questioning of myself – What could I have done differently? I would often ask myself if she ever thought of me and I would wonder what was happening in her life?

If I had been gifted a wish in those days it would easily have been that one day my phone would sound and it would be an unexpected message from her realising she felt the same sense of loss as I did. But as time progressed, it became obvious this would not happen. So, what next? How did I move past this and go forward in life? After all, she had moved on and my life felt like it was passing me by.

Most of us will have to face this type of situation in our lives at some point and many people deal with this common problem in a few ways. Firstly, they could choose to feel anger towards the other person and get it out of their systems by telling everyone close to them how bad that person was as a partner and they are better off without them. In some instances, it is true anyway, so on the face of it this method seems to work well.

Maybe another solution would be to get straight back out in to the World and have some fun; go out with your friends, party, and try and meet new people. This could lead to finding a new partner and rebuilding the lost happiness – which is great. Perhaps you decide to take some time out travelling and see the World while finding yourself. Or, do you deal with the confusion and loss by stopping it from happening again and withdrawing away from romantic encounters altogether – Telling yourself you are better off alone and it's easier not to look for anyone new ever again?

You could tell yourself, that if in the future someone finds you and there is some attraction between the pair of you, and that person chases enough, maybe then you will consider letting your guard down – but for the time being, it's just you. All of the above strategies have pros and cons attached to them, but they all have something in common too. They discredit any of the good that came before, focusing only on the bad and telling the mind that the situation needs to be prevented from ever recurring in the future.

Eventually, I settled on a different method that now helps me overcome a wide variety of life's negative situations. It occurred to me that I did not want to forget this person but I also wanted to move on. The relationship was for the most part the best thing that had happened to me up until that point in my life. Why tarnish that person and what we shared as 'bad', because of how I felt after it was over?

Why rush into a new relationship to forget that person and the resulting feelings I experienced at the end of our time together? I liked my life and had responsibilities, so I did not want to run away; off around the World in order to find myself. It was also outrageous to consider that being so young the answer would be spending my life in solitude.

So how did I move on in a way that allowed me to find peace and not subject any future partners to suffering in an attempt to make sure they didn't treat me the same? **The answer for me, was to give 'thanks'.** Sounds simple? Maybe so, but let us look at exactly what I mean by this.

After some reflection it occurred to me that I had experienced things and felt emotions during this relationship that I had never known existed. These memories are wonderful and I could not have experienced them alone. Someone took a genuine interest in the story of my life and wanted to listen to me speak.

She looked into my eyes in a way no one before her had. When we held hands for the first time I experienced goosebumps and felt lighter because of how much energy this person gave me just being around them. I felt excited to be alive and looked forward to each new day. With her presence, I felt like I was better at life. If I was once a toad, I then felt like a prince. This was a special person who was able to reveal something to me that was hidden for the whole of my life prior to their arrival. When I saw it from this perspective, thanking them for the time we spent together seemed like the most natural thing I could do.

There was no rush to grab the phone in a bid to thank them personally. I am speaking of an internal *thanks*. As this idea grew within me it developed to a point where I decided to spend the moments before I fell asleep one evening replaying all of my favourite memories and sending thanks outwards for everything I learned from our time together.

I realised at the core of it she did not mean harm to me, just that there was something else calling at that stage of her journey. In my mind's eye, I began to thank this person for all that they had given me. It also helped me to realise what a wonderful thing it would be if in the future I could ever help someone else feel new and positive emotions they had not previously known existed.

The longer I pondered on this concept, the more I realised the importance of it. What if someone managed to inspire new feelings in my former partner? Did she not deserve to share these experiences as well? Some of you will feel your ex-partners have not earned the right for that. But are your ideas or intent about how they should live or suffer stopping them from seeking out chances to try and have the new, happy, exciting experiences they desire? Most likely not.

Wanting them to pay for the past hurt they caused you just makes it more annoying and upsetting if you find out they are having the positive experiences they are searching for. We all know the feeling of watching someone close to us open the gift they wanted for ages and it was us that finally brought it for them. There is an uplifting feeling we get to experience when seeing the happiness on their face as they open it and watching this can make us feel great too.

If you could choose to have more of the above two types of experiences in your life, which one would you pick? Would you choose to increase the feelings of frustration at watching someone get something you feel they don't deserve, or is it more appealing to you feeling an increased sense of joy each time you give an unexpected gift to someone?

Giving thanks – if done correctly and sincerely – offers liberation and empowerment in a way that is massively over-looked in my opinion. First and foremost, it offers a solution to the mind's instinctive protective power that we have previously spoken about towards the end of Chapter 2. We can tell the mind: I accept a bad and unwanted situation has occurred, but look at all the good that we experienced as well. If it was not for meeting this person how could the good moments have happened? Do I want to live a life protected from the bad if that means I am also denied the good?

This thinking also offers us the chance to stop any negative feedback loops that are the result of the mind attempting to understand why this particular bad thing happened and how to avoid it repeating in the future. Using the method of giving thanks allows you to develop the power of calming this defensive mechanism. Therefore, *thanks* has the power to free yourself from some of the common and persistent personal mental turmoil, that we can all experience throughout life; by offering the mind a solution, it can understand.

As you begin to adapt your thinking using this method, it will become clear that most of the deep suffering you experience at points in life can be considered as a side effect of the investment you made to improve your happiness. More often than not, if we look hard enough we can see that this side-effect is small in comparison to the happiness experienced.

Using this line of thought I came to a powerful realisation: Why should I focus on a month of misery at the end of that relationship while doing what I can to prevent that pain from ever happening again, when the rest of the relationship provided me with years of amazing memories? Why should I be scared of the past repeating in the future? Should I fear one month of sadness or be excited I might be able to have a new relationship that offers me many more years of happiness and new experiences?

Mastering this approach takes time, however, I feel it is much easier to start with the most painful situations in life as they are usually complex. That complexity actually offers an easier root to finding the upside. The bigger the situation, the more chance we can recall a moment that was good and therefore give thanks for it.

I should like to point out here that this is not the typical half-empty/half-full glass analogy. What I am trying to explain, is that the power of this method lies in a deep and truthful *thanks* for the good you felt and received. It is as much a shift in perception as it is learning to feel the gratitude as well. Eventually, as we develop this ability to recognise the good and how the best bits of any given situation made us feel, it is possible to apply this thinking to even the most minor of life's irritations.

A simple example of this in action; you drive to town, park your car and pay for parking (or 'parking meter' for our American readers) you go shopping and end up in a queue at the checkout, which makes the trip longer than you planned. Upon returning to the vehicle you find a parking ticket stuck on the window.

The annoyance of the fine is compounded when you see the time it was issued is only three minutes over what you had paid for and only two minutes before you returned to your vehicle. What do you do? Try and find the parking attendant and reason with them to please cancel the fine? But those that have tried this know that is rarely successful. You return home agitated and plan to appeal it, or maybe you just accept the inevitable and begrudgingly pay it?

I found myself in this exact situation many years ago, not long after I began using the approach of giving *thanks* and it was one of the first moments that I used it effectively to deal with one of life's minor aggravations.

It was a very hot Summer's day and instead of using any of the above strategies, I simply realised driving the distance to the shop was much more preferable to walking, especially in the heat. After this, I realised that I was thankful I could afford a car and I was extremely thankful it had air conditioning to make my day that little bit more comfortable. Next, I began to smile when it occurred to me that I probably would have paid more money than the ticket value to stay at home if I had to face making that trip on such a hot day without the car and having to carry all the heavy bags home by foot. Finally, I realised at least a small portion of the money from the fine would more than likely end up going back into maintaining the carpark ('parking lot') and that it would benefit me in the future because I planned to visit again. This was my local shop and the facilities had always been clean and safe, I did not have to worry about crime or damage to my car while it was parked and there was never any rubbish or debris on the road that might damage my tyres. A punctured tyre is more costly to replace than a small parking fine.

So all things considered, there was plenty more for me to be happy and thankful about, and this event did not have to ruin my day or allow my frustrations to ruin someone else's day. I decided to set a reminder in my diary to post the ticket payment a few days later when I knew I had some spare time and I moved on putting the experience behind me.

As time has gone on I have developed this way of thinking into an effortless part of my day-to-day living. The result is not only that I am happier and calmer, I am also rarely bothered by the normal hiccups that occur every so often during our daily routines. Most importantly, I barley ever experience recurring thoughts of what I could have, or should have, done differently in any given situation.

A progression of this type of thinking taught me a new level of acceptance to this World that was not present in my life before. I learnt to accept that we cannot always control the events affecting us, but we can control our approach to how we deal with them. You are fully in control of how frequently you use the two techniques we have just spoken about. The **inherent mindfulness** present in childhood and an ability to **give thanks** are qualities each and every one of us have access to.

These might sound like simple ideas, but I can assure you that taking a disciplined approach to developing and integrating these methods as part of your approach to life will transform how you view old traumas and solve current problems. Once we begin to weave these techniques into our daily routines it eventually allows us to see that no matter what the issue is, we do not need to explain to ourselves or anyone else why we don't feel good.

Blaming people, situations, circumstances or the past, only holds us back and prevents us from finding what feels good. As we expend energy on that stream of thinking we can believe that blame holds the answers to what is keeping us from being where we want. In doing this, all we are achieving is forgetting to ask an extremely important question: What can you to do to feel better right now and start attracting into your life all of the positive feelings and amazing experiences you desire?

Practising gratitude and mindfulness in the way outlined within this chapter, you can begin to sow the seeds that will eventually break down all barriers of separateness with others. You will start to radiate positive feelings as you show your appreciation for all that life has to offer. As a direct result, you will begin experiencing a new connectedness that can build new bridges with people and an increased happiness within your life. Ultimately the removal of these barriers will serve to not only better connect yourself to others, but also to the universal energies surrounding you.

CHAPTER 4

Accepting Your Origin

IF THE CONCEPTS OF the previous chapter can help reveal a fresh approach on how our mind's are better able to tackle the problems of life going forward, how do we find true peace with our deepest and most persistent memories of the past suffering we have been subjected to? Many of us will feel that there is a limit towards how much thanks we can give, and at some point we will want deeper answers. Why did it happen to me in the first place?

Over the next few chapters, I will share with you some of the things I have come to realise over the years about my personal situations and also what I have come to learn about the universal rules that influence every single living being. These are the lessons that brought me complete acceptance with what I experienced growing up. What has been revealed to me has created the space for some of the most powerful and rapidly transformational years of my life, while at the same time teaching me how to overcome any new struggles that might appear. As I have said at the start of this book, if it works for me, I believe it can do the same for you.

Have you ever heard someone say: I like to get up in the morning and find bad things to do? I like to plan all my bad deeds for any given day and set to work as quickly as possible inflicting pain and spreading misery. Only once I am suitably satisfied that enough people have been hurt by my actions I will be able to return home calm and happy with what I have achieved. I sleep better if I know I have upset someone and I try my best to be nasty each and every day.

I know I have never personally met someone who thinks or speaks like that. But I have also heard numerous stories that our prisons are full of people who feel misunderstood and those who believe they are innocent. People who have committed frauds and justify their actions by saying they were only trying to support their family. People who have committed violent acts out of self-defence or because they had feared for their own safety. People who have violently abused others because they experienced it themselves and had known no other way of life.

What about the people who believe they can assault women and children in the most heinous ways possible? Even these people will often attempt to offer a defence that tries to convince others they had little ill will towards their victims. I have read the apologies of these criminals and they often explain such things as not having been able to think straight or they had mistakenly felt their needs came above everyone and everything else.

Those people will speak of not being able to empathise with others, that they felt detached from society growing up and didn't realise that what they chose to do would impact their victims as deeply as it has. We have all heard the stories of how the guilty attempt to rationalise and justify their actions, but how many of those guilty people feel they are actually nasty or evil?

How many times have you heard stories of a judge slamming a convict for showing a lack of remorse during a trial? Considering this, raises some interesting questions: Where exactly are all the bad people? If we have never heard someone saying they live to do wrong and those who are proven to have done so, regularly protest their innocence, then why are our prisons full? Many criminals will try to convince us all that they are not bad and will prove it to us if we just give them a chance; so where do the bad people of this World reside?

The answer is simple, there are very few if any people who truly believe they are nasty, evil or wrong. In fact, the vast majority of us believe we are good. People wake up in the morning not feeling like a bad or evil person. They go about their day-to-day activities with their own set of rules, believing they are making the best of their lives with the circumstances they face. The problems occur when their rules and morals contradict those of others or of the wider accepted ideas and laws of society.

Let me ask you for a moment to consider what exactly is the term soulmate describing? Meeting someone who is the perfect romantic match! I think that's a little vague; to me a soulmate is someone who perfectly understands and accepts you for who you are. They do not try and change you because they share the same values and ideals as you. It is widely accepted as a great thing if we are ever to meet such a person and many of us might wait an entire lifetime and no such match ever comes along. This isn't to say we will be lonely, just never with a partner who truly and completely understands us.

Why does this matter? One moment I was talking about criminal behaviour and now I'm taking about soulmates? Well, I think it perfectly demonstrates the massive variety of human individuality. Each and every one of us navigates life using our own set of guiding rules and belief systems. The differences between people can be minor or they can be vast. However, many of us accept that meeting a perfect match is such an exceedingly rare and lucky event in life it might not even happen.

So if we take this down to its bare bones, it reveals just how rare a single person's ideas and rules about how life should be lived are. You might grow old and never meet another individual who shares the exact same set of ideas, rules, beliefs, habits and personal behaviours as yourself. I believe this offers a small, but significant insight into why others can sometimes behave so appallingly towards each other.

Those of us who woke up in the morning feeling like good people only to end the day discovering that certain actions hurt or upset someone – rarely set out to do so. This is not an attempt to suggest we should all just let people do whatever they want to others. I would simply like to offer a point of view into why people subject others to situations that can feel so personally painful.

A lot of our suffering in life comes down to a perception that someone deliberately set out to personally hurt us. What we know to be good and true is so obvious to us that surely everyone else knows and understands our values? Therefore if they end up hurting us, it is easy to assume it can only be through a deliberate and personally targeted intent. This realisation can pave the way to a powerful truth: **We judge other people on their actions but we judge ourselves by our intentions.**

Good people go about their days being good in the personally unique way that best reflects whatever ideas of how they should and shouldn't act. Each and every one of us spends a lifetime developing a specific idea of what 'good' actually means. The trouble begins when one version of *good* goes against what another person's understanding of good is. People can be very stubborn and will fight to ensure the survival of their individual understanding of the World – Sometimes even in the face of overwhelming evidence disproving what they believe to be true.

If we really think about it, situations that threaten or disrupt another person's core values offer one of two choices: To accept what they thought was wrong and change their ideas, or fight to prove they are right and you are wrong. Now ask yourself which is the easier path to take?

Do you think it is easier for someone to change their own mind or dig in and fight? On the face of it, you might say, 'well, they could choose either option'. At this point, I ask you to imagine that the said person has held a particular view for many years or even the majority of their life. Perhaps it was taught to them by someone they greatly admired and respected, therefore further compounding the strength of how *true* it must be.

Faced with those circumstances, it is inevitable that some people would choose to try and disprove each and every threat to that belief system. If someone is in love with an idea or belief and another person accidentally encroaches on what they feel is to be true then trouble is inevitable.

In these instances – when the problems occur – there are a number of responses we can typically expect. From the minor, such as telling someone to shut-up or just plain ignoring them, right up to the extremities of one country invading another. History is littered with stories of people carrying the most widely varied ideas and seemingly good beliefs imaginable, but still committing all sorts of atrocities.

All of this bad is done in the name of defending various idea systems, and research has demonstrated that it is common for the people committing these acts to truly believe their actions are righteous and acceptable. It is unfortunately also very common and very convenient for people to arrive at a conclusion that if another person does not agree with their doctrine that they must be mentally ill. This sounds extreme, but there are a number of studies that validate this claim.

I feel we can learn from this attitude though. To my mind, this shows that sometimes there can be no attempt to discover if someone with conflicting views to another is a reasonable person. There will be no attempt to offer the person with opposing views the opportunity to demonstrate or validate their claims. I frequently encounter this in my spiritual work with certain people who express an attitude that those people working this way are charlatans, fakes, steal people's hard earned money and should be ashamed of themselves.

The language they use is fascinatingly similar, which shows they are not thinking for themselves but instead, reciting words that they have previously heard, perhaps coming from an ideology they have found security in. There is never an invitation to show them how spiritual work can be of benefit, only unprovoked attacks. I see the pain and mental suffering many people acting this way feel, therefore, I try to live my life to the opposite of this approach and allow people a chance to explain their reasoning no matter how conflicting the idea might be to my own beliefs.

When reflecting upon my early circumstances and the way I was treated as a child I came to realise I simply would not respond to discipline in a way that perhaps many other children would have. I was in no way disrespectful to adults either, I certainly never screamed, shouted obscenities or disregarded what I was being told. I think it was just a perfect storm in which I was born with a temperament that could not be subdued into a world of adults who believed children should be controlled and needed to show respect to those adults' rules without complaint.

A moment ago I spoke about how we judge others on their actions and ourselves by our intentions. I believe that my early challenges reflect the importance of remembering this. A child who appears unruly can be acting in a way that is completely different to what they intended in their own minds. Before we brand someone as wrong, bad or evil based purely on their actions, and then punish them accordingly, it can certainly be a powerful exercise to attempt to understand what their intentions were.

I was never once fearful of my situation growing up but I believe that certain people around me felt that children should fear those responsible for them. Unfortunately, physical discipline was the method of choice for attempting to control my temperament. The result was a situation in which progressive violence was the only path. A child under the age of five was certainly not going to challenge the tried and tested belief systems of those adults. Did they think they were committing wrong towards me? Of course not! They had to fight to preserve the validity of their own way of thinking.

When we look at it from this angle, we can see that I was in fact more of a threat to them than they were to me. Other forces were obviously at play as well, I believe frustration towards their own pasts and the living circumstances they faced at that time, created a high level of pressure that was too much for all involved.

Does any of this make it right? Certainly not. To my mind, it just demonstrates the importance of understanding yourself and how your mind responds at certain moments in life. If we have no idea about the processes occurring in our own heads; how they got there and why – then when we face the correct set of pressures we could become capable of committing the most deplorable acts.

The lessons I have taken from those early years and watching how all of those involved have dealt with it in the coming years, has taught me an important approach to life. I would rather be ready to drop a belief that I felt strongly attached to than face the remorse of how I have acted towards others trying to defend it.

Ultimately though, the way people are capable of behaving when fighting to protect an idea has taught me a simple truth. Enlightenment requires the development of the self; it is easy to decide that you wish to pursue this path, but you will have to release your mind from past traumas and question the ideas and beliefs that you hold true from growing up.

You will need to be prepared to question what you know, drop ideas that limit, control and distract you from discovering the path to your own happiness. I have found that those of us who find comfort and security in subscribing to a group ideology are those of us that are furthest away from the personal happiness we all desire.

Once we begin to accept and understand why good people can be driven to do bad things, it is natural that another specific set of questions might arise: Why did I meet those people? Why was I born into that life? What could my life have been if I had been given a different set of more loving people to care for me in my early days? My answer to these is more philosophical than the answers we have given to the previous topics because I feel these are more philosophical questions and therefore the following answer is warranted…

This concept came to me in meditation many years ago and I have used it in my work with helping others ever since. It is an important cornerstone in the approach I use to quietening the mind's questions about the injustices of the past.

I will always begin explaining this by asking: Let us consider you have decided today to open an account with a credit card company; they accept your application and give you a large credit limit. You proceed to spend some money on the card over the next few months, but all is well as you only spend a small amount overall, and can cover the repayments with no issue. Then one day, you decide to buy a new car. You find the one you want and the dealer allows you to drive it away with only a small down payment, the rest can be financed and you will only have to pay a small monthly amount. After your calculations, you realise this is not a problem and you agree to the terms. Everything is perfect and continues this way for some time. Eventually though, you wake up (on another day) and realise you are not happy with your life. This feeling begins to grow and it isn't long before you need to act; it is time to change life for the better.

So what do you settle on? How about moving to the country your best friend's family relocated to a while back? Yes, that sounds great, you have seen the pictures of how wonderful their life is and it would be great to live near them so you begin to make the arrangements...

After organising a visa to stay in the new country you search online for a property and find a great deal; the estate agent says it's in demand, but no worry a deposit will secure it. Money is starting to get tight because of all the preparations, so you put it on the credit card. Next you leave your job so you can focus on cleaning the home and packing your possessions. You start spending more on the credit card as your last pay cheque has gone.

A few weeks go by and you are nearly ready to leave. Only a week to go until the big day. Then the phone rings and it is the credit card company. They want to make sure you are aware there has been some unusual spending on your account – 'It's OK!' you say, I am moving to a new country next week to start a new life.

The caller responds saying, 'I just need to speak to my manager, are you available for the rest of the day?'.

'Yes, I certainly am, feel free to call later,' you respond and then put the phone down.

Later another person calls: 'Hello I just wanted to make sure all is well as we have not received the last payment for your car.'

'Yes it is fine, sorry I forgot about that, I have been really busy getting ready to move to a new country, I leave next week.'

The caller is nice and chatty and the conversation eventually leads to them asking, 'How do you plan to travel to your new home?'

You reply, '-In my new car, it is really comfy and reliable.'

The caller changes their tone and says, 'I just need to speak to my manager, are you available for the rest of the day?'

'Yes, I certainly am, feel free to call later.' You then put the phone down.

I imagine you have a good idea of what happens next. For the next week the car and credit card companies are going to employ every tactic available to them, to seize the car and whatever assets possible to recover the money spent on the credit card before you leave and before they have no more power over the situation.

It is my belief that when we announce to the Universe we are going to live by a different set of rules to what is traditionally expected of us, a similar situation occurs in our lives. There are a number of ways we can announce this intent to live differently, certain life style choices such as embracing a spiritual path can be met with very turbulent waters. If you are going to change your cycle of karma the universal bank manager is going to use all the tactics at his/her disposal to collect what is owed from you.

I believe we can make this announcement of intention to change our path in many conscious and unconscious ways, either in this life or immediately before we enter it. The result will always be the same; we will be tested in ways that are specifically designed for us to see how much we are truly willing to embrace that change.

If I had chosen to harbour hate and anger towards the perpetrators of my abuse and never moved past what had happened to me, then where would I be today? If I had chosen a path of self-pity and comparing my losses to how easy I thought everybody else had it, then it is possible I could have used my early experience in this World as the perfect platform for various destructive behaviours and who could have judged my choices? In light of my early challenges, would anyone blame me for embracing a negative lifestyle?

Yeah he takes drugs all the time because he was abused as a child. Of course he could never get close to someone emotionally and love them, he didn't know love himself. Why do you think he is violent to others, all he knew growing up was violence. It's terrible he thinks he can steal from others, but I guess he never had anything, so he just decided to take it. Isn't it tragic he treats his children like he was treated because he thinks that is the correct way to parent?

By looking at karma as a credit system, we can see it is not what happened to you, but more how you interpret the challenges you endured. This realisation can prevent us from falling for the delusions of the mind and you can begin to see that as fortunate events come your way, it isn't due to luck. On the opposite end of the scale, you will begin to understand that when difficulties present themselves in life, you will not feel hard done by or unlucky. Those of us with the strength and courage to face up to this, will find that karma is, in fact, a powerful contemplation tool that can be used for spiritual advancement.

I believe every single one of us are tested but not every one of us will find the strength to truly overcome and use these moments and experiences as a precursor to genuine and lasting happiness. However, when we reflect upon the reality that there are no events as such, and that everything is connected through the river of time, powerful realisations will arise.

Considering this can allow you to realise somewhere along the line of – time karmic seeds were planted and you are experiencing the fruit of their growth today. Finally, we can accept that if we have repaid our karmic credit while making sure not to run up more debt, freedom from that cycle is all but assured.

I like to view this Universe as a place of the upmost balance, I will explain this in more detail later, but for now I think it is relevant to remind you of the many rags to riches stories you would have no doubt heard during your lifetime. The stories of the homeless becoming the rich; the people who lost everything only to rebuild bigger, better and more fulfilling lives. The immigrants who fled war-torn countries and started again with nothing in unfamiliar lands only to end up living the life of their dreams.

It is easy to focus on the cycle of material loss and gain when listening to this type of story, but when I hear or read about these situations I see two important factors. Firstly, the importance of never giving up and never allowing self-doubt to creep into your mind. We are all capable of achieving things today that seem wildly impossible. Many of us can relate to this at points in life when we look back and realise how far we have come.

Secondly, I see the universal forces of balance at work. Whatever the depth of suffering you have experienced, it will eventually equal out and the opportunities that can allow you to create your version of complete happiness will begin to arrive. I believe the greater the suffering one has to endure will be met with an equally greater opportunity for success and happiness later in life.

Issac Newton said, 'For every action, there is an equal and opposite reaction'. These words can perhaps seem difficult to believe when we are in the thick of a crisis, but anyone who has endured and come out the other side will eventually begin to agree how much things can change.

Disruption can feel like it is the most difficult and unbearable thing while it is happening to us, but we should never forget how rapidly positive change can come into our lives if given the chance. Studies have shown we tend to overestimate what we can achieve in a year, but we wildly underestimate what can be achieved in two years. You could be poor today and unhappy in your job, but working for a company you have never heard of, being paid a salary you are amazed by in two years. You could be single and lonely today, but married to the love of your life with a child on the way in two years.

In summary – of how I believe we can begin to release burdens the mind can inflict on us – we must understand the adjectives that define us are only temporary and we should not become overly attached to them. You are far more than a name, a career choice or someone's other half. It is true there are a number of words that when uniquely arranged can reflect a large part of who you are – But, it is also true that the deeper your attachment to anything that has a temporary nature associated with it, will leave you exposed to facing future emotional struggles if those identifiers are disrupted or taken from you.

Next, we should be sure to reflect on the potential impact of realising some of what you thought was OK in childhood actually turned out to be bad from adult perspective. If we try to overcome this change in perspective by trying to discredit childhood because we were somehow weak or vulnerable, it becomes easy to forget the natural mindfulness skills we all possess that were learnt during this stage of life.

There is not a single person alive who can undo the past, but if we overly worry about the pains of that time repeating in the future, it is likely we will stop ourselves from entering into new situations unless the outcome is assured. The result of this approach is that we will certainly stop the bad from happening, but it is highly likely we will miss out on new positive experiences as well.

Mindfulness can stop the fear of the past repeating from holding us back heading into the future. You can use all of your experience to monitor the present and adjust the course if appropriate, but it should not be forgotten that adapting to the present moment is preferable to preventing all future difficulties by limiting your choices. Instead of building defensive walls, learn to trust in your own wisdom. The difficulties of your life – if accepted and embraced – will reveal that you have the ability to spot warning signs in future. This foresight can be used to stop negative situations from escalating beyond control.

Understanding the mind wants to protect you by finding answers and solutions to problems is the next key. Your mind will find it relatively easy to teach you about preventing physical pain, but the complexity surrounding unexpected emotional pain is difficult to interpret and predict. Therefore social withdrawal and creating a smaller world can feel like an obvious answer. We must resist letting this innate protective nature escalate into negative and restrictive thought patterns that can pull us away from society.

A simple way to begin doing this is by reflecting on the past with new eyes and learning to use this approach with the intent of finding the good, and giving thanks for it. I understand this can feel counter-intuitive to begin with, many of us feel defined by our pain but as you will come to learn later in this book, the weight of this energy will only serve to hold back the development you seek, it must be released for you to achieve what you desire.

After this, we should remember the competition that slowly arose when becoming an adult can stop you from wanting to share any negative experiences. It is easy to assume by sharing the bad you might come across as being weak, or that you have failed in dealing with your emotions, therefore you must have lost the competition of being a happy and balanced person. This is a restrictive approach that only causes emotional isolation, which in turn can leave a person feeling alone and detached from the World. I ask you, if by me sharing my early disappointments in life has made me seem weak or vulnerable to you?

Are you less likely to take my advice now I have shared memories of personal trauma? Or do you feel that knowing this makes me more relatable and you would be interested to hear how I overcome the difficulties of my early years?

I believe any guilt you hold, shyness or anxiety towards other people's responses will quickly evaporate when you begin to consider what we have spoken of so far. It is important if you choose to share with someone that you trust them. Even if you do not know anyone personally there is always a support group or free advice line where you can find someone to speak with.

We should remember even the worst of people think they are good, so try not to take someone else's actions towards you as a personal and targeted attack on you. Even in the rare instance that someone has set out to attack you, we should not forget to consider how deep their problems reach within their own lives for them to be behaving that way. It is important to keep in mind that you typically judge other people on their actions while judging yourself by your intentions. You are not alone in this and teaching yourself to ask what someone's true intentions are can help to shine a new light on why people behave in certain ways. Be sure to consider your own actions in this World and ask yourself, 'do these actions reflect my truest intentions?'.

The karmic credit system I have spoken about does go some way to explaining part of the early suffering you could have experienced and you should keep in mind that the harsher the beginnings, the higher the potential for good to appear later in life. There is an eternal balance within this Universe that I will explain at length in later chapters, but I want to finish this here by reaffirming your power to consciously alter your path in this World.

No matter what others believe or say, no matter what they subject you to experience, right is still right, even if the whole World is doing wrong. However difficult life gets, your decision to do right will be rewarded with peace of mind later in life. I have seen firsthand the regret and sadness holding onto and blindly attempting to defend a belief system is, so I finish this chapter by inviting you to consider the benefits of being prepared to have your mind changed if ever the opportunity arises.

CHAPTER 5

Good vs Evil

NOW, THROUGHOUT THE PREVIOUS chapters we have spoken about the various methods and philosophies I believe, if used correctly, can build a framework to help overcome some of the frequently encountered problems and scenarios that plague many of our lives. As you no doubt understand, these common difficulties can easily create long-lasting misery, while distracting the mind from bringing in the lasting happiness and success we all deserve.

Acceptance of the past is essential to progressing spiritually and developing the self. However, many of us will have very likely experienced another form of discomfort in this World; namely the frustration and often sense of helplessness we experience when hearing the stories or witnessing the various forms of suffering others also have to endure.

This empathy can often extend beyond those closest to us, spilling out into many other areas such as strangers, animals and environmental issues. Many of us cannot bare to see the weak and defenceless suffer at the hands of others or befalling tragic circumstances that they do not deserve.

The feelings of you being powerless to intervene and alter these situations can inevitably lead to asking one of the biggest questions of all: Why is there so much evil in this World? By extension, if we cannot suitably answer this question then how will we ever experience long and lasting peace of the mind?

Some people refer to themselves as an 'empath' and for those of us unfamiliar with this term, I will briefly explain. An *empath* is someone who is highly aware of the emotions of those around them. This can bring empaths a different perception of the World as they seem to be aware of all the pain, suffering and emotional needs of those beings they encounter.

It is my belief that as we pursue this journey of awakening our personal enlightenment we will undoubtedly become more sensitive to the suffering others endure. So, how do we prevent ourselves from becoming emotionally overwhelmed in the face of all the bad presence within this World? At times, this form of negativity is almost inescapable. Turn the TV on for a moment, read a newspaper or open your Internet browser and within minutes you will likely be faced with some type of tragic story detailing and reminding us of the unfair suffering this World holds.

These constant daily reminders raise the obvious question: What is the point of overcoming our personal suffering if we are then destined only to have this replaced with living a life feeling the pain of all of those we share this World with?

Some years ago at one of my stays with the seventy-plus-year-old third-generation Shaman I visit in the Peruvian Amazon, a beautiful solution to this challenging question appeared before me. During a traditional Amazonian spiritual ceremony I was deep in meditation, sitting secluded in a wooden hut facing the pitch black of night absorbing the Shaman's songs, when I experienced a wave of information rush over me that helped to change my perception of how I view good and bad forever.

For a long time afterwards, I felt it to be almost impossible to find the words to explain the concepts revealed to me that evening. But over the years, I have managed to refine what I was given that evening into something people can relate to and comprehend. This answer is long and winding, which is why I decided it deserves a dedicated chapter. I believe this powerful concept can offer you the framework to finding your own peace with much of the suffering this World contains.

As I sat perfectly still listening to the endless sounds of the rainforest outside, blending with the traditional Icaro being sang next to me; I began to feel, and then see a stream of images and ideas rise through my mind. It began with a vivid vision of our beautiful solar system. I found myself watching a microcosm of all the chaotic and brutal processes that have been at work every second of this Universe's existence since the first star was born.

I then began to focus on the unimaginably hot furnace of our Sun: The glowing yellow, orange and red plasma twisting and turning, trying to tear itself apart while simultaneously spitting pieces of its own matter with bursts of radiation into the piercingly cold and dark black depths of space. Among these unforgivingly harsh processes I began to sense the absolute chaos that is required from the Sun to create and sustain life on our planet.

This chaos intensified when I was taken back to witness some of the many violent processes that unfolded to shape and create our very own planet billions of years ago. A time when asteroids and comets smashed unrelentingly into the rock we now call home. This essential period of disruption in Earth's history delivered the water that eventually formed our oceans, which in turn became a nursery for life on this planet.

I saw the harshness of the toxic and unbreathable gases released from the early volcanic eruptions that helped create the basis of what we now call our atmosphere. As my consciousness drifted back and forth I began to become aware that this essence of chaos was in fact present everywhere within our Universe, and it is absolutely essential for the creation of life. Like a veil being lifted from my vision, this idea that chaos is around us at all times no matter where we look became clearer with every passing moment.

Chaos is present right down to the atomic scale; material particles are simultaneously created, smashed and transformed into something else every fraction of every second that time passes. Stepping up from the atomic scale to a microscopic scale brings no relief from this inherent chaos. Viruses and bacteria are trapped in an endless war of competition and destruction, fighting for their chance to survive.

Next, we have the visual scale of matter that we can feel and see with our own eyes. But what do we observe in this World? Nature is often so beautiful that we forget this planet we occupy is dominated by chaos. Plants are fighting to grow in every vacant space and competing to steal whatever light they can access from their competitors. Insects trapped in a race to consume food and reproduce as fast as possible, without any awareness or capacity to think of the effects overwhelming their environments would cause if the chance presents to them.

How many times have we seen crops destroyed by pests or invasive species killing off entire populations of rival insects? Are the larger animals exempt from this chaos? Certainly not, they do not escape the race for survival and its associated chaos that is often needed to ensure their right to live. We have all seen the various lengths animals are prepared to go to if those actions in turn ensure their survival.

Stepping away from life for a moment and examining the environmental processes at work around us reveals even larger scales of chaos. We are all familiar with the difficulties weather forecasters experience when trying to predict conditions for more than a few days ahead. The weather systems are so notoriously difficult to analyse; we just accept that there is little chance of planning ahead for how to dress next weekend and instead are simply thankful when we receive pleasant conditions. Fisherman and beach life guards try their hardest to monitor water currents and wave heights, but ultimately find themselves at the mercy of these chaotic unstable systems.

Escaping Earth offers no relief from this state of chaos. Our planet's protective magnetic field is bombarded by cosmic rays that would strip our fragile atmosphere away if it didn't exist. Prolonged unprotected exposure to these rays is certain to cause us various cancerous conditions. We know of no other survivable place away from this planet. The unimaginably cold vacuum of space or the ferocious heat of our Sun are incompatible with human life.

The toxic gasses of Venus and Jupiter and the baron rocky landscape of Mars offer nothing but certain death if we somehow found ourselves in any of these places in our natural human form. You will see the further we look, the more chaos is revealed. Much of this however is either accepted as the laws of nature or just dismissed as some ignorable byproduct of the natural order of things.

As my mind explored the chaos around us even deeper, I began to see that the bad within this World can be classed as another sub-form of chaos. People who suffer immensely due to accidents or catastrophes of various descriptions; natural disasters ruining the lives of countless millions throughout history; freak occurrences of people being in completely the wrong place at the precise moment for something tragic to befall them and change the course of their lives forever – Are all simple examples of this: The unfair and unforeseen suffering that can feel like it came out of nowhere or even the shock we experience one day finding out something we did with the very best of intentions in fact caused harm to others around us. I began to become acutely aware that chaos is unescapable, whatever I saw and wherever I looked, chaos was present in some form or another.

It was at this point, a truly pivotal moment of realisation occurred. All of my life, I had been asking the wrong question. I had been so distracted by the bad around us, I was constantly searching for answers and solutions to overcome the various difficult and negative things we all have to experience in life. In my endless attempt to try and prevent the *bad* from happening I had missed the point all along…

My whole life I wanted to know, why does bad exist within this Universe? When in fact, the question I should have been asking is: Why is there good? As this concept took hold, the visions highlighting the various forms of universal chaos began to subside and were replaced with a scene that demonstrated a much more favourable view of the Universe. This realisation was given to me in an extremely vivid and detailed vision. I will attempt to explain how I have come to understand what was seen and what practical advice it offers all of us.

After spending what felt to be an eternity rapidly flipping from one form of chaos to another; a moment of absolute silence took ahold inside my mind. In that instance, I was taken away from the Shaman's song and the sounds of the rainforest. I then began to feel as if the air temperature around me was slowly rising. My mind reminded me this was a similar sensation to stepping out from the shade into the sunlight on a hot Summer's afternoon.

This feeling was then followed by the visualisation of standing in what looked to be a vast and barren desert. As this image began to sharpen, I could see endless rolling sand dunes as far and wide as the horizon extended. After a moment, I realised this desert was the embodiment of chaos itself. Each and every grain of sand represented some form of what our human understanding would recognise as some type of negativity.

Once I had grounded myself in the energy of this desert, my attention was then drawn away from the dunes to a tiny anomaly in the distance. This shape broke the endless flow of sand and I felt instantly drawn towards this point of difference in the otherwise overwhelming heat and humidity. As I made my way towards this tiny shape, it became clearer the closer I got – it as the most beautiful oasis one could possibly imagine.

This lifeline in the otherwise barren space had everything I could possibly need to sustain myself. A crystal clear freshwater spring surrounded by lush vegetation – producing all the fruits, nuts, vegetables, shade and shelter I would ever need. It was instantly apparent this oasis represented the embodiment of good.

I had been shown a simple yet powerful representation of good and bad. After I began to recognise the obviousness of these opposing forces existing side by side I was given a number of simple, yet profound questions to ponder upon. Now, at this point a lot of people will ask me, who asked these questions? It is a natural and obvious question to ask, but the answer is equally as long and winding as what I am trying to share. I do plan to address this at length in a future book, but for now I want to focus on the what, not the how.

I was then asked: Because you now understand the symbolism of this desert and the oasis it harboured, what would you do if you found yourself stranded there? If you woke up one morning in the middle of this desert, alone with no provisions and unsure of how you got there, what would you choose to do? There was no electricity and you had absolutely no means to contact anyone you knew in order to ask them to mount a rescue. In that situation, what should you do?

Should you climb the tallest dune and attempt to survey the length and width of the desert? Should you use bare hands to dig as deep into the sand as possible and see if there were any usable resources while trying your hardest to stop the sand refilling the hole?

Even if I could answer all of these questions, would it improve my situation? No, is the simple answer. No person is strong enough to walk the length of this desert without provisions or equipment. Even if I could work out the precise length, width and depth of this place, I would still be alone and stranded with no hope of escaping the heat and sand. After I was shown the hopelessness of these questions and by extension, realising that in this situation accepting 'I would be trapped in this desert', was the only answer, I was next asked to walk into the oasis.

I obliged and found a spot in the shade to sit. As the temperature began to lower another set of questions were asked: If you had to accept that you are to live the rest of your days surrounded by these unforgiving sand dunes, should you focus on learning how to build a comfortable shelter that protects you from the harsh conditions of the desert? Would it be helpful to learn what you can about each of the plants that fill this oasis? Do you think that it would improve your situation to nurture these plants and help them to flourish and bear more fruit? If you could harvest enough seeds would it not be possible to use them for growing new plants to expand the size of land this oasis occupied?

What is the more beneficial question to ask: How did the desert come to be? Or, how did the oasis come to be? Does the size of the desert or the size of the oasis improve your well-being? If you had to choose one option, would you shrink the size of the desert or, should you grow the size of the oasis?

Reflecting upon the nature of this analogy allowed me to find a peace that had previously been absent from my life. If we really think about it, then we can begin to understand human beings are the only life form we know of that have the conscious ability to do good. Each and every one of us possess a duality inside of us, we can behave in a way that coincides and complements the default chaotic energy of this Universe…

We can give into impulse, spread negativity and then spend our time here trying to convince others our choice was the right one. Or we can consciously choose to behave in a way that to our knowledge no other species is capable of doing. Every single person alive has an apparently universally, unique ability to do good, to create positivity in the lives of others and the wider World. Chaos, bad, evil and negativity are the normality, these forces are present everywhere at all times, it is inescapable and to ask why this force exists, only leads to creating more of what we want to avoid.

Thinking about the chaos more often than not brings sadness into our lives. Focusing upon why criminals do the most unimaginable things to people does not undo their deeds. In fact it is possible to compare the worst acts a human can inflict on another human with those that animals do every day.

Animals murder each other, abuse each other and have no respect for the boundaries between family or friends. It can be said that the worst behaviour a human being can engage in, is just as chaotic as what occurs within the animal kingdom daily. I believe the reason good people are so disgusted by witnessing others act this way is because, they understand humans are capable of more. We have choice on a level other conscious life does not possess, therefore, it is deeply worrying and upsetting to see someone ignore this and choose chaos over order.

The other side of this however, is that nearly all of us will feel an improvement in our mood when we do good deeds. If those positive actions benefit someone else in the process, the recipient usually feels an improvement in their mood to some degree as well. Behaving this way is comparable to growing the oasis of good against a backdrop of chaos.

As you are born into this World you are thrust from a non-material space into a place that is inherently chaotic. As your consciousness develops while you age, the realisation that chaos is everywhere can become so overwhelming it can be easy to forget you have the unique ability to counteract this energy through consciously creating energy of opposing polarity.

Should you ignore the bad? Certainly not. Should you just accept that certain people choose to do bad things to others? I don't think that is beneficial either. In fact, there is a hidden gift in the chaos many of us miss. Every bad deed you receive or witness in this World, every negative action you see and experience, offers you a barometer to develop what your idea of good can be.

If we never saw or experienced one bad event in this World how would we decide what good is? There has to be a benchmark in which we can work to counteract. I believe the deeper one suffers, the deeper their perception of good can become. Once you understand what exactly you don't like, you can then begin your work to create positive opposition.

In light of this, I have spent many years now trying to **grow the size of this energetic oasis of positivity in the desert of chaos.** At a minimal level, we all possess the ability to improve the day of someone else. It does not have to be some grandiose gesture or volunteering all of your spare time to charity. A simple heartfelt and honest smile can brighten the day of a total stranger, and this type of positive action should not cost you anything.

Armed with this knowledge, you now have a decision to make, which path do you wish to pursue going forward? Do you continue treading the same tried and tested route of questioning all of the evil in our World, feeling awful at the overwhelming suffering we are all surrounded with, or do you take a new direction? Another and perhaps previously unknown road also exists, and to begin exploring this, all we need to do is ask ourselves what our personal understanding of good is.

Waiting for the next negative experience to unfold keeps us in a reactionary state. While in that state, we give up our ability to direct the course of our lives. Remaining in a state of reaction prevents us from creating the action we desire within our World. **Focusing on what positivity we can manifest switches our state from that of reaction, to one of action.** Therefore instead of simply waiting to respond to events around us, we can begin to start influencing our own paths in a much more favourable manner.

Action is most certainly going to be required to awaken your enlightenment. So I ask: What good can you do for yourself and what good can you effortlessly do for others? **We all have the ability to become an expanding oasis of good in the desert of chaos.** Any one of us can choose to transform fear into acceptance, switch suffering into opportunity for change, and use desire as the seed of action.

Jacob Braude elegantly touched upon this line of thinking when he said, 'Life is like a grindstone; whether it grinds you down or polishes you up depends on what you're made of'. I believe our difficulties can make us tough, but once we understand the universal rules of suffering, true strength can then be developed and cultivated through compassion and openness.

Ever since this was revealed to me, in the face of experiencing or witnessing suffering, instead of asking: Why is there bad within this World? I now ask: Why is there good?

CHAPTER 6

Panoptic Mapping

THOUGHTS ARE TRULY POWERFUL things, some of them feel stronger than others; particular types can be enjoyable, and I am certain some of them you would rather ignore. We all know that it is not possible to hold or bottle a thought. Yet, this nonphysical energy has a potential to elevate or depress your emotions, help you to succeed or sow the seeds of your failures and ultimately direct the course of your life. Perhaps most importantly of all, thoughts have the ability to shape your perception of both the internal and external world.

Are you harsh and overly judgmental of yourself in the aftermath of making an error? Perhaps you think more kindly and understand your last mistake is your best tutor. When someone else gets it wrong, do you think their actions were deliberate, maybe you feel they even singled you out? Or, are you naturally trustworthy and think other people should be given the benefit of doubt regarding of their behaviour? How we think about what we do, and process the things that happen to us can vary dramatically between different people.

This chapter will differ slightly from the previous topics. So far, we have focused exclusively on what you are aware of, and the various methods I use to help alter our relationship with that in which we can consciously perceive. Over the course of this chapter, I plan to begin addressing our unconscious mind, and more importantly how you can transform your relationship with this extremely powerful force.

I have spent a number of years creating a potent, highly effective method that, if implemented with discipline and determination, can truly alter the course of your life for the better. My technique blends ancient and modern knowledge from around the globe, with my own understandings developed through achieving particular meditative states.

Panoptic Mapping might sound too good to be true, it might even sound too simple to be real. However, I can assure you that the information you are about to read has already changed lives. It has helped suicidal people to find happiness and created abundance of all forms in numerous people's worlds.

Ninety-five-percent of all your brain activity is beyond conscious perception. In short, nearly everything that happens inside your head you have absolutely no awareness of. Within these hidden realms, I believe an energy exists so powerful, it has the ability to give you the life of your dreams, or perhaps make each day difficult and uncomfortable. In extreme cases, this unseen power could even make you wish you were no longer alive. Some of you might be thinking that these are bold claims, but by the end of this chapter, I am sure you will reconsider that view.

Have you ever wondered who or what is the creator of your thoughts and ideas? Where does the inception occur? We have all experienced thoughts 'popping' into our heads. This process is so natural that it is rare many of us would ever ask where does it all begin? If a magician could conjure a thought for you and then asked the question; What type of new thought would you like to receive? How would you respond?

Do you already know what seeds of thought or ideas you would like to have planted in your mind? Or, would you over-think this question until you became trapped trying to work out what you wanted to think? How challenging would it be for you to choose a single thought? Now, consider how it would feel having to choose each of your individual thoughts every day. I am sure even a moment of pondering this will reveal that it would be an almost impossible task.

If the challenge of conscious thought selection is now becoming apparent, let's take a moment to throw the true depth of our external environment into the mix. Have you ever paused to completely immerse yourself in what is happening around you?

The full details of our surroundings are so complex that we only realise what we are absorbing if we stop all activities and direct our entire focus to the moment. Let us assume you are sitting while reading this book. Perhaps on a chair, so why not take a moment to look at it more deeply. Really focus and take in all of the chair; the textures, colours and materials it is made from. Can you see the individual weaves within the fabric threads? What about any patterns? If it is wooden can you see a difference of shades from one side of the grain to the other?

Wherever you are, I invite you to really pause and examine the scale of your surroundings. I am certain that the longer you do this for, the more details you will notice hidden from view just a moment ago. If you take even a single minute to do this, it can begin to teach you that objective reality is in fact, an illusion. Discovering you had missed the full details of an object as common as a chair begs the question; What else is passing by unnoticed?

This illusion is based in the truth that you are only ever aware of a tiny fraction of the environmental depth surrounding you at all times. In fact, even if you could handle consciously processing all of what is happening around you, there are clear limits to what your biology can perceive. For example, the human eye can see less than 1 percent of the electromagnetic spectrum and the ear can hear less than 1 percent of the acoustic spectrum. Each of our five main senses are severely restricted in what they can perceive compared to what the environment offers.

In recent times, various scientific studies have demonstrated that the brain reconstructs our world within the mind. It has even been suggested that we hallucinate our external world, and human reality is a collective of these hallucinations in which the majority of us agree upon. When we take all of these points into consideration it becomes apparent that the vast majority of reality must exist beyond what we can consciously perceive.

Reflecting upon these understandings have raised some interesting questions within my mind; If we are only ever shown a fraction of our true reality, who or what decides which pieces we see? How, when, and why, are we shown these tiny segments? Perhaps most importantly, is it possible to expand this internal filter to see more of what is available?

My attempt to answer these questions brought me some surprising realisations that eventually lead to a reframing of how I engage with myself on a daily basis. What I discovered was a little unsettling at times, and for a short while, it even made me a little fearful of this passive power that exists within all of us. However, as I began to accept this knowledge, I was then able to begin shaping this power for my own benefit and the results were almost magical. I believe this important knowledge, if understood correctly and implemented regularly, can become an essential tool in building the reality of your dreams.

I am in no doubt that you will have heard of the term 'higher self', but what exactly does this refer to? Searching for answers online will yield many different results. The *higher self* is widely accepted to be a term that is associated with many belief systems. At the core of these ideas, the higher self is a term one might use to describe a somehow separate and intelligent being that exists deep within us. Perhaps this is even the root of where the real *us* resides.

Within yogic philosophy the higher self is also known as the transcendental self, or Purusha, in Sanskrit. Some people consider the higher self as the divine self and even a part of the cosmic consciousness. Now, as you will learn, I do not doubt some of these ideas to be rooted in the truth. But for a moment, let's examine the effect of using some of these adjectives has on your perception of the higher self.

To my mind, using words such as 'higher' and 'divine' invoke connotations of inaccessibility. If something is higher, it feels to be out of reach. The word divine is even harder to personally relate with. We are all beings who get angry at times and have passions that might be less than pure. People automatically think that someone who is divine would be infallible and therefore, how could we possibly relate with such purity. An extension of this means it would be natural to think, '-surely if we start believing a higher and divine being exists within us, it won't be long before we are revealed to be big fakes'.

Adding the words 'transcendental' and 'cosmic' creates a further layer of inaccessibility. These words have an ethereal feel about them that is distinctly separate from the Earth we all call home. It is my belief that using such terms to describe the higher self has resulted in a widespread, deeply-rooted attitude that this part of us should be left alone.

Many of us live a life of trying to prevent others from negatively judging us. Keeping our relationships, careers and home lives on track is difficult enough. Why would we want to risk being judged by an omnipotent being on top of this? The answer is simple, if we think the higher self will see the truth of our inauthentic existence, perhaps hiding from it will spare us some potential negative judgement, making life a little easier.

I believe that regardless of your belief system, you are fully aware that some of the World's dominant religions are under-pinned with another version of this fear I am speaking of. Like it or not, we are conditioned from a very young age to integrate the idea that a powerful god-like force could exist.

This entity might be watching us in secret, judging our every move and determining what our eternal fate will be. Those of us living in a democracy and casting votes on how we are governed, will likely feel unsettled by the idea that a monarchy, or king could be in control of the Universe. If this king turned out to be a dictator, the outcome would mean we would have little control over our destinies. Therefore, it is common that when we encounter situations or beings with those traits, they could be seen as unpalatable and should be resisted.

Climate change, sea level rise, pests destroying crops, food shortages, natural disasters, alien invasions, even the idea of an artificial intelligence are all things that could exhibit a version of these traits. The individual can feel very unsettled in the face of absolute power that has the potential to sweep us aside as if we are meaningless. When this happens, it is not unrealistic to expect some form of fight or flight response to be activated.

I feel the language we use to describe the higher self and the characteristics we unconsciously associate with it, have disconnected many of us from the truth. Suggesting there is something within ourselves that is hidden and made from pure and eternal energy, is a concept that might not feel relatable to some people. However, I believe the reality is that this energy does live within us, but it is not interested in judging you. In my view, it can be also said the higher self doesn't really care how you feel.

Sigmund Freud developed a model of the mind, whereby he described the features of the mind's structure and function. Within this model he included the ego and the superego. Although I just expressed a view where the higher self is disinterested in your feelings, I do believe the mind does have a lot of love for you. However, those emotional traits exist within the ego area of the mind. The superego is where, I believe, the *higher self* resides, and my experiences have taught me that this part of the mind is emotionally neutral towards you.

A car can take you where you want to go at a great speed while protecting, entertaining and keeping you comfortable. The same car can also drive you into a wall. If you understand how to maintain the vehicle it will serve you for longer than if you neglect it. It is also true that although there are many complex components within motor vehicles, we do not need to know how each of these work to effectively drive. A car does not judge you if you do not use it correctly, it only exists to serve you, how well it does that, is down to you.

It is my belief, that your higher self behaves in a similar way. The problem is that too many of us attach mystical traits to this part of ourselves and therefore only want to engage with it when we are in particular mental state. I believe this part of you is non-judgmental and rather neutral to how you are feeling. To my mind, it is both the unconscious gatekeeper and an unconscious gatekeeper. This is perhaps a complex concept to grasp, but I am sure that if you put the principles I am about to share into action this idea will eventually become apparent.

Earlier I spoke about the mind hallucinating our reality, and the fact that the true depth of what we can perceive is hidden from us. I believe the higher self is the gatekeeper that decides what this hallucination consists of. I feel that function is primarily a protective one, but not necessarily in a capacity you are used to. External threat identification is part of this function but as you know, you can also choose to harm yourself if that's what you desire.

In filtering out what we don't want or need to see, more capacity is available to focus on what we do want. It would be utterly overwhelming to see every single morsel of external stimulus the Universe offers and so this function is totally necessary.

Although much of what this part of us does, works on a kind of autopilot, continuing with the car analogy, it is not in control of you. Some of the most modern vehicles available today have the ability to transport you from A to B with minimal input from the driver. But even these vehicles still require instruction of which destination you wish to travel to. By understanding this, we can begin to learn that although the higher self has a lot of power, it still requires input from you. In essence, your higher self is programable to a degree and I truly believe it is crucial to accept this.

Have you ever woken up the morning after a night out with friends having drunk far too much alcohol with an awful hangover? Some of us who have done so might tell our friends never to let us drink that much again. The friends might laugh at this and its likely next time you all go out a similar fate awaits. Now, imagine that you had an extremely determined friend who took those requests completely seriously.

There are two interesting outcomes of that scenario: You could be grateful the next time you went out that they only bought you soft drinks, saving you from another hangover; or the second scenario, you could become quite annoyed that they did this because it stopped you having the fun and enjoyment you had hoped for. Remember, it was you that gave the instruction, but it might not actually be what you wanted and therefore conflict could rise as a result.

Fortunately, our friends do not take everything we say seriously because they take feelings into consideration when making decisions. The higher self is observing your spoken words, conscious thoughts, feelings and monitoring the depths of your emotional responses. It knows what you laugh at, what tastes good or excites you, what scares you and what makes you sad. It behaves like an eternal stenographer, but at the same time it is neutral about how you feel. Think about the voice activation feature available on some of today's mobile phones, this listens but takes your instructions on face value and executes commands without a second thought.

I believe that the higher self wants to construct the version of reality that you ask for, regardless of whether that's what you actually want. Like the magician from the start of this chapter, the higher self wants to conjure you a thought or idea, but it does not know how to associate truth to what you want. Therefore, it needs deeper instruction if you have any chance of getting what you truly desire. It is programable to such a degree that it can cause problems if you do not understand that it works in this way. Many of us are unaware of this and I believe it goes some way to explaining why a lot of the internal conflicts we can face in life occur.

'Know thyself' is a concept that many of the greatest philosophers to have ever lived understood an obeyed. There is a stoic idea that to be able to free yourself, to live with virtue, to become who you were put on this Earth to be, you must first know yourself. It is said that part of achieving this, is you must become the master of your mind. Learning that the higher self is programable; for the good and the bad, was a crucial part of my development that was both unsettling and liberating.

There is an old saying that states if you say either, *you can* or you say *you can't*, you are right both times. We already know the version of reality that we see barely even scratches the surface of what is available. Your higher self will effortlessly find the evidence to support your ideas. True reality is overflowing with potential stimuli and I believe there is enough support, validation and evidence within the Universe to create whatever you want.

Pretty much anything you ask to see, feel or experience can be filtered into the hallucinated reality the mind constructions for you. If the magician can seed thoughts and ideas, it is you who creates the composition of the soil these will be planted in.

Have you ever found yourself in a situation at work that made you say 'I hate my job', and then shortly after this moment, things became worse and worse until you could not bear to be there anymore? As soon as you started thinking you didn't like it, more and more evidence proving that *fact* leaked into your reality, until finally you were undeniably correct.

What about when we found someone to be untrustworthy or disinterested in you? People are capable of such a wide range of behaviours – both good and bad – yet when we associate a dominant trait to an individual, there is likely to be an abundance of evidence following any assessment we can use to verify all of our beliefs.

The more you understand this is happening, the more it becomes apparent. Most of us know a person who is able to spot the good in anyone. Perhaps you have seen the amazing variety of people on the Internet who can create art or music from seemingly useless everyday objects? I believe the artists' eyes and musicians' ears have all been programmed by the higher self. People with those traits wanted to enhance them, and the higher self obliged.

A far more sinister example of this can be sometimes seen in the way society's teenagers talk to themselves. If you think hard enough, I am sure you will be able to recall seeing or hearing a teenage boy indirectly make fun of an older male. The older man might have some undesirable trait such as being overweight, stuck in a boring job, have a partner that doesn't care for him etc. and the younger male might choose to mock those things. This can go far enough to hear the teenager make careless throwaway remarks, something along the lines of 'kill me if I ever end up like that'.

Before he knows it fifteen years pass by and the boy is now a man in his mid-thirties. Perhaps life was tough and didn't turn out as expected and he woke up one day to find himself in a similar situation he had mocked all those years prior. Obviously, he would have long forgotten consciously instructing what to do in those circumstances, but the higher self certainly would not.

It is well-publicised that there is a suicide epidemic among men between the ages of thirty-fifty-years-old. There are multiple facets to this issue, but to my mind, one of them is attributed to incorrectly understanding and instructing the higher self. I think it should not be dismissed that our aspects of mainstream society allow the broadcast of teenage boys behaving in such a way. There are numerous examples of this that I can refer people to throughout our TV shows and films.

When I made this connection, I initially found it very unsettling to consider what we say today has a potential to hurt us in twenty years. It took me some time to learn how it is possible to reverse these types of effects. I now believe through by understanding the basics of these processes occurring deep within the mind and employing some particular techniques, we can correct any negative orientation created from incorrectly priming this part of ourselves.

Through my studies I have become aware of various different ideas surrounding how to instruct the higher self for our benefit, some of which span back to the Victorian era. Much of what I researched I went onto try out myself. Some things were more productive than others. Typically these ideas were originally created by people who wanted to increase financial wealth. But, I began to see certain things could be adapted and used for personal growth and spiritual purposes.

To keep this chapter to a manageable size, I will focus on explaining a few of my most effective findings. These are simple, easy techniques that you can start using today. I believe this potent blend of different methods, used by a variety of people over the last century can bring powerful positive change to your reality and redirect the course of your life for the better.

Auto-suggestion

This is a psychological technique that was developed by Émile Coué at the beginning of the twentieth century. At its core, this term refers to understanding how to use different stimuli through our five main senses to induce self-administered suggestion into the subconscious, or higher self. It focuses on developing an understanding of communication between that part of the mind in which conscious thought takes place and how this can then transfer into the subconscious.

It is my understanding that Coué was trying to teach us that no thought either positive, negative or neutral can transfer into the subconscious mind without the aid of auto-suggestion. I will mention here that I believe thoughts and ideas picked up from the collective consciousness are an exception and can bypass auto-suggestion. I will touch upon this in later chapters, but to simplify my understandings for the moment I will primarily focus on what you are able to control.

I believe evolution has brought us to a point in our development where we have an extremely high level of control over the thoughts that can enter our subconscious. The issue is that very few people seem to be aware of how to use this gift we have all been blessed with to their advantage. In my interactions with people, it appears the vast majority are oblivious to this fact, which perhaps explains to some degree why many people experience life in a way that displeases them.

A large number of people have some intuitive awareness that what they say and think can potentially shape their reality. I am in no doubt this is why mantras and affirmation practices are so popular. In recent years, various manifestation techniques have also become somewhat mainstream. I expect you will know that all of the above ideas seem to produce very mixed results. Some people swear that these things produce amazing results while others find them to be a waste of time.

I believe the reasons for these varied results are quite simple. Firstly, the language used to describe these techniques is quite mysterious and therefore, perhaps not very relatable to certain people. Secondly, words without feelings to back them up are hollow and ineffective. Remember earlier I wrote your higher self is akin to an ethereal stenographer, recording everything you think and feel? Well, the things that cause the biggest ripples in your life, both good and bad, always have the highest levels of feelings attached to them. There is no exception to this rule in my mind and understanding this is key.

For you to begin using auto-suggestion to program your higher self for the better, you absolutely must understand the importance of attaching emotion to the things you say, do and want. I believe the higher self recognises and prioritises listening to emotional feelings over all other forms of stimuli. The lack of understanding surrounding this fact is why I believe manifestation, affirmations and mantras are ineffective for many of the people who attempt them.

If you use spoken words to ask for what you want, but do not truly believe you deserve, or feel these things to be true, then they are just words. Hollow words are easily forgotten because the real meaning when using language comes from the attached levels of emotions.

Realistic Belief

Before I explain how I have adapted an easy-to-follow and highly effective method to instruct your higher self for the better, there are two more points I must explain. The first is one I simply call *realistic belief*, and it is a straightforward but essential concept.

If you set yourself a massive goal and get to work every day trying to achieve it, but results come slower than expected what happens? Typically after some time of hard work you will naturally become tired. Then perhaps you decide it's time for a break away from all that effort. Finally, once you halt the routine to rest, it is common that you will not want to pick things back up. It doesn't matter what you had achieved, the idea of getting back to all of that hard work now seems impossible.

I am sure we have all been there at some point in life. Realistic belief addresses this by asking that you do not aim to be a millionaire next month neither an awakened Buddha by Christmas. It is not to say these things are impossible to achieve but realistic belief invites you to focus upon an entirely believable target that can be achieved in a manageable timeframe. The magic happens when you begin to see that just as with climbing a staircase, each small achievement takes you closer to the scaling heights that might seem unobtainable when starting the journey.

Now, I believe repetition is essential to programming the higher self. The method I am about to share will require you to dedicate a few minutes each morning when you wake, and then again before bed. If you follow these steps I am certain there will be subtle but powerful alterations in the way your higher self constructs the hallucinated reality that is shown to your conscious awareness.

Subliminal Priming

This a technique used by the biggest marketing agencies around the World for decades. It was discovered that certain forms of stimuli can occur so quickly you will have no conscious awareness they have occurred. Yet, this stimuli can still influence you and your decision-making process.

It does not take a genius to work out how this can be of huge benefit to companies wishing to sell you their products and services. In recent years, people have been developing dieting methods that integrate this technique to help people eat less. I also believe certain self-help gurus have used this idea to help people become more individualistic. It has also been suggested that some of the World's most successful sports teams have developed methods to help build better teams through priming individuals to be more collectivist.

This is an extremely deep topic that I could write an entire book on. But for now, I would like you to know that you actually have the power to prime yourself for whatever life you want. This can be done through words and numbers, sensory priming and physical actions.

Auto-suggestion was on the right path when it was developed, but adding realistic belief and subconscious priming, in my opinion, turbo charges what Coué discovered. Integrating all of these methods into your routine will begin to train your higher self to effortlessly notice and prompt you to take advantage of every single opportunity that will aid in achieving your dreams.

I have broken this down into a five step, easy-to-follow process I have named Panoptic Mapping. My intent here is to explain a method that is so simple and easy to use that everyone from skeptics to absolute beginners will create positive results very quickly.

The Panoptic Mapping Method

1: Language selection

It is time to immediately stop talking negatively about yourself. Not even in jest. Self-descriptive phrases that are loaded with any form of negative orientation must be eliminated from your way of life, right now.

For example, sometimes when we make silly mistakes we might ask, why am I so stupid? Making errors can often be met with a sense of emotional discomfort such as frustration. Asking a question or uttering a phrase loaded with negativity and strong emotions will enter into the subconscious with ease. The higher self will respond by showing you all the reasons you are an idiot. This can trigger a cycle of perpetual self-loathing much faster than you might initially think.

However, while you are adjusting to only speaking and thinking kindly about yourself there will likely be slip ups. If you find yourself accidentally saying or thinking something negative don't panic. Instead pause, smile and apologise to yourself while saying or thinking two positive things.

Select your language in same way you would choose a fine wine. Sample what feels good and make sure you enjoy your thoughts and words. Do this for thirty days and I assure you there will be an improvement in how you feel about the World.

2: Rewrite Your Map

If you do not know where you want to go, how will you get there? If you have no idea of what you want how will you achieve it? Society has developed a perfect map that you have been lead to believe shows the path to a happy life: Go to school, work hard and get accepted to a university; graduate, maybe take a year out and see some of the World. Then it's time to start a high-flying career. Along this phase of the journey we should be open to finding the partner we will marry. Once that is ticked off then surely a mortgage and children are not too far into the future.

You have done well to this point, so now it's time to start saving for those lovely family holidays and material trappings that will further validate your happiness. Once we have achieved that over the course of fifteen years or so, it's then time to start planning and building towards your retirement.

Does any of this sound familiar? Are there parts of this map you want but feel pressured to accept those bits that don't appeal? Have friends and relatives spent years reminding you of their ideas for your own future? Maybe you feel guilty that you are half way down a particular road and have decided it's not for you. Do you see it out or turn and run in another direction?

Wherever you are and whatever has brought you to this point, it's time to pause and think. No matter if you love life or want something new, today is the day to sit and write your own map. I do this myself every three months. I would not jump into a boat and sail out to sea without either a map or compass, so why would I attempt to blindly navigate life!

So, four times a year I take an hour or so to sit and reflect on where I am, what I have achieved and what I want over the coming months. I use realistic belief and kind affirmative language to detail simply and clearly what my desires are for the next three months. Émile Coué spent years developing his auto-suggestion method and although I have adapted it by blending other concepts, I will always write the first line of my maps using his famous phrase.

'Day by day in every way, I am getting better and better…'

This language, although simple, has been designed specifically to empathise to the unconscious or, higher self that you consciously desire both physical and mental improvement. Below is a the framework of a map that I regularly use that you can simply adapt and fill in the bracketed sections of to match your current desires.

Day by day in every way, I am getting better and better…
I choose to feel (*realistic desire*) more and more.
I want to see (*realistic desire*) more and more.
I wish to build (*realistic desire*) day by day.

As your confidence in this method increases and the results begin to show themselves you will start to see that your definition of realistic belief shifts for the better. There is no point in writing I wish to see one million in my bank, if you are overdrawn and in debt today. You will likely not believe it is possible and your words will therefore lack the emotional stimulus needed to enact the change.

It is absolutely possible for you to attract the finance, lifestyle and mindset you wish for. However, I often feel that incorrectly understanding the mechanisms behind realistic belief blocks many people from achieving this. Success in all forms comes from a long-term mindset, often mantras and affirmations are only used for a short while.

My quarterly map method allows you a chance to effectively survey the terrain ahead of you. It offers you a chance to pause and look ahead before you take a new path. When you find success in this technique it will activate a powerful positive feedback mechanism that will drive bigger and more dramatic changes heading into the future.

3: Shift & Repeat

More than once throughout this chapter I have spoken about the importance of emotions and feelings. I believe spoken words and conscious thoughts are like small parcels waiting to be delivered to the higher self. As with all parcels that we send, they need the aid of a courier to reach their intended destination. Feelings and emotions effectively provide this delivery method.

As with all postal services different options are available. You can pay out and use a priority service or you save some money and select a basic option. Obviously, the less you want to pay the slower the service will be and the longer the delivery will take. Every single day for your entire life you have been unknowingly shipping various packages to the higher self, using different services.

This chapter is designed to reveal how you can start sending a few each day that are of your own choosing. Once you have written a map for your next three months, you will need to understand how it will be delivered to your higher self. The answer is quite simple and can be broken into three stages.

First: You must understand that a positive emotion will deliver to the higher self quicker than a neutral or negative one. So before focusing on your map, you must take a moment to recall something pleasant. You must really get into the vibe of feeling good. This can initially be very difficult if you have never attempted to do this before, but I assure you that practise will make perfect.

Second: Once you are in a state of feeling good you must read your map out loud. This process needs to be done first thing in the morning before you start your day and again just before bed. You must truly believe you deserve what you are asking for. It helps to believe that you deserve it so much it has already happened, you are just reminding the Universe to give it back to you.

If you lost a wallet and heard one had been handed into the local shop, you would have no hesitation in going to ask for it back. The shopkeeper would likely know just by looking at your face that you truly believed it belonged to you and it would take minimal effort on your part for them to give it back.

Ask for what you want with this level of intent and determination. Blend that with being in a positive state of emotion and the Universe will absolutely relent to your wishes. Everything you want is already rightfully yours, you have simply forgotten this fact. There is no shortage of energy in this Universe. Do not fear that there isn't enough to go around, because there certainly is! Abundance exists everywhere, and is available to everyone – including you, but you have simply been distracted from this fact up until this point.

4: Totems & Notes

The final stage of delivering your map to the higher self regards the principles of subliminal priming, specifically sensory priming.

Take a moment to list in your mind five to ten of the most common spaces you visit daily. Bedroom, bathroom, garage, car, workplace; the options are endless, but I want you to think about the places you have some influence over.

Within these spaces it is essential you load cues that will continually prime your higher self to recall what you want added to your hallucinated, reconstructed reality. For example, if you are trying to bring more money in and have written a total on your latest quarterly map, you can also write that amount on sticky notes and place them around in subtle locations.

This is distinctly different from manifestation boards because the prompts must be much smaller. The aim of priming is to use small objects, notes and numbers that trigger the higher self into searching out the opportunities you require. Notes and totems placed about areas you frequent daily in a way that you can observe them, but don't consciously pay attention to is essential. It is a powerful form of reinforcement that will help increase the speed that you are able to achieve your various targets.

Play with sticking notes on your computer or leave them in the centre console of your car. Get creative and try to locate places you see but rarely pay attention to. Perhaps you can buy some fridge magnets and leave single words relating to your desires on display. Tiny little photo clippings left on the corners of shelves or reoccurring reminders on your gadgets are also effective. There is no limit to the creativity you can deploy in loading your frequently used spaces with sensory primes that keep your higher self on track.

5: Balancing The Equation

What would you do to receive one million in your bank account tomorrow? This is a question we have no doubt all frequently heard throughout life. Some of the answers are entertaining, others are obvious, certain people have also provided hilarious or shocking responses.

This question highlights a very deep process that occurs within the mind. That is, how we analyse the cost and reward ratio of many things within this World. We are almost continually making assessments about ourselves and our environments. Research points to us having an entire system within the brain that is dedicated to coordinating the multiple aspects of thinking that help us to make decisions.

At the centre of this reward system is an area of the brain called the striatum. Action planning, reinforcement, motivation and reward perception are all functions that are said to originate from this place. It has also been shown that notable changes can be observed within this centre among people who have addictive behaviours. Particular habits that have become deeply ingrained are also said to influence the structure of this system.

I draw your attention towards these points for the purpose of highlighting two important truths. First, many of us naturally expect, that to gain something, we must give something. We work for the outcome of money, then we can exchange that money for something we want or need. Sometimes we help others in exchange for favour at a later point. These are basic examples of an important principle; the mind often reasons in a transactional nature when considering what is the best path to acquiring certain things in life.

Second, I want to demonstrate that it is actually possible to rewire the area of the brain that processes the cost and reward of any given situation. Research has clearly demonstrated this can be done in a negative way. However, as I have already spoken about earlier, many of us live our lives on autopilot and therefore, are not often setting out to make positive change within the brain.

The final point of my five step Panoptic Mapping technique is designed to appease the cost-reward system while working to rewire it for your benefit. If you find yourself often assuming good won't happen for you, or that you somehow don't deserve things in life, this method can eventually reshape these orientations for the better.

Once you have completed the first four steps, it is time to take care of the little voice that reminds you nothing comes for free. Many of us believe that in order to get what we truly want, there must be a cost. Eventually, as you rewire your mind and expand the consciousness, these illusions will begin to evaporate. However, before a person reaches that point, it is extremely important to provide the mind with the fee you are prepared to pay for receiving any of desires you have requested within your latest quarterly map.

Fortunately, this is not a complicated process. I invite people to refer back to realistic belief – but this time, use the principle to decide what reasonable, believable action should be exchanged for what you have requested. This need not be a massive commitment, and again you can use as much creativity as desired when thinking about the fee. So, I will always add this additional line below the map.

In exchange for receiving what I have asked for in this map, I will be happy to (insert fee)

In the past, I have made commitments to volunteer my time to a number of charitable and environmental causes. I have also offered a number of free spiritual services and donations to my local food bank, in lieu of receiving the map requests I have asked for. It is no hardship for me to offer these things in exchange, and it satisfies the natural transactional thought structures that often come alongside making requests for our benefit.

Many years ago, when I first experimented with affirmations, mantras and manifestation techniques, I lacked belief. I often felt that I was an imposter, asking for things I neither deserved or had earned. It was not until I considered the true effects of our brains' give and take nature that things really changed.

Feeding this important system will go towards eliminating any doubt that you might not deserve what you have requested. This final step is often the energy that dictates the speed in which you receive what you have asked for. Believing that you deserve is essential, offering a suitable fee for your written map requests to be granted, increases the energy of belief almost instantly.

As you become comfortable with Panoptic Mapping, you will likely discover your reward system changes your belief orientation. The result of this change will be; Instead of worrying you don't deserve, you will instead become comfortable in your belief that you are allowed to ask for what you want.

When I teach the importance of writing and enacting these quarterly maps, I will always invite people to take care and accept the responsibility of asking for what they want. We often think we want something or someone and then live to regret it.

This technique is extremely powerful, beneficial and straightforward to use. But if you end up with what you thought you wanted and it wasn't good enough, you might discard this method as useless and search for something else.

For millennia, the happiest and most successful people have all understood the importance of knowing thyself on a deeper level and taking control of undesirable mental processes. I lost a dear friend to suicide as a younger man and there was no more of an important indicator to how much the mind and the higher self should be respected and understood.

The Buddhists ask us; Do you know what kind of world you are shaping for yourself and people around you? Every single day each and every single one of us use our words to shape the World around us while announcing our intentions and desires.

Harsh language is often used so flippantly we are unaware of the true extent it can affect us. It is said that your language has the power to destroy you and poison the World around you. Or, more importantly the spoken word can be used to plant the seeds of beautiful flowers in both your mind and that of others. Words that improve the feeling of yourself and invoke positive feelings in others can bear fruit for years to come.

Thankfully we all have the power to undo any damage accidentally caused by using language, thoughts and feelings that are not useful to us. You can begin correcting your path today simply by writing a positive map for the next three months and using the techniques I have described daily. If you have never tried anything like this before I would urge you to be patient and make a determined agreement with yourself to try this method for at least three months.

At the beginning of this chapter I asked you if a magician could plant an idea or thought in your mind then what would you choose? It took me many years to connect the dots and realise that I am both simultaneously the magician and the person he is entertaining. It's as if I wrapped the seeds and left them out but did not know the postman took the parcels and delivered them. I then act surprised when things grow that I had not really wanted.

Perhaps we made an agreement before birth that I would forget the dynamics of this relationship. Maybe I thought he could better perform his tricks if it was a surprise. Relearning the power *the magician* has to reconstruct reality in front of me, and my role in this act, has resulted in changes to my life that can definitely be regarded as magical.

Buddha himself said; 'Happiness comes when your words are pure, bringing about kindness and benefit to yourself and others.' This quote is a beautiful simplistic reminder of what our words can do. I feel the topic of our higher self could easily consume an entire book, but for now I hope you can use this information to begin taking powerful steps forward while reconnecting with this part of yourself from a fresh perspective.

Every single thing you witness within this World that was created by a person started as nothing but an idea. Ideas at their best, power the development of human society for the better. At their worst, ideas have the power to create widespread destruction and misery. We are all capable of programming the higher self to deliver an abundance of either type.

Using the methods I have described in this chapter, can give you increased control over the orientation of which ones you receive heading into the future. All that you observe in this World can become destinations you gravitate towards. Study these things, but remember, the best thing about a map is if you don't like one path you can choose another.

There is a free to download, printable map template available on my website at the link below. You can simply print your copy and begin your Panoptic Mapping journey today: www.TheTheoryOfYou.com/Assets

CHAPTER 7

Living With Your Mind

I BELIEVE THAT ON some level, we all have an inherent desire to be connected with others. At times, today's society can almost feel like a giant popularity contest that is trying to draw us into participating with, regardless of if we want it or not. It is natural to seek emotional comfort and self-confidence through others' approval, and we often enjoy the feelings of support that our personal relationships can deliver. Many people will use the feelings that social validation and acceptance from others delivers, as a way to measure if they are on the correct path.

With all of the wonderful shared experiences, material distractions, goals and achievements the external world can offer, it is of no surprise that our societies have slowly moved away from improving the self, through discovery of knowledge that cannot be seen or measured.

Throughout history, numerous cultures not only accepted the quest for introspective knowledge as a natural and noble pursuit, but they actively encouraged creating systems to identify and support individuals with the traits required to potentially take this journey.

The ancient Greeks were famous for the philosophers their culture produced. They set up systems of development to encourage people to journey within themselves to find unique answers to the common problems that many people faced.

Today this type of inner personal development has been cast aside by much of society. As a result, we can find ourselves on the path looking for the deeper answers to life in the external world instead. Maybe if we travel, live with monks or have a particular experience, the answers we seek will show themselves?

Society promotes competition as an attempt to prove one idea or way of thinking is better than another and the winners of these numerous competitions often use their victories as a platform to dismiss others' methods or ideas as wrong.

This is part of the reason why I believe we see people struggle to find long-lasting happiness. At this point I would like to state; happiness is not something that can be won. I believe the pursuit of true happiness comes from a system of thought and understanding that allows us to be prepared to acknowledge and receive the previously unknown.

Thoughts and ideas should be treated like oxygen. We don't compete for breath, we just trust that there has been, and always will be enough air to sustain us and every other living being on this planet. We can breathe faster or slower than someone else. We can breathe deeper or shallower than others.

Fish use their gills, some whales can survive on two breaths per hour, and a particular species of turtle can live on one inhalation every seventy-two hours. Certain snakes only have one lung and some salamanders can absorb all the oxygen they need through their skin alone. All of these methods are right; all of them work and it wouldn't matter if we tried to prove our way of breathing was the best.

As a young boy, I was given a set of encyclopedias that had been printed some years before I was born in the early 1970s. I often spent extended periods of time alone in my room, and with the absence of technology to distract me there was little else to do but read. I developed a keen interest in these books and found lots of the information written to be fascinating.

I was not very interested in school during this stage of life, but reading books of my own choosing at my own pace felt very rewarding. At the time, I was enjoying these encyclopedias they were already around twenty years old, but I saw no reason to question the knowledge they contained.

One of my particularly favourite volumes was a fairly detailed atlas and over the course of about two years I picked up a reasonable amount of the countries names and locations.

As I grew older and was introduced to more complex subjects at school, I remember very clearly the day we started learning geography. Our teacher gave us books that contained current maps of the World at that time and set us some work to do.

I started flicking through this newer atlas and after a while I began to notice some things didn't seem right. Where was Zaire? I had studied my atlas at home many times and knew exactly where it *should* be. Why was the Democratic Republic of the Congo in its place? As I scanned that page, I grew even more confused to see Rhodesia was called Zimbabwe. After a while, in the absence of any logical answer I asked the teacher who was a little surprised to hear I knew of these countries. She then explained to me how revolution and war can cause the collapse of one country and the birth of another.

It was at this moment I learnt a very important lesson; Information that can be so true it is published in an encyclopedia one day is possible to be changed, disproven or improved upon a few short years later. In my adult life I have looked over these books and found more and more outdated information. One volume speaks of the World's most powerful microscope, which in 1970 is a fraction of what has become available forty plus years later.

Within the books are also terms used to refer to ethnic populations that would cause outrage if printed today. Through all of this, I realised at a very young age the importance of having an open mind. Understanding since I was a boy that, what can be true one day can just as easily become incorrect later down the line – this became a cornerstone to my perception of this World.

As the years went on and I developed my mind, I realised this attitude towards the truth and how it is possible to discover something new had an unexpected positive side effect. By conditioning my mind to accept that a change in what I believe to be true today is highly possible in the future, I was in fact telling myself there is always more to come. This might sound like a small and inconsequential point but, let me ask you – how do you feel when you realise something is finished?

How do you feel when your favourite TV program finishes after years of watching? What about when the last few days of an amazing holiday or vacation are closing in and you know you have to return home? How about when you visit your favourite restaurant and realise your favourite dish is off the menu and you are unlikely to ever taste it again?

Fundamentally, it is in our nature to want. We want to be warm and safe, we want to have the right job, we want the right friends, to be with the right partner, we want to achieve a whole host of things in our lives. Everything we do can be considered in some way connected to our *wants*.

So ask yourself, what actually happens when you decide that some belief or attitude you subscribe to is undisputedly correct? Take it a step further and ask what actually happens if you prove any idea you have to be right over another person's viewpoint? I would invite you to consider for a moment the after effect of winning an argument.

In my view, a win is just a way for the mind to say 'that's it', now we don't need to learn anything more on the subject. We won, so our views and ideas are the best, and now we have beaten those who tried to dispel us, we can hold onto this way of thinking forever.

Well, isn't that attitude in direct opposition to the very core of what it means to be human? The want to be *right* has the power to override the basic want to learn and have more in life. To me this paradox, absolutely has to be overcome if we wish to bring in personal enlightenment. I will always be thankful for those early memories of the incorrect encyclopedic information. What I once believed to be the undeniable truth, only to learn that outdated ideas had been replaced with new information, helped shape my mind to have an advantage in later life.

Every time the urge to prove someone wrong stirs deep within the core of my being, I just smile and remember that what I know today is a fraction of what I will know in five years time. Proving someone wrong today does not mean they won't prove me wrong in the future. This open mindset has made me continuously ready to hear fresh viewpoints and I am excited for what knowledge the future will bring.

Now, it is possible you have read all of what has been written so far and not a single piece of this information is new to you. It is also possible that over the years you have developed your own highly effective ideas and coping mechanisms. You might already have a power system in place to help accept your reality and find the mental stillness needed for developing the self. The opposite is also possible and you might be feeling trapped in this World, feeling everything is too much for you to cope with.

Maybe you have tried various methods to help bring the calmness to your mind you seek. Wherever you are on your journey I would like you to understand that all of the ideas I have talked about are simple, free and available to anyone, anywhere, facing any circumstances. With some discipline and routine you can easily add all of the techniques I have discussed into your life, whatever is happening.

You do not need to have any drastic upheaval of living, neither should you turn your back on everything you already know and do. There is no one who can change a single second of any of our past experiences and you are free to hold onto them for as long as you wish. However, I do believe, although we will all have undoubtedly experienced a lack of control in preventing some of the most difficult days of our lives from occurring, each and every one of us has the ability to control how we perceive these moments heading into our future.

There are numerous other techniques I use that are available to fine-tune your experience of this reality as you develop and head forwards in life. For me though everything we have spoken about so far – if factored into your daily routines – will provide the basis for a quieter and more disciplined mind. This increased discipline will then allow you to start using the power of your mind in new and exciting ways.

We all have our own perceptions of this World we exist in and I feel that my work is to demonstrate how to open a door. I want you to understand there is no rule that says you need to be bound to anything in this life. There is no rule to my knowledge that says you must be trapped by your current or past circumstances. Nor should you remain stuck; trapped in a cycle of questioning yourself or the events of the past.

Every single waking moment you are here within this space can be the moment you decide to turn everything upside down and choose a new path. It is up to you to decide whether this is a door you wish to open and, if you wish to walk through it or not.

Many people will claim to tell you what every stage of your spiritual development will hold, the signs to look for and what to expect when it happens. I feel this not only takes the excitement out of what is to come, but it also preconditions you to look for certain things. Therefore, instead of telling you what to expect I choose instead to share the fuel I believe can prime the mind to function in a more beneficial state. The resulting freedom can empower you to decide what comes next.

If we put petrol in a diesel engine, the vehicle will still tick along for a while – The driver will still be able to decide which direction the car should travel in. But we know at some point, the engine will experience difficulties and then eventually, be unable to continue without being repaired.

If we want to reach our destination of choice in life, it is essential we prime the mind with the right fuel to make sure there are minimal difficulties along the road. The knowledge I have shared so far is the exact same framework to developing the tools and ideas that allowed me to coexist with my own mind in harmony.

It was not always easy to look back at certain parts of my life but I decided very early on that taking a journey of discovering how to accept what had come before and look towards my own future with excitement was much more preferable to becoming trapped and defined by the past. Accepting that there is no real way to control the external world while understanding, I do have power over my own mind helped me to find a strength that I believe we all possess.

You should be aware that when making alterations to the way you engage with your mind, particularly the higher self, there is a potential to experience what I call an energetic hangover. If you have not exercised for years you would not expect to run a marathon tomorrow. Training is required to get fighting fit, so I invite you to have patience with the process. There are no rules to how long change will take, but I can assure you that sticking to a path of change will absolutely bring it into your life.

If you choose to combine and implement all of the techniques I have discussed in this first section, and you apply a disciplined approach to making them part of your routines going forward, I believe an almost magical transformation can begin developing. Eventually, you will discover a fruit of this growth will be concentration in its purest form.

Concentration provides us the focus needed to actually recognise what the mind is doing. A secondary consequence of this will be, that no matter how often the mind wants to recall the past, imagine lofty future goals or distract you with pointless thoughts, you will be able to ground it back in the present moment.

After a while of living this way it will then become possible to see that a deep connection with the present moment causes the forces of fear, worry, anxiety and depression to evaporate. Finally, at this stage, you can discover in your own way that explaining things by the past is actually an avoidance of explaining them at all. All it serves to do is postpone you accepting and moving past that which does not benefit you. This journey might not feel easy or comfortable at times, but I believe the most difficult paths lead to the greatest destinations.

Learning to understand my mind was an essential part of unlocking the puzzle to discover who I am. But as I mentioned earlier, this is only one part of us. There are two other distinct and equally fascinating systems we must explore to complete the picture. I believe these first chapters have offered the foundations to explore the mind from a powerful perspective. I am certain this information, if implemented into your life with determination, will not only help you to live with the mind in a new way, but additionally will lay the foundations to answer some of life's most challenging questions.

PART 2

The Body

CHAPTER 8

The Dust That Holds You

WE ALL UNDERSTAND THAT it is not possible to physically dissect the mind. If we open up a brain, it is not possible to extract the mind because it can't be seen. It is the bridge between the unseen consciousness and the material observable physical self. The mind is made of something we all know exists but no one can explain what it is built from. A different set of rules apply to the body though, we can all see our bodies. It is possible to sense and feel the physical self and science has a pretty good understanding of what materials we are made from.

But what exactly is our body? Unlike the mind, the physical being is made from visible matter, so this naturally lends itself to being understood in a much more scientific way. I believe the body has a lot to answer for, this physical arrangement of matter can bring us a diverse range of both positive and negative sensations. Things can feel painful or pleasurable; we have all felt too hot or too cold. Some people love the taste and benefits of garlic while others are physically allergic to it, and therefore it would ruin a dish for them.

The physical self can drive us to behave in some unpredictable ways and I decided many years ago that if I could better understand this system, then logically I would be able to live more comfortably with myself.

What exactly is your body? On the face of it, this is a simple question and for me understanding what exactly we are made from started as a personal curiosity to try and improve my physical health. As this knowledge began to develop, I ended up discovering powerful lessons about how I could harness this system to live a far more comfortable life.

As the years have passed, more and more people began to ask me, what they can do to develop spiritually. It progressed to the point I now receive messages almost every single day requesting this form of support. It is fascinating to me that nearly every single person I have ever spoken to about this topic either wants guidance on interacting with spiritual energy, validation that they are on the correct path or what they need to do during meditation to reach their aims.

When I speak with people to discover how I can help, I can guarantee they have overlooked the importance of working with the physical self. To highlight the significance of this I will often use the following question: If I were to ask you to light an incense stick in your home while being sure to create an atmosphere that would allow the smoke to fill and remain in a room of your choosing, how would you go about this task?

Would you open all the windows and allow a breeze to circulate? Obviously not; any draft will cause the smoke to rapidly dissipate. In this analogy, the smoke represents spiritual energy and the house represents your body. We can buy and burn all the incense we want, but if we do not learn how to create the correct physical environment there is little chance of us enjoying its effects for long.

So where do we start on this next stage of our journey together? Well it turns out that before we can get to the bottom of how and why this system influences us in the ways it does, there are some pretty interesting questions that need to be addressed.

I imagine many of you are familiar with the connection that our physical bodies at their source come from the stars themselves. There are numerous well-documented quotes from various high-profile scientists and astronomers from the last one-hundred or so years highlighting the link between the deaths of ancient stars and the building blocks of life itself. One of my favourite and simplest ways to sum this up was written in 1973 by Carl Sagan. He said:

'Our Sun is a second – or third – generation star. All of the rocky and metallic material we stand on, the iron in our blood, the calcium in our teeth, the carbon in our genes were produced billions of years ago in the interior of a red giant star. We are made of star-stuff.'

Is this idea not beautiful? To consider that stars dying billions of years ago are directly responsible for life on Earth today, is to my mind, almost a form of universal poetry. I certainly remember the fascination I experienced when realising this as a child. In my mind, after this revelation took hold though, some other questions began to arise.

If we are alive and we are made from stardust when did that dust become alive? The dust from the death of stars isn't floating around in space alive so how am I alive? Eventually, I learned that to the best of our knowledge everything in the Universe is made from the same materials. This only lead to further questions: If everything is made out of the same things, is it all dead or is it all alive? If I am made from dust that is not alive can I ever die because am I even alive to start with? What is actually being alive and at what point did I become alive?

You can see the obvious difficulties these types of questions can raise. Personally, I am grateful for the philosophical rabbit hole that enquiring about these things presents, and even more-so for the eventual answers they gifted me. The next few chapters will be dedicated to sharing with you the process of discovery that brought me a deeper understanding of myself, which then eventually revealed to me why we can all be prone to certain behaviours in life.

It is natural for us to think in a linear fashion, so I will start answering these questions by beginning with the atomic scale; as this is the building blocks of all physical matter. We will then work upwards from that point. If our atoms come from the stars themselves how is this dust arranged inside us? How are we actually made of stardust? The answer to this is relatively straightforward. A quick search online will show various scientific and mathematical calculations demonstrating exactly how the physical matter that makes-up our bodies came about and what percentage of our cells, is made up by this.

But to very simply summarise, our cells take in the elemental matter that itself comes from material created in the ancient furnaces of long dead stars. OK great, so our cells contain atomic particles made from stars! So what is a cell? Again referring to simple online searches will provide numerous in-depth answers, but in summary: A cell is the smallest structural and functional unit of an organism.

Most of us will understand that we are made from trillions of cells. Cells provide our bodies with structure, they take in nutrients from the food we consume and convert it into energy. Various types of cells also carry out specialised functions in an attempt to keep our bodies working as efficiently as possible. This information is widely known and accepted, if however we probe a little deeper; to me, the function of cells becomes somewhat confusing. We accept we are alive and that we are made of cells. In fact, all life as we understand it is made of cells. Just one problem though, no part of a cell is actually alive.

The individual cell has many characteristics that we associate with life, but is unable to perceive itself or experience feelings and emotions. Instead, the cell's function is to create chemical reactions and change matter from one thing into another. It does this in an attempt to create more of itself and therefore ensure its continued survival.

Although no part of the cell is alive it would seem the only goal of the cell is to prevent death by producing new entities. I would like you to note this seemingly small piece of information, as once I discovered this it eventually revealed some very insightful answers to some big problems that many of us face in this World. This ultimate function of a cell's goal to ensure survival, offered me some deeply personal solutions to some of society's big issues.

If we return back to the hunt for the point in which life becomes alive, the next logical step would be to look at DNA; after all, this is what our cells produce. If the cells are the building blocks of all life as we understand it, DNA would be considered the building blocks of *you* as an individual. Each and every one of us has a unique DNA code that separates us in some way from everybody else, so is this what makes us alive? Well although it is complex, I doubt many of us would argue DNA is alive. Very much like the cells, DNA cannot perceive or feel itself so therefore it is not alive.

As we climb the ladder of what a physical body is made of, the answer to where life begins remains elusive. For example, we can lose blood and receive a transfusion from someone else but not become them. If we lost a limb that part of us can die but we are still alive, even before the death of the limb it would not be considered that there was temporally two of us. Eventually, along the path of analysing various bodily functions, we can reach a point where the brain would perhaps seem highly significant in the question of life - as we consider this the seat of our personality.

But, ultimately the brain in all its complexity is still made from cells that are made from things that are not alive. The more we probe this question, the more apparent it becomes that at a point we have to accept there is some unseen additional force that takes us from being a collection of cells, DNA, muscles, organs and a brain, to something that is alive.

I believe this is evident when we consider the effect of the nervous system on the body. The nerves and brain can be physically seen, but they do not work without the input of electrical stimuli. Our entire nervous system is built around transmitting unseen signals to a brain that has an unseen force operating within it that is able to process and interpret these signals almost instantaneously.

It is entirely possible to preserve the physical body after death through freezing or perhaps embalming, but it is currently impossible to preserve this unseen life-force that powers us as a person and individual. Originally, I wanted to try and analyse the physical body and all of its components in attempt to build upon my knowledge of both myself and where life for all of us started. These are natural questions that I am sure many of us have thought about periodically throughout our lives, but the answers have provided many surprises for me.

What I found, took me on a tangent of discovery that helped to uncover some techniques that have allowed me to experience the longest period of uninterrupted good health in my entire life. As a child, I began experiencing what would later be diagnosed as chronic migraines. These migraines only intensified in both pain and frequency as I grew from a child into an adult. Eventually after many years of suffering, I ended up having to take medication daily in an attempt to keep them under control.

This cycle continued until I began to practise what I discovered. I can now happily say that since the age of thirty, I have not taken a single pain relief tablet. Neither have I even so much as had the flu. I have not needed antibiotics or other such medicine and went from visiting the doctor every few weeks to not needing an appointment for over five years. The last appointment I attended was for some travel advice and I spent most of the time with the doctor answering their questions about how my health had changed so drastically.

I have adapted what I have learnt over the years into some techniques that allow for me to truly help others overcome certain issues that severely hold people back in achieving a happy and fulfilling life. Again, I believe my understanding of working with the physical body could fill an entire book alone and I feel that in the future I will attempt to collate everything in one place. For now though I want to work with a few of what I feel to be, the most useful techniques that will allow almost anyone to induce and effectively maintain a calm and balanced state within the body.

CHAPTER 9

Overcome Your Anxieties

AFTER SOME DELIBERATION OVER which technique to start with, it felt like a good place to begin would be where the early realisations about how the physical processes within my own body could be harnessed to create a more comfortable way of living. In the wake of years spent attempting to understand and develop myself, eventually one day, things clicked and I was able to start seeing the dots of how one thing directly affected another within our bodies and what could be done to bring balance to the entire system.

One of the first common problems we all face, that I began to put these lessons to good use with, was anxiety. I discovered the principles I used to overcome this issue, also have additional benefits. Overcoming anxiety and depression can help create part of the physical conditions that I believe are essential to opening the doors towards increased spiritual connection. Anxiety is a complex and difficult condition that is unfortunately a blight on the lives of millions of us worldwide.

Anyone who has experienced it, will understand the range of negative emotions this can bring into daily living. Worrying about leaving the house, fearing interactions with strangers, sleepless nights, low energy and moods, constant self-doubt and questioning every single choice, are a few of the problems people have to face.

At the extreme end of the scale – amongst other troubling symptoms – people can experience unprovoked panic attacks, cold sweats and heart palpitations. It is common for the people I work who experience this condition, to feel defeated and that they somehow are not good enough or are abnormal. This is as far from the truth as one could be, nobody is 'not good enough' for this World and anxiety-related problems are a normal and understandable response to the difficulties of life. It does not make you or anyone weak for experiencing this. In fact, to my mind, it shows that you are alive and living!

It is my opinion that the World today is fixated on winning, beating, overcoming or defeating any obstacle; big or small. The aim of the game is to correct whatever is bothering us and rapidly move on. I feel people rarely pause and take the time to ask what is actually happening or for the reasons why. Even fewer of us will pause to reflect and look if there is something valuable to be learnt when faced with something uncomfortable.

I believe it is important that we all ask, what is the point of overcoming a problem if we have a lack of understanding about the conditions that brought the problem into existence to begin with? Anxiety is seen as something completely negative that must be removed from our life as quickly as possible. I agree that we should not have to accept feeling anxious long-term, but I feel it would certainly benefit all of us to pause for a moment and actually observe what is happening when we feel this way.

One particular woman I worked with felt the best way to fix her anxiety was to just avoid the thing that made her anxious. On the surface, this is quite a natural and logical response, remove the problem and move on. She had a fear that something bad would happen if she went for an evening out with her friends, if there was alcohol involved the issue was only heightened.

This anxiety escalated to the point that if she socialised at the weekend she would worry for the rest of the week that something bad had happened that she had forgotten about. Every day was a countdown waiting for someone to call her and tell her how awful she was. She revealed to me that she had started going out less and less in the hope it would stop the anxiety escalating. This problem had reached the point of physical discomfort and minor panic attacks in the days prior to and immediately after spending time in public with her friends – and it was time to tackle it as opposed to avoid it.

I listened to everything and then asked her, did she think it was fair that she should limit social contact with people she had known for years and miss out spending time with them individually or as a group? The answer was obviously 'no'. I then discussed with her that it was my belief that this method of dealing with the problem by removing the triggers only displaces the anxiety from one scenario to another, and I would expect that she would soon find herself struggling with a new fear to replace the old one.

She confirmed this was already happening and that she had felt worried about going to the shops alone in the days before we spoke. If we had not worked to break this cycle it wouldn't have been inconceivable to see her in a place of never leaving the house in an attempt to stop and control every possible situation that she was worried about.

I believe the simplest way we can begin to restore balance when faced with escalating anxiety is by returning to the question at the start of the previous chapter: What exactly is our body? This time however we need to dig a little deeper. You will recall we already discussed the fact that we are a collection of cells that are made-up from matter born in the centre of ancient stars, and that we also briefly spoke about some of the cells' functions.

We then touched on the magical ability of the brain to harness some unseen energy that is known to be the mind. It is the brain I would like to now talk about in more depth. Your brain is incredible, but because it has been with you since the start of your life it is easy to forget just how amazing it truly is. Right now you have one of the World's most powerful supercomputers inside your head. I suspect in the not too distant future computers will eventually surpass the human brain, but we are not there yet and can all enjoy our status as a top information processor for a little longer.

Your personal supercomputer right now is quietly sitting inside your head, monitoring everything about you and your surroundings twenty-four-seven. It does this to try and keep you and your cells as happy and safe as possible. Presently, you are occupied with reading this book but in the background your brain is effortlessly working on dealing with an endless stream of information while also working to regulate your heartbeat, breathing and temperature.

It will tell you if you are hungry or thirsty, it will let you know if any of your joints are aching, your blood pressure is being taken care of to the best ability your body can handle, and if the kidneys, liver and intestines are all being silently instructed to do their work as efficiently as possible. Hormones are being released as and when they are needed, while each time you do something the brain likes, it rewards you by releasing endorphins. To sum it all up, we could easily say your brain loves you. It takes care of you the best it can and wants to use any excuse possible to make you feel good.

Now, for a moment let us move away from the talking about these functions and get back to the topic of anxiety. It is at this point, I like to introduce a concept that is possibly a little controversial: Anxiety is good for you, I believe it serves a powerful and important role in life. Every single person I have ever heard of, helped or spoken with that has experienced persistent episodes of anxiety, all have one thing in common: That being the first attack can be traced back to having a perfectly valid reason behind why it occurred.

Perhaps someone experienced financial problems that escalated and got out of hand. Maybe they found themselves in difficulties with a partner and their behaviour. They might have worried about a situation at work getting out of control or a whole host of other unfortunate problems that can occur from time to time. Whatever the root cause, once we identify them, it is important to understand and to refer to these situations as legitimate anxieties.

When something comes along that has the power to disrupt the path of our lives, the brain responds by activating an early warning system to inform you that something needs to be done. I believe legitimate anxieties prompt the brain to kick this system into gear and tell you that *now* is your opportunity to try and rectify something for the better. I believe all of the classical responses we experience during an episode of legitimate anxiety are simply you being told by your brain that now is the time to act.

We should remember that if life was completely comfortable all of the time, would there be any reason to do anything at all? If we had all the money in the World, a fully stocked kitchen in the house of our dreams, how much motivation would we need to get up and do anything? I believe that discomfort and necessity are powerful driving forces behind action in this World.

During my work I have discovered there is another thing nearly everyone has in common relating to their first bout of anxiety, which is how good it felt once the problem was finally solved. What happens when we reach that wonderful moment and finally realise the problem is over? Usually a feeling of elation begins to rise within us, we walk around with a smile on our face and finally get to sleep easy again.

However, as people experience these welcome feelings they are prone to primarily focus on the emotional aspect of what is happening. Very few people take the time to ask what physical processes are unfolding within the body at these moments in life. I believe this oversight is precisely where the problems of persistent anxiety can begin. With this in mind, let us take some time to think about the physical side of anxiety as opposed to the emotional.

At the moment you realise any legitimate anxiety has been resolved, your brain responds physically to this external situation by releasing a rush of feel-good hormones. The larger the perceived anxiety, the bigger the problem solved, therefore the more of these mood enhancing chemicals are released. All who have experienced this will know this sense of happiness feels great and can last for days. Typically, a person will be so thankful the problem is finally sorted they will just want to enjoy the moment, and rightly so.

I doubt any of us would actually want to slow down and ask what is happening within our brains and what it all means for us long-term. Taking a moment to do this however, can have a profound impact upon how we view the nature of anxiety.

At this point in creating an effective long-term strategy for dealing with anxiety, the relevance of the brain's role starts to become important. Remember how I wrote about the fact that your brain wants to make you feel great? Well, the brain is on constant standby waiting for any excuse to release these feel-good neurotransmitters commonly known as endorphins.

Studies have demonstrated this and shown even the most simple of things such as laughter, eating spicy food, dark chocolate, exercise, meditation, even acts of generosity are all valid enough reasons for the brain to reward you with an endorphin release. Endorphins activate certain receptors within the brain that have been identified with pain and stress reduction, improved sense of general well-being and euphoria.

Research would point to the brain having a preference to achieving these states and by fixing that legitimate anxiety you offered a perfect reason to release a substantial amount of those chemicals to enhance your positive feelings. As with all chemical reactions though, the effects eventually subside and your mood will begin to return back to its natural baseline. Quite simply after a while the amazing feeling of fixing your problems wears off and life returns back to normal. I believe what happens next is where anxiety conditions can progress to the next stage – I call this transition the birth of the illegitimate anxieties.

Over the coming days, weeks and months, as life settles back to normal and the disruption that caused all of the original problems turns into memories you would rather forget, something odd beings to happen. This process is slightly different for every one and there is no set time-limit for these events to begin. None of us know if it will be a few days, a week, six months or perhaps a year, but the way in which long-lasting anxiety creeps into our World is nothing more than a whisper to start with.

A typical scenario of how this unfolds is surprisingly simple. For example, one day you wake up, you are not expected to be overly busy; it is just a normal day in the routine of your life. However, shortly after you get out of bed and go about your activities you become aware of a feeling, like a small knot is in the pit of your stomach. You ignore it at first, but as the day progresses so does this feeling.

Finally, you pause and take a moment to ask yourself, what is it? Something you ate yesterday? No not that! Did you leave the lights on at home or is the back door unlocked? Did you forget to engage the parking break in your car? There is a particular relative or friend you have not heard from for a while, are they OK?

After fifteen minutes of worrying; a quick trip outside to check the car; you send some messages and make a few quick calls – The result is, you realise everyone and everything is perfectly fine, now you can relax. You breathe a sigh of relief, the knot has finally gone now that you have checked everything out and found everything is ok. This whole scenario can be put down to you being a worrier. Maybe you even have a laugh about it.

I imagine you are not aware that in dealing with this feeling of a knot in your stomach this way, your brain has released a subtle, yet significant amount of endorphins. That is precisely why the feeling is now gone and that is also why you felt the sense of relief that allowed you to breathe easier and to relax.

Earlier, I said that the brain is truly amazing and this is one of the scenarios that reminds me of the fact. The brain is perfectly capable of creating physical conditions within the body that you must respond to, that is why you reach for a drink to quench the physical feeling of thirst. Feel hungry – you eat;

feel hot – you take a cold shower. Your brain creates physical stimuli every day that can only be resolved by you carrying out a specific action to appease that particular feeling.

Each time you respond to a particular feeling of something ever-so slightly uncomfortable, the brain rewards you with a little release of the good chemicals. We all know how great a full stomach feels after the physical discomfort of feeling hungry all afternoon. The brain loves to reward you by improving your mood and if left to its own devices, it can easily fabricate a fictitious scenario that needs to be resolved in excuse to offer you the chance to feel great.

I believe this is what illegitimate anxiety is, your brain will happily create a physical feeling within your body that your mind will race to try and address. One easy way to make you feel great is to give you a problem to worry about and to solve – check the lights are off; check the car is parked safely; check the doors are locked – then release endorphins once it's over. If we start down this path of solving small and silly problems, the scenarios will eventually become more and more unreasonable. There is no limit to the brain's creativity in convincing you that an anxiety is real and must be observed and addressed.

In my experience, the longer we indulge the requests of illegitimate anxieties, the more unreasonable they will become. One of the most notable examples of this, is when I worked with a man who had a fear of flying that extended back into childhood.

As he grew older and wanted to travel to other countries, he decided to use hypnotherapy as a method to overcome this worry. It worked well and he was able to start travelling on planes. Unfortunately, the root cause had not been addressed and eventually the fear of flying was replaced with a new fear of using the tube in London. This became a huge problem as he lived in one part of the city and worked some miles away.

He did not drive, nor did he own a bicycle, so to his mind, the only answer to this problem was to walk to work. It would typically take him two hours walking in the morning and a further two hours in the evening to walk home.

Each time he arrived at his destination he experienced a huge sense of relief that he had avoided a catastrophe. He is an intelligent man and his brain gave him perfectly valid responses to anyone who told him the tube is a safe reliable and usually quick method of travel. Unfortunately, he could not see that there was an equal level of risk walking through the city as there was using the tube. Through responding to his worry in this way, his brain had created a situation that allowed him to be given a large release of endorphins twice daily every time he went to work and then again when he returned home.

The fact that he was unnecessarily walking for at least twenty hours a week – although a major inconvenience – was to him, essential to his well-being. This is one of the worst and most persistent cases of illegitimate anxieties I have seen. It was further compounded by his attempt to keep it from his partner as he did not want her to think there was something wrong with him.

This is no way to live, so what can we do to remedy anxiety that is controlling the way we engage with the World? The answer is surprisingly simple and it only requires a little more understanding of the physical body. Once we pull back the curtain on some additional processes that occur within each and every one of us, I believe anybody can begin the journey back to a life lived on their own terms.

Before we delve into these processes, I always like to make people aware of an important truth I dearly believe: When we are in a state of negativity, specifically fearful negative thoughts and feelings, the mind is extremely efficient at finding a problem to every solution. I truly believe that whether you think something is right or wrong, true or false, good or bad, your mind will give you every shred of evidence available in your surroundings to validate you are correct.

Often the biggest obstacle to embracing change is our own perception of the World. It is common place to hear people say things like, *if it was easy everybody would do it, or if it's too good to be true then it probably is.* These phrases are catchy and it certainly is prudent to be cautious in life sometimes, but I have always been willing to do my own research, from as neutral a standpoint as possible, before making my own decision on what is right or wrong. That is how I discovered the ease in which the brain releases endorphins and that is how

I discovered a solution to counteracting the brain's attempt to put us into the stress/reward cycle that persistent anxiety often brings.

The shamanic cultures of South America have known of these techniques for millennia, but unfortunately this knowledge has been forgotten in the West. If we briefly look at the history of Europe for example, it is easy to trace back countless examples of war and revolutions for the last two-thousand years. There is a phrase that states *history is written by the victor*, and I believe this explains why we are disconnected from ancient knowledge.

Each time a new leadership model arose in Western culture, the previous model was often erased to some extent. This resulted in valuable knowledge being discarded in a way that is much more difficult to achieve in the Amazon. If shamanic cultures where pressured through threats and changes to leadership structures with war or revolutions, they could simply vanish into the jungle until things settled down.

As a result of this, I have found that certain knowledge, attitudes and behaviours are so ingrained to those cultures that they think little of the relevance these things have to today's World. Mixing my understandings with particular ancient Amazonian techniques has allowed me to reconnect with ideas I believe, have been lost to a large extent in the West.

I will always remind people that the knowledge I offer is given from a position of experience, everything I share is simple and easy to add to any daily routine. You do not need to ignore your doctor or therapist and there are no extreme lifestyle changes needed. If you can accept that there is nothing to lose in trying any of the techniques I speak of and you are willing to give them a trial, I am sure you will be pleasantly surprised.

So far it would seem like the mind is at the mercy of the physical body. The brain gives you instructions when to eat and drink, tells you when to sleep and when to warm yourself up or cool down. It could even be argued that we are just here to make sure the collection of cells that house us, meet their goals of producing new entities to ensure the genetic material they possess lives on. Maybe you will also be aware that you have very little, if any say, over the complex reactions occurring in your physical system every day. We are unable to instruct our kidneys to work or ask the liver to work a little harder so we just have to trust everything will function correctly.

But all is not lost, yes there are many things happening within the body you have no influence over but there is also something important that you can control. You have a hidden gift that is so natural and so effective at bringing the physical system into check, that any idea we are simply slaves to, the brain will quickly disappear. This unsung hero is **the breath**.

Now, I understand how anticlimactic that will seem on the face of it, but if you allow me to explain, you will begin to see what I am talking about. Out of all the essential processes occurring within your body at any given moment the breath is one of, if not the only thing, you have the ability to consciously influence. There is no way you could stop you heart beating for just a moment, nor do you possess an ability to stop your cells carrying out their production of complex proteins. You can curiously however, hold your breath if you choose to do so. Why then is this such a gift?

Oxygen is absolutely essential for your survival, but if you choose, then you have the power to regulate how much of this gas you breath-in and also how frequently. I am sure most of you are aware that when we take in a breath it has more oxygen than when we exhale. This is because we use some of the oxygen that enters our blood to burn the sugars and fatty acids our bodies need to produce energy.

Many of us are also aware that when we exhale there is a slightly higher rate of carbon-dioxide in the breath than what was inhaled. This is because carbon-dioxide is produced as a byproduct of energy production within the body. Too much of this gas in the body can become toxic and cause a range of negative effects.

I am sure you are all aware of this, but I draw your attention to all of this, as a refresher to this basic knowledge that you perhaps have not thought about for some time. The reason this is so important is because each and every one of us has the ability to consciously change the levels of oxygen and carbon-dioxide within our own bloodstreams. If we learn the correct way to do this, it is possible to begin using the brain's natural processes to our advantage in dealing with illegitimate anxieties.

No doubt you have seen or heard of people experiencing panic attacks being given a paper bag to breathe into. After a few minutes of using the bag they will generally begin to calm down and the panic attack will hopefully subside. I remember seeing this when I was young and asking why this method worked. The answer I discovered was simple, containing the gases a person exhales within the bag serves to increase the amount of carbon-dioxide that is being inhaled. So the next question I asked was, why does that matter? I found this answer was not so readily available to me as a young boy.

Life often provides the answers in the most unexpected of places and eventually I discovered the answer to the second part of this question years later through a totally unrelated activity, yoga. When you begin to practice yoga regularly, as you progress, there are a number of different breathing techniques you will learn. These breathing patterns have various different purposes and it was in my research on this topic that I found the answer to the carbon-dioxide question I had asked all those years ago.

Pranayama is the specific yogic name that describes the regulation of breath through certain techniques and exercises. I began to learn that there is a philosophy in yoga surrounding the idea that to breathe less is to live more. For some time, while I was learning these techniques, I read various books about this and one day I discovered a scientific journal that offered a factual account of the brain's response to specific forms of breathing patterns and more importantly carbon-dioxide retention.

What I learnt is that through breathing in a controlled manner, we can prevent the lungs from exhaling the same amount of carbon-dioxide as they would do so through unregulated natural breathing. When we breathe on autopilot the brain effortlessly instructs us to breathe as deeply and as frequently as required to keep the carbon-dioxide levels at an optimal level. This is such a natural process that a healthy person will barely notice any variation in the way they are breathing.

However when we consciously take control of our breathing patterns, we also take control of how much carbon-dioxide is allowed to exit the bloodstream. One of the brain's extremely important functions is to make sure those levels do not rise too high. If the brain detects even the slightest increase of this gas it will immediately investigate. What the brain does next has a side effect that I ultimately realised can be extremely beneficial for a number of purposes and also can stop anxiety in its tracks.

I will explain the pattern and then explain why I believe it works. Once you learn this method – the reasoning behind it and how to identify when it should be used – you will have a powerful tool at your disposal for bringing calm into your life whenever required.

Breathing in this set pattern for no more than three minutes is all the time you will need to start bringing illegitimate anxiety into check. The pattern is extremely simple, you can inhale while counting to four in your head, then pause, and slowly exhale while continuing up to ten. It looks like this

Inhale 1,2,3,4
Pause for around 1 second
Exhale 5,6,7,8,9,10
Repeat

If you take note of the time you start and preferably set an alarmed stopwatch, to allow yourself three minutes to breathe in this way, I am certain you will begin to feel calmer and more in control of your body and emotions. Setting an alarmed stopwatch allows you to remain fully focused on the breath and nothing else. At first, the effects will most likely be minimal but with persistent repetition, positive feelings will be enhanced. The reason this method is so effective is quite simple: When you slightly increase the carbon-dioxide levels in the blood, the brain enters a low level of alert.

While in this state the very first thing the brain does is, begin to pause and ignore all the non-essential processes that happen to be going on at that time. This includes any non-essential thought sequences that can be occurring within the cerebrum. I compared the brain to a supercomputer earlier and what the brain does in this situation would be comparable to you freeing-up more processing memory power on a computer by shutting down any programs or browser windows that you are not using.

Anxiety at its core is a strong worry, nervousness, fear or unease that something bad is going to happen in the future. It is only possible due to the amazing complexity of higher thoughts that the cerebrum is able to produce. In the case of an illegitimate anxiety, there is usually little, if any, real evidence that the thing in question is actually going to occur at all. While the brain is in a low state of alert induced by consciously regulated breathing, it will focus its energy on fixing the immediate problem at hand rather than fixing something that could happen in the future.

This means that within three minutes of you starting and sustaining the breathing pattern outlined here, the feelings of anxiety will begin to subside. In a nutshell, while you are breathing in a regular and controlled manner the main goal for the brain is to investigate why this change of gases in the bloodstream has happened and then monitor the situation until the carbon-dioxide returns to natural levels – during this time of alert everything else nonessential can be forgotten. This is the exact same process I witnessed at work all those years ago with the paper bag. The only difference is that the bag increases the carbon-dioxide levels in a different way.

I would now like to mention a few other important points. It should be understood that if the pattern detailed above feels uncomfortable then you can simply try breathing with different number combinations. Inhaling to the count of five and continue to ten on the exhale, or inhale to three, pause and exhale to six will all work as well.

Comfort is an important part of the process, so you should take the time to work on what feels right for you. The key here is the regularity of the breathing combined with allowing yourself three minutes to keep the routine in motion. Another important thing to mention is that there is no limit to the amount of times a day you can pause to breathe like this.

Typically, I have noticed that the more severe and persistent the anxiety has become, the more quickly the brain will return to telling you it is time to worry again. In the first few days people try this method out, it has not been uncommon to hear that they needed to use it a few times every hour. It should be remembered that breaking a persistent cycle of anxiety requires retraining the brain to understand you are not interested in receiving the feel-good endorphins it wishes to offer you for solving fictitious problems.

I like to also invite people to begin reconnecting with how they view anxiety to start with and remember that it is a powerful tool in dealing with the legitimate problems life can throw at us. Anxiety is not all bad, it should not be considered as something that needs to be completely eliminated from life. Instead, we should all understand that this powerful alert system has the ability to escalate into something negative if we do not understand what is happening and why. So how do we identify illegitimate anxieties?

Identifying whether an anxiety is legitimate and needs to be addressed or is illegitimate and should be tackled, is an important skill that needs to be developed and refined. This process of learning is a journey that has no set time limit and will vary from person to person. I have explained that when we are in a state of negativity, it is easy to find a problem for every solution. I feel that remembering this – and that many of us are prone to this way of thinking at certain points in life – is an important step to overcoming the thought patterns that hold us back.

Your brain will offer you almost unlimited reasons that an anxiety is real and needs to be addressed. You should always remember the motivation of the brain is to make you feel as great as possible and that it wants to do this by releasing endorphins. With this in mind, I feel the very easiest place to start with identifying the validity of an anxiety is to question the evidence available.

Is the evidence physical? For example, you have received a letter about some type of action towards you that has made you worry. Is the evidence circumstantial? For example, the brain is reminding you about something negative that happened in the past to you or someone you know, while suggesting you don't know if it will happen again or not? All anxiety, will at first feel legitimate and perfectly reasonable. Realising something is not as you want it to be, is actually you being given an opportunity to do something about it. The quicker you embrace that fact, the faster you can begin to find the solution.

The longer you observe the anxiety and the longer you focus on how much you don't like it, the longer it will last. If you take an approach of breathing to reduce any unwelcome thought loops or other unwanted physical sensations, this will help to reset your emotions so that you can question the evidence available from a place of neutrality.

What do I mean by resetting your emotions? *Emotions* is a word we have all heard of and they are something we all experience every day. The definition of this word is: 'A strong feeling deriving from one's circumstances, mood, or relationships with others.' This is a pretty straightforward and understandable explanation, but if you think about it, every single emotional state we are capable of experiencing can be classed into one of three categories.

These are simply either positive, negative or neutral. I imagine we would all like to exist in as positive of an emotional state as we can for as long as possible. It seems the object of many of our lives is to create personal happiness and try to avoid negative emotions the best we can. In my experience, in dealing with emotional states many of us tend to focus on achieving positivity and avoiding negativity.

This is normal enough, but thinking in this way means we often overlook the third state, emotional neutrality. Some people will class emotional neutrality as perhaps feeling surprise, astonishment, boredom or even the sense of feeling drained. I however, feel those feelings can be either positive or neutral depending on the context or situation they are being experienced in.

When I talk of emotional neutrality, I like to use the example of talking about the feeling one can sometimes experience when they first awaken and open their eyes after a night's sleep. Those mornings after we had slept relatively well and there is nothing pressing happening in our lives. We open our eyes and just feel calm, there is no dominant positive or negative feeling, we are simply just there in that moment.

It is on days like this, we might not realise but we have the power to decide how we feel for the majority of the day. For example, if the first thing you did after waking in that state was to get out of bed and stub your toe then this small inconvenience has the power to sway you from a neutral state towards a negative state, which can then develop and persist throughout the day. Hence the saying 'someone got out on the wrong side of the bed this morning'. The inverse is also true and maybe you remember that there is an event you are looking forward to that day. This creates a positive state that can also develop and grow. When I talk about resetting your emotions, what I am explaining is the importance of finding this neutral state.

With this method to reset yourself and understanding you can choose where you go from there and is the final part of this puzzle. The ability to do this effectively will have positive repercussions throughout many other areas of your life aside from anxiety. This is precisely why I have taken so much time and attention to explain this breathing method in such detail.

Understanding what my physical body actually is, on a slightly deeper level to that which is common among many people in society, and what drives each part of this system forwards was a turning point in my life. This knowledge empowered me to reflect on how I deal with unwanted feelings and emotional states with a much higher level of control. You could possess all of the spiritual connection and gifts that are universally possible, but if you are not able to bring the body into check there is little chance of being able to understand, harness and develop your connection with this energy.

If I gave you a radio that was able to tune into a wide range of frequencies, but told you it required that you keep the aerial down, you would instantly understand that you would most likely not be able to tune into every station the device was capable of picking up. Sure, you might be able to listen to all of the stations on a perfect Summer's day, if perfect atmospheric conditions were present, but if you experienced some static or unfavourable weather, the list of frequencies you could choose from will quickly become restricted.

In my mind, the aerial represents emotional neutrality, without it you are vulnerable to unfavourable conditions and will not be able to tune into your favourite stations and listen to the music that makes you feel positive. The breathing patterns I have detailed in this chapter once understood and developed, can bring about a state of emotional neutrality within three minutes.

Once you have achieved this state, you are free to choose which emotional orientation comes next. You can tune into the frequency that makes you happiest and focus on all of the good things you want to do with your life if you choose. But it is also your choice if you wish to revisit the negative thoughts and feelings of the past, to continue battling and questioning why they happened, whilst worrying about something happening in the future.

Depression from replaying the past in your mind and anxiety created due to worrying about the future often trigger overwhelming feelings. People often forget that the more they feel, the less they are able to think. A reduction in ability to think clearly creates a situation in which it is not possible to clearly see the true reality and potential available within one's life.

I have also found a common attitude expressed from many people that if we are feeling negative we must get back to positivity as quickly as possible. In this instance I ask people to consider they are standing on the banks of fast flowing, wide river with very powerful currents. The side of the river they are standing on represents negativity and the other side represents positivity. It is not possible to jump or swim to the other side and so the only solution is to find a bridge. This bridge is the energy of neutrality and it is all too common that people forget this is the only way to safely; the reliable journey from one side to the other.

Cleansing yourself from illegitimate anxiety and learning the ability to find a neutral state when life becomes difficult are extremely powerful tools in the journey towards happiness. Sustained happiness eventually allows you to tune into the universal energies that will awaken the enlightenment this book speaks of.

I understand the simplicity of what I have spoken about in this chapter could at first seem too good to be true, but I would like to remind you that it's free to try and can be easily implemented into any lifestyle. Quite simply, what have you got to lose from trying?

CHAPTER 10

The Essence of Addiction

WHEN WE HEAR THE word addiction, more often than not it will conjure up images of substance abuse and misery. Compared with those experiencing other misfortunes or illnesses, society seems to take a dim view of those in the grips of particular addictions. People are quick to point the finger of blame solely at the feet of those it is happening to, and people can express little sympathy as they believe that it was their choice to get into the mess to start with. It is common to then see them being further negatively judged for not having the willpower and strength to stop.

As a young man I experienced the helplessness that can occur when witnessing people you care for slip into the grips of addiction. Although I wanted to help, I observed some interesting paradoxical behaviour regarding how society deals with this topic. For example, if a person is addicted to smoking, then develops lung cancer as a consequence, broadly speaking society will be sympathetic. Any disease caused by the addiction will typically be treated without judgement. The same can be often true of someone who develops heart disease, hypertension or diabetes due to a lifetime of poor diet and lack of exercise.

This lead me to surmise; it appears you can be addicted to something that is bad for your health, but if you have not bothered others along the course of that journey, (directly or indirectly) anything negative that happens to you as a result, will usually be treated as an unfortunate effect of chance that was not your fault. If a person develops cancer as a result of their own lifestyle choices it is extremely rare to judge them harshly, instead we are more likely to console them on their bad luck.

Many of us understand that addiction plagues every single segment of society – no particular group of people are immune – rich, poor, old, young; it does not matter where in the World you live or what ethnic group you belong to. As I began to see this in my teenage years, some simple questions grew within my mind; What exactly is addiction and how can it have such a wide variety of effects, both mentally and physically on people and society? How can one person be judged negatively for being an addict, but another can be accepted as someone expressing their right to live how they wish?

As the years passed, I discovered more around this topic until, one day during meditation the essence of what addiction is, and how it impacts each and every one of us was revealed to me. I believe the concepts that have developed in my mind over the subsequent years as a result, are valid to all of us, and the knowledge I wish to share over this chapter I believe to be an important cornerstone to your own spiritual development regardless of the life you have lived.

Addiction has many faces, it is a complex and often confusing subject which has divided the opinions of many people for many years. We all have our own set of beliefs surrounding the how, what and why it even occurs in the first place. Depending on what your own experiences have been and how your particular character has developed throughout your lifetime will most likely dictate how you approach this subject.

A simple example that demonstrates these extremely varied viewpoints can be seen when examining how people choose to give up smoking. One person with outstanding willpower might simply quit by going through the process of what is commonly referred to as cold turkey. Another person might need to use nicotine gum or patches and people with certain personalities will find hypnotherapy to be the best solution. There are an almost unlimited range of individual ideas and approaches surrounding this topic, but when we step away from the individual level and observe how society views addiction, things begin to change.

I believe that on a personal basis, we focus on the addiction itself and what can be done to overcome it. This applies when we are trying to help ourselves or another individual we might know and care for, break a cycle of engaging in detrimental behaviour. We will often try and research solutions, share advice or recommend some form of supportive help to the individual in need. As a society however, I feel instead of focusing on the addiction we are prone to focusing on the addict.

At a societal level, I feel instead of trying to understand what is happening with the addict, we switch our focus, and become more concerned with the effects their often negative behaviour could have on us and other people we care for. This is more noticeable the more culturally undesirable the addiction is. A person addicted to crack cocaine or heroin is unlikely to find as much non-judgmental support compared to someone who is addicted to smoking.

Perhaps this judgement stems from the instinct to protect ourselves from potential threats, and we feel an addict who does not know us and has little regard for themselves also has no reason not to steal from or cause us harm. Sometimes unpredictable behavioural traits are associated with certain forms of addiction and I feel this is perhaps where the direct fear of an addict can originate from.

I believe we can also be indirectly affected when facing the uncomfortable reality, that sometimes there is nothing possible to be done for a person choosing to live their lives spiralling out of control. Many of us want to help friends, families and colleagues where we can. Lots of us also give to charity where possible and some of us even volunteer our time to various causes in the attempt to help others. Therefore, if we face the lost and helpless soul of an addict and have no answers to how we can fix them, it is sometimes easier to hope the problem will just disappear.

By extension, this can then create a situation where certain types of addicts are labeled by society as 'bad people'. I believe those trapped on that side of the fence often react to this negative judgment in a way that only perpetuates their situation, causing them to spiral even further downwards. Nobody wants to be frowned upon and maybe an addict will even use that judgement as a validation that nobody cares for them. If they are alone, even labelled as a bad person, it's possible they will feel there is nothing to lose by continuing to live with their problematic behaviours.

Personally, I see both sides of this argument, drug addicts who lie, cheat and steal, or alcoholics who endanger others by driving under the influence should not be excused. It is completely natural and understandable that society frowns upon those who act in this way. There is perhaps no stronger instinct than wanting to protect you and your loved ones. We are always searching for potential threats to some extent, and people engaging in those behaviours are certainly dangerous to others and themselves.

No doubt you will have heard numerous stories of people committing unforgivable acts while in the depths of addiction, which only serves to deepen the worries many of us can have. When I began reflecting on this line of thought I eventually asked myself; How do those people arrive at a point of neglecting themselves and their responsibilities to start with?

After all, surely at some point in their lives they would have been aware of exactly what society thinks and how people can treat addicts. Yet, they still choose to take that path regardless of the risks. It could also be suggested, that at least some of the addicts out there would have also been previously judgmental of the very behaviour they ended up engaging in.

So if their old views surrounding addiction could be corrupted, how is it possible for one to arrive at that place?

What needs to happen for a person to ignore their potential fear of how society would view them for acting in such a way?

As I have dedicated the start of this chapter to talking about the most obvious and possibly most severe types of addiction, let us begin by addressing those. Drugs and alcohol are probably the most famous of the various things a person could develop a dependency towards, but what exactly are they? I myself, have known people with these addictions, and I have experienced the long-lasting damage their actions leave in this World.

Drugs are defined in the dictionary as, '-A medicine or other substance which has a physiological effect when ingested or otherwise introduced into the body'. Drugs can usually be classed as one of two categories, either a stimulant or a depressant. These categories help to define what type of effect a drug will have on the person taking it. However, if we take a closer look, we see that these definitions focus almost exclusively on the physical effects that taking such substances will cause.

Although many of us are aware that drugs have a wide variety of measurable effects on the body, we should not forget or overlook the importance of what happens to the mind when a person chooses to induce these states. Unfortunately, we only see hints of this point in how the dictionary defines addiction: 'The fact or condition of being addicted to a particular substance or activity.' The word 'substance' in this definition would point towards drugs, while the word activity is perhaps the result of a mental process causing an addiction.

Either word is relatively vague and is open to a number of interpretations. I think defining *drugs* primarily by the physical effects they cause is a result of how we have developed our societies over the last few hundred years. It is my belief that this small point is actually an extremely significant obstacle we have given ourselves in relation to understanding, and therefore overcoming this global problem. I will explain how I came to realise this as the chapter develops.

Now, in my mind it is clear, right from examining the absolute core of this topic how complex the problem is. Straight from the beginning with only a little objectionable thinking, it is possible to see that we can barely even describe what a drug actually is. If you take the above definition, that I have quoted straight from a dictionary, and apply it to food for example you can perhaps see what I mean.

Alongside the fact the dictionary definition focuses mainly on the physical effects, is it not possible to suggest that even the vitamins and minerals found in the food we consume could be classed as substances that have physiological effects on the body? In short, the nutrition we ingest into the body could be classed as a drug using the dictionary definition above.

With this confusion alone, it is no surprise to my mind that society has not developed an effective strategy for combating the problem of addiction. Trauma is often regarded as a gateway to addiction, but I feel this is a weak attempt to explain a complex problem. There are many people who experience trauma and do not become addicts (myself for example). Other people experience no real notable trauma yet still find themselves hooked on illicit substances.

How then, can we fix something we do not fully understand? The difficulty answering this question is perhaps a reason most of the World's governments have decided the simplest approach to controlling the problem is to simply ban the use of the substances with the worst reputation.

Unfortunately as you will see, this approach of passing laws to restrict what is not understood has many weaknesses. This can then cause confusion and frustration among the populations living under such rules. In the UK for example, during my lifetime, cannabis has been both upgraded and downgraded in the guidelines surrounding how serious an offence the law views its possession and consumption. Cannabis would now appear to be on the path to legalisation, which we see is already happening in other Western countries.

This push and pull system of upgrading, downgrading, legalisation and criminalisation, will surely only create division. I say this because, certain segments of society who have grown-up where conditions made them fearful, and therefore judgmental of such substances will most probably hold onto their deep rooted views. Others who grew-up surrounded by more relaxed laws, will likely find the existence and use of such substances completely normal. This only serves to further compound the division in the arguments to who, or what, is considered to be right or wrong.

Cannabis use in the USA offers us the perfect example of this division in action. Many states have now legalised its use under certain conditions, but there are also politicians of a particular age who remain convinced it is still a 'gateway drug' and want to see it re-criminalised.

As the chapters within this section of the book relate to the physical system of the body, I am focusing towards the issues surrounding physical substance addiction. Obviously there is a non-physical side to this debate, and as I have just used the term 'gateway drug', I feel this would be a fitting point to briefly talk about mental addiction. Some people refer to lower potency substances as gateway drugs, which supposedly leads the user onto more addictive or dangerous drugs. While this might be true in some cases, I feel this focus on the physical hides another gateway – mental addiction.

People can just as easily become mentally addicted to activities such as sex, gambling, binge eating or even exercise. Mental addictions in their early stages can broadly go unnoticed by society. These addictions might easily be dismissed, as it could be argued little harm is being caused.

However, I believe that people displaying mental addictions are still activating physical mechanisms in the brain in an attempt to distract themselves from their deeper problems. Eventually in certain people, the endorphins the brain releases in response to these activities will no longer be enough, and they might consider taking the path to substance abuse and bigger highs.

I believe that the techniques I have discussed earlier in the book for accepting the past, and reprogramming the higher self can offer some help in dealing with the roots of mental addiction. So, going forward, this chapter will work on understanding physical addiction.

Now, I feel that understanding the contradictory problems surrounding drug control and legislation, offers us a small foothold with how to get to grips with the complex problem of physical addiction. To delve into this I ask; Who is it that advises a government on which substances should be restricted? The answer is typically that this guidance would come from a combination of trained medical professionals and leading scientists.

Obviously, this sounds logical on the face of it, but if we examine the background of the people making those decisions we can begin to see the first hurdles. These types of professionals will have no doubt undertaken years of the relevant training to be classed as experts in their corresponding fields.

The problem is, that they likely will be experts in using legalised medicine, drugs or other related chemicals. Usually for the sole purpose of treating and curing physical illness. If they are met with a substance that has no value in improving a patient's physical condition, or extending their life, it falls outside of their training. Therefore, the substance being reviewed is of no use.

This lack of understanding the properties of things outside their training, is why I believe psychedelics are banned in most Western cultures. Further problems occur when a substance is allowed to be used in a medical capacity, but not by a member of the public. Opiates are a prime example of this, people understand morphine and heroin to be closely related. However, one can be prescribed by a doctor, while the other is illegal.

This unfortunately creates a precedent in which someone could think they are being lied to. How can one substance be bad and illegal if someone is using another form of it safely elsewhere? I also think the potency of a drug has an influence as well. For example, alcohol is legal throughout many countries and in normal conditions it would take you a long while to consume enough in one sitting to overdose. It certainly is possible to cause damage from alcohol, but certain other drugs are far more potent when consumed in much smaller quantities.

There are many stories of ecstasy being consumed in a simple tablet form and causing much more damage in a shorter timeframe. All of these factors combined, quickly muddy the waters of how we define one thing as right, and another as wrong. Despite our best intentions, society is still in a position that has resulted in our best experts having to make decisions about certain substances that fall outside of their training.

We also have medical professionals administering drugs to people who meet certain requirements, while telling others they are dangerous and illegal. Our governments ban some drugs to protect us, but then they allow the sale of alcohol, which is widely accepted to cause health and potential addiction problems. Governments not only allow us exposure to this particular substance they also put a financial tax on every alcoholic beverage sold. You can perhaps now see the level of confusion and contradiction is rising the longer we ponder this topic.

I believe for the most part that democratically elected governments are usually trying the best they can to reflect the views of those who voted them into power. Sadly, they will often still face criticism at every turn regardless of the control measures they implicate. Entire populations look to a few elected individuals for leadership, but when we analyse what is happening, it would certainly appear our governments are just as much in the dark as the average individual regarding this topic. I believe if we are distracted with the allocation of blame for failing drug policies, the deeper debates needed to enact real change will not happen.

During these discussions, I will usually bring up a specific analogy around this point. I like to ask this, if I brought you a brand new TV with every channel available, what would you do to ensure that you did not waste all day and night watching it and ignoring your responsibilities?

The answers I receive will always vary, but whatever response is given I will reply with the following; I have listened to your ideas but I am still unsure that I could trust you to limit the viewing time yourself. Do not worry though, all is not lost as I have a solution, I will help you by allowing you to have the TV, but I will keep the power cord. Therefore, you own a beautiful new TV and I can be guaranteed you will not watch it too much. Is this not a win-win situation for us both?

Obviously not. If I take the power lead I am not controlling your use of the TV, instead I am removing your ability to use it altogether while telling you it's for your own good. People usually smile at this analogy, but I feel it is similar to how we are governed in relation to drugs. The way many substances are classified is not drug control as we are lead to believe. Instead it can be argued it is drug suppression, and this strategy itself brings in further problems.

Firstly, your control of anything in this World does not come from you being told by someone else what to do. Control only ever comes from the self. Building on this, I feel long-lasting control comes from a place of being told the truth, understanding the facts surrounding the topic, combined with a healthy self-discipline. The second problem is related to how we react when we feel we have been lied to. Cannabis is a prime example of this, one year it is dangerous and a few years later it is being legalised. Is it safe or not?

Many of us who were told it was dangerous by teachers, parents and the government when young, went on to try it anyway. Nearly all of those who used it for the first time discovered that they woke up alive and perfectly well the next morning. At this point anyone experiencing that situation could easily have asked a simple question; If I have been lied to about the dangers of cannabis, what other drugs have I not been told the truth about?

In some people this can create a lack of trust and leave them deciding to ignore what they have been told, instead choosing to make their own minds up through trial and error. Some people will then go out to discover the truth with an extremely risky hands-on approach. This is a path of potentially choosing to try anything they feel interested in and learn through experience. The third problem of banning a substance completely is that it instantly becomes more exciting and attractive. There will always be certain personality types within society who will then work towards acquiring and trying it.

Now, please do not think I advocate the use of all drugs as the answer, or that I want everything to be freely available. My intention here is to help get to the bottom of what is happening and why, so that we can discuss how it impacts you. There is a lesson here that helped me along my path of spiritual development, and I believe can be of use to you as well.

Most importantly, I hope what I have pointed out so far demonstrates that drug suppression actually equates to increased levels of danger within society. Suppression does not eliminate problematic drugs; it allows a chance for the unmonitored criminal manufacture and supply of such substances, which we all know today causes terrible suffering globally.

Before I share any of my further understandings, I would like to circle back to the way we define drugs to start with. Now I have explained how we categorise them and some of the most obvious problems this causes. I would like to explain why

I feel we arrived at the point of focusing on the physical effects. I believe that as a society we have chosen to pursue a path that values scientific findings above all other forms of knowledge.

Most of us understand that many years ago religion was the dominant belief system in the West, it was thought to offer knowledge and guidance to all problems. Fast forward a few hundred years and it could now be argued that people from the scientific community can occupy spaces in our belief systems once previously reserved exclusively for religious figures. Today, the widespread respect given to names like Charles Darwin, Albert Einstein and Stephen Hawking would have not been possible in the past.

If we go back further into the time when religion was the dominate school of thought, we can find some more interesting and relevant points. There is plenty of evidence to demonstrate that centuries ago, priests would not only act as spiritual advisors but also as medical practitioners. At some point however, as the field of scientific study developed, the church decided it was unholy. Their response was to instruct priests to move away from anything that could be classed as scientific and focus primarily on the spiritual aspect of worship.

This separation between the fields created two distinct systems that in my opinion, have spent numerous years trying to disprove each other. Scientists will argue reasons to prove God does not exist, while religion responds in kind by fighting to disprove many scientific ideas, such as the theory of evolution.

I could write an entire book on this subject, but for now I wish to highlight one particularly important point – science focuses exclusively on what is measurable and observable.

Applying science to a biological and medical perspective, there is a clear and understandable objective to use scientific knowledge for developing methods of extending physical life as long as possible. Doctors will spend years training with this aim in mind, to keep patients alive and do no harm.

Pharmaceutical companies spend billions trying to develop drugs attempting to combat every disease and illness we know of. All of these share the same goal of extending how long it is possible to physically live. We all know this is great, and the scientific knowledge discovered in recent history has both improved and extended the lives of countless millions globally.

However, when faced with the most obvious universal truth – that all physical life eventually dies – difficulties begin to arise. We see this in the way doctors sometimes interact with terminally ill patients. If a doctor and patient who both devoted their lives to believing in science meet at the end of the patient's life, both can behave in interesting ways when addressing the impending death.

First, a doctor might take the family aside and warn them the patient has little time left. The family are then advised to try to make the patient as happy and comfortable as possible. Eventually when the patient finds out the inevitable is soon to happen, in many instances they will begin to wonder what if anything happens to them after the point of physical death. Perhaps they go as far as to ask the doctor what has happened to other patients, or if he/she has seen any proof of the afterlife.

But, typically the doctor has no real training in what comes next. His background and training is firmly rooted in the measurable and observable. The energy that powers the body is nonphysical and unobservable, therefore beyond scientific principles of measurement. Likewise, the patient knows the doctor has no answers to these questions and it is at this point either the doctor, patient, or indeed both, might consider the services of a priest. After all, the priest has devoted his life to the pursuit of answering the question: What comes next?

This paradox is perhaps why a hospital is one of the only places you will find science and religion coexisting peacefully. I have not visited a hospital in the West without a chapel. Trying to work out how this stalemate between opposing ideologies, coming to exist side-by-side peacefully, is another of the small points that helped me to develop my understanding of the difficulties surrounding addiction.

We will come back to this towards the end of the chapter and I will weave it all together, but for now I will leave this point by reassuring you I am not going to advise you that religion is your saviour. I appreciate that I am bouncing between various points at the moment, I do this in an attempt to best share with you the order in which these things were revealed to me.

It is my belief that sometimes we ignore certain thought sequences. I try to help people learn, that if we allow these things to play out, it is possible that profound answers can be discovered as a result. That said, I would now like to go back to the point in the earlier paragraph where I began to talk about the various types of people who abuse substances and their motivations.

Throughout history, culture has always been full of people who are willing to try anything. This attitude has lots of positive benefits and it could be argued that in its most desirable form, has shaped the innovation and progression of human culture. The first person to drink cow's milk, eat cheese or an egg are amusing examples.

People with these curious and risk-taking traits discovered things that helped all of us in the long-term. The downside to this attitude is that sometimes these people can be drawn towards jumping into new situations without assessing all of the available information. Some can be prone to naively assuming that the worst wouldn't happen to them, or they can outsmart the system.

Like it or not, ultimately people with these personality types – living in a society that has confusing and conflicting standards regarding drugs – are vulnerable. This is in the sense that, if they choose to indulge in any of the particularly potent and physically addictive substances, it can be hard to stop once started. Another at-risk group are those who have suffered traumas and as a result, decide that self-medication will help them to forget. Trauma is given a lot of attention as a powerful driver behind addictive behaviours, but I feel there are other equally important things to consider.

We all understand the mind is very strong and therefore attempting to silence it with drugs is a difficult task. A person trying to do this will usually have to experiment with a number of substances before they find something that is potent enough to have the desired effect.

People entering into the pursuit of consciousness suppression, perhaps face a worse challenge than the people willing to blindly jump into something new. Someone who ends up realising it is only the most potent and addictive of substances that can quieten the mind, probably will not care as long as it is having the desired effect.

If we don't care about ourselves and feel we must try and silence the mind, trouble is almost always guaranteed. These are the most dramatic of scenarios and therefore, the most noticeable; when we see someone displaying the telltale signs associated with hard drug abuse.

Years ago, I wondered why these people would be judged so harshly for their choices. After all, certain risk-takers are rewarded in society, the investor who's portfolio came good is a great example. Our blockbuster movies are littered with examples of risky behaviour paying off, so it is obvious some forms of risky behaviour are accepted, and even welcomed by society. I know I already detailed some of the reasons we frown upon those who risk falling into addiction. Perhaps it's associated with our fear of the damaging behaviour those addicts can display, but I felt this answer was only part of the reason.

Eventually, a deeper and far more important answer came to me, I realised the substances with the largest stigma around them curiously all fall into the same class, that is that they can be labeled as depressants. After some consideration, I reached a point of understanding that the drugs society will not tolerate people becoming addicted to, are the drugs that cause the consciousness to quieten.

If we look back throughout history it is possible to see that human culture has an almost eternal fascination with achieving altered states of consciousness. The Egyptians were doing this 4,500 years ago and there is evidence Amazonian tribes were doing this up to 5,500 years ago. Most importantly to my mind, the most accepted form of this fascination is firmly pointed in the direction of altering consciousness for the purpose of expanding awareness.

If drugs are taken for the purpose of seeing something new, previously hidden or accessing mystical knowledge, society has a certain level of tolerance. There are numerous methods of awakening the mind to induce these altered states and in my experience I realised that although not everyone will want to take psychedelics or engage in prolonged periods of meditation, many people still have an interest in hearing about the experiences of those who do.

I have traveled to the Amazon rainforest on a number of occasions and altered my own consciousness with ayahuasca. I have studied with the shamanic practitioners and healers while there in order to help shape and develop the awareness of myself, other people and this World we all reside in.

The plants I have worked with and learnt from are poorly understood in the West. Yet, everybody who speaks to me about these experiences will always ask the same types of questions, which at their basis are; What did you see?

There is much I am happy to share surrounding this question, but for the purpose of this chapter I bring this point to the discussion to demonstrate how I am treated.

If I consumed these plants in the West I would be in breach of local laws. In contrast, it is perfectly legal and socially acceptable to do so within the Amazon, but when I return to the West where the opposite is true, I am not greeted with people judging me. Instead, more often than not, I am met with a sense of wonder, curiosity and intrigue, with people asking that I share what my experiences revealed.

I will mention, I am in no way addicted to these substances and have only taken them a handful of times, but the point remains. There are more people who are likely to be negatively judgmental towards someone who had taken heroin a few times compared to someone who had experimented with consciousness expanding substances. Even though both parties are taking substances that can be classed as illegal in certain countries; people can often be tolerant of one while frowning upon the other.

I believe today, this deep interest in consciousness expansion is being enhanced by the path society has chosen to embracing science. There is very little, if any, scientific research surrounding what happens to those people drinking ayahuasca. The reason for this is simple, there is very little for science to measure or observe. Although there are a few physical reactions – I would suggest this is only around 10 percent of the experience. So 90 percent of what happens does not fit in with mainstream scientific testing methods, because it is not measurable or observable.

As a result, the simplest way for science to deal with this problem is to dismiss what is happening, and then advise governments to restrict the usage of such substances. A common explanation for this choice is citing that there are no physical benefits or no improvement to length of life. There is also often an attempt by certain segments of society to tarnish those who engage in these journeys and label them as some type of misfit. The fear of the unknown has been said to be, *the fear that rules them all*. Science is held in such high regard in modern society, that people can become very fearful of the questions scientific methods fail to produce answers with.

In my opinion, this attitude is reminiscent of how the church treated the subject of science all those years ago. My research, observations and experiences have resulted in a personal belief that both the discipline of science and religion have important lessons to teach us all with the subject of addiction. By learning to accept both belief systems having parts of the answer, yet that neither have the entire answer, revealed to me a gap within society that I believe needs to be addressed.

To my mind, medical science wants to extend your physical life as long as possible, religion wants to prepare your soul to live in eternal paradise – but neither are devoted to helping you live for today; in the here and now! Depending on your personality, life experience and how deep your desire to find a way of living in harmony within this precise moment is, I believe has a direct correlation to your level of attraction with exploring experiences via consciousness altering substances; both negative and positive.

I ask, what path is a person who has suffered long-lasting and persistent trauma throughout their lifetime going to take if they decided enough is enough? Sometimes we reach a point in life that our problems must be tackled head-on. But what is a person who has reached this point to do, if there is a lack of understanding about how to explain and deal with what has happened to them? Most importantly; Why do they feel the way they do?

If we factor in the personality types we have discussed, the variations in willpower and emotional states, then mix this with confusing legislation, it is possible to see how *bad* choices can be made. At this point, it can then come down to chance. What support, or substances are available to a person wishing to find answers or forget something can dictate what happens next. Someone with a mindset that they are willing to do anything to overcome their problems could just as easily be prepared to try anything that might help them, or to simply switch the noise off.

In the previous chapter, I detailed the role of the cell within the physical body and that it could be suggested its sole purpose is to create more of itself by ensuring the survival of its genetic material. I was reminded of this small piece of scientific evidence during the meditation I spoke of at the start of this chapter. The purpose for this, I believe, was simply to show me that **we are physically hardwired to be addicted to life itself**.

As this realisation developed, I began to see how important the relevance of this small point is to the topic of addiction. Each and every one of us is born housed within a collection of cells that exclusively work towards the sole purpose of staying alive. A natural question at this point could be to ask, why suicide exists then?

The answers to that question are very complex and I will cover my understandings in a future book. For the moment, I would like to briefly talk about how I realised this addiction to life to be true, even in the presence of suicidal thoughts. In 2004, a documentary film was released surrounding the topic of people jumping from the Golden Gate Bridge in the USA. The filmmakers wanted to raise awareness of the people who choose to end their lives there and the devastating effects their choice had on their families and friends.

During the course of the film the producers were able to interview some people who had miraculously survived the jump. These survivors came from many different backgrounds and demographics, but all had one thing in common. As soon as they took the jump from the bridge, they instantly regretted it and fought with every piece of strength and energy they had left, to try and survive.

Unfortunately, too many people tragically lose their struggle with life. Over the years, I have listened to the stories from many people who have all survived various attempts to end their time here. Nearly all of them report the same feeling of being close to the end and then experiencing a wave of desperation to fight and live. To my mind, this shows the deep attachment and influence the physical body has towards living and that in a sense, know it or not, we all have an addiction to life itself. This for me, was a small, but significant realisation because I believe our best ideas and techniques to help heal addicts, all focus on trying to make them stop being addicts altogether. This strategy unfortunately is in direct competition with the physical laws that govern our cells. How can someone simply stop being an addict, when addiction to survive is wired into the fabric of our cells?

Before the medical treatment of addiction even starts we try to make people stop being addicts. This is typically done by first ostracising them while they are exhibiting the unfavourable behaviour. We all know stories of people losing relationships with families, friends and colleagues due to addiction. The next stage might come only at a point when we feel they have demonstrated a willingness to accept they are living in a way that is considered to be wrong. If a person has been outcast, part of their journey back to society is convincing others they have truly accepted they need help and understand their actions to be wrong.

At this point, after the addict has made those realisations, typically a program of detox, often at a rehab centre is offered. This is usually away from mainstream society and often the philosophy of a rehab program is to first stop being an addict before true recovery can start. I ask the question, how can any of us stop being an addict completely, when every single cell we are made from is at its very essence coded with a basis to be addicted to something?

Science wants to treat the physical symptoms of addiction because science deals with the measurable and observable. Our rehab centres are based on medicine and, as we already know, medicine is typically based in science. So how do we address the mental side of addiction? The reasons people become addicted to anything, can just as well start in the mind and then spill out into the body, as they can from consuming an addictive substance.

This is a perfect example of the unmeasurable meeting the measurable, and exposes the flaws with our current way of looking at the World. It could be argued that science is well on the way to winning the battle with religion, but this creates the problem that our society now is set up to primarily deal with the measurable, due to a widely accepted belief system that science is always right.

Psychotherapy tries to bridge the gap of working with the unseen mind, but I feel it falls short by having a tendency to focus on triggers, as a trigger is something that can again, be measured. But what about the addict who uses our best current scientific techniques to overcome their problems, and then fails? Perhaps they recover but then feel as though life going forward is a tightrope between sobriety and addiction. Eventually, at a random point they wake-up one day feeling fine, only to relapse for no apparent reason by the evening.

After mainstream scientific and medical recovery techniques are exhausted, alongside failing, maybe the person next turns to religion – as the church works with the unmeasurable. Is religious spiritual healing the answer to an addict's problems? In some cases this can be true, but again other people taking this route will then run into a new set of problems.

As Carl Jung said, 'All spiritual disciplines are preparation for death'. I believe Jung was partly correct in saying this, but only when we look at the work of the church. Religion would certainly seem to have a solid basis in preparing us for our inevitable death by outlining a set of rewards or consequences in the afterlife, depending which path we have taken through our life on Earth.

The problem here, is that although a person might seek the forgiveness religion promises, they also know that many of the World's religions view addiction in a negative light. The only way to achieve forgiveness using this method would be to follow a strict set of guidelines as laid down by the religious texts. Additionally, there is a cloud hanging over this path that suggests maybe even following these rules are not going to be good enough. True peace and forgiveness might never be attained, so is it worth the effort to begin with?

Once I understood the core roles of science and religion within society, and after I identified the obvious void in-between the two, I arrived at possibly the most important questions of this topic; If a person wants to get on with the business of living – not preparing for death – if they choose to seek a deeper understanding of why they exhibited persistent negative behaviour; damaging their happiness, health and acceptance from others, where do they turn? How do we truly free ourselves from the mental chains that physical addiction imposes?

We live in a challenging world full of conflicting attitudes, personalities and healing strategies. At times it can feel almost impossible to tell right from wrong. We lead busy and hectic lives, there is often little time available to address the big issues, especially if there is no guarantee of results.

I believe this is partly why society has chosen to control what is difficult to understand through suppression. Therefore, anything that is confusing in the absence of obvious benefits is outlawed. This is a simple and easy to deploy coping method that frees our minds to focus on other tasks. However, as a result, if someone chooses to engage in it anyway, they risk isolation from society.

Sadly, due to this, those who perhaps need the support of society the most, are also the most vulnerable to becoming ignored and expelled. Once excluded if they are let back in, we often then attempt to force them into being healed by listening to people who have often not experienced those same difficulties or traumas.

If you want advice on anything in life you naturally have a predisposition to seek it from an expert, preferably one with experience. How is an addict going to take advice from a highly-educated therapist who is likely not to have experienced the same struggles or life conditions? I believe we have lost connection with the fact we are born with an addiction to live at the core of us all. Forgetting that means we have lost sight of the fact this system can quickly get out of balance and turn against us if certain pressures are introduced.

Our fascination of altering our state of consciousness is rewarded if it brings in new exciting information, but frowned upon if the alteration subdues or closes it down. But what is a person to do if they cannot find answers to help solve their unmeasurable and unobservable problems? If there is nobody with comparable experience to turn towards, should they instead add even more complexity to their lives by following difficult and uncomfortable rules? Those rules are often set by people who have not experienced the circumstances that took the person who is suffering to that place of deep misery and confusion.

This chapter has revolved around the specific forms of addiction that have spiralled out of control in a person's life, but the answers I found from asking these questions bring lessons for all of us. Instead of judging people who have succumb to a system that exists in all of us, that sometimes unfortunately falls out of check, should we not be asking; Why do so many of us have a fascination with changing our conscious states to answer or ignore the most difficult questions?

Does this not demonstrate a desperation within certain groups in society that it is time to look for answers in places outside of the old norms? I also ask; Why is it so easy to change our consciousness to begin with? Even smoking a cigarette, drinking alcohol or high-caffeinated drinks can prompt small changes in how we perceive the World. The list goes on and on and even something as small as a sugar rush will offer a temporary change to our cognitive processes.

Through my experience of this World, I have come to believe that a middle way is necessary if we hope to overcome these problems. Currently, broadly speaking, society is not prepared to control the use of certain substances and so suppresses them instead. In recent history, our priests used to be doctors and religious healers until the church eventually split from this dual role when it began to disapprove of science. When doctors became doctors in their own independent sphere; away from the rules of the church, religions then instead focused exclusively on preparing us for spiritual acceptance of death.

I do not believe we can have one without the other, a sick priest will still call a doctor and a dying doctor will still be asked if they want their last rites read. The competition that arose in this separation between the church and science has unfortunately created a confusion within society.

To me, one of the most damaging results of each system trying to prove each other wrong means medical professionals do not understand the role of substances that can be used without the presence of physical disease. Unless something extends or improves a physical quality of life, sharpening or expanding the consciousness is seen as novel or to be discarded.

Many people with a scientific mindset mock the pursuit of exploring nonphysical phenomena, even though they understand their awareness of reality is based in energy with those properties. When the nonphysical energy that powers the mind is referred to as a spirit or soul, the mind might make religious connections. Science wants religion disregarded and so people who heavily subscribe to this way of thinking miss the option of a middle path.

I believe both science and religion disregard the underlying desire society has to alter its consciousness. From my travels, I have discovered that there is a small pocket of people hidden in the World who have found a fascinating middle way. The shamanic cultures of South America have helped me realise that if we treat certain substances with a healthy respect, we can fulfil the desire to expand and awaken our consciousness. We can then strive to find the deepest answers to life while observing that we all have the potential to become addicts if subjected to a certain set of situations.

Learning about how our bodies work on their deepest level has allowed me to find answers to the biggest and most persistent questions humanity repeatedly asks. The result of this knowledge, is that I have found a route allowing me to get on with the job of living in the here and now, instead of trying to live *forever* in some capacity. I am neither obsessed with being young forever or preparing my soul for eternal paradise.

Additionally, I now have little desire to suppress my consciousness, neither do I have an infatuation to continually expand it. I have discovered a balance between each side of the scale and this way of living has brought in peace and acceptance of my natural state of mind. Instead of asking how I can become something different – to think or feel differently – it has allowed me to ask the question; Why do we return to this fragile state of mind that can be so easily altered? I now also regularly ask; What lesson is there to be learnt in living in our natural state of consciousness?

I believe finding the balance between suppression and control of the mind, allows us a healthy attitude to approaching each altered state. For example, many of us will still want to enjoy drinking alcohol on certain occasions and there is also most definitely a use in bringing forward new knowledge from meditation. It is my understanding that if you can find the path to using altered states of consciousness sparingly, it is possible to remove some of the common distractions that prevent many of us from embracing the *here and now*.

The journey of exploring addiction has produced a result I could not have expected when I started down this particular path of discovery many years ago. Science wants to save our physical bodies and prolong our lifespan, while religion wants to save our souls and grant us eternal happiness. Unfortunately, neither of these pursuits help any of us with accepting who we truly are right now in this moment and how to find lasting peace and acceptance with past difficulties.

If we are continuously looking to the future, how can we overcome the physical and mental mechanisms that if not fully understood, can stop our personal journey of enlightenment? Yes, science could find the answer to eternal youth and who am I to say if religion's various versions of the afterlife are right or wrong! I have certainly developed my own clear ideas on what happens when the body ceases to exist, but should I push these ideas upon you? Or, would it serve you better for me to offer the foundations of the path that provided me with this knowledge? Is it more appealing for you to explore a new path yourself, or have someone do it for you?

So, what about the right now? How can we begin to reframe our preconditioned ideas about this complex subject? To my mind, the problem of addiction within society can partly be related to a belief that answering the deepest of questions about life cannot be done alone. We are taught from a young age that there are people in society who can fix our physical and spiritual problems through the use of practices we are not trained in. We all know that doctors are needed to fix our bodies, and we are told from a young age religion might hold divine answers to this World's wider problems.

The problem is that, on the face of it, many of us feel there is no single institution that offers all of the answers. Therefore, nobody is available to teach us how to take control and do this important work of self-discovery independently. This can create confusion, which at its worst means some of us can find ourselves in vulnerable states searching for answers to the difficult questions.

If we attempt this type of journey without understanding the basics, often at first glance, the results can have conflicting answers. These conflicting ideas and information can then lead onto mistrust, which in turn, at the extreme end of the scale can result in poor decisions being made.

I do not claim to have all of the answers, but I can share with you the knowledge and ideas that have brought me the longest period of good health and happiness in my entire life. The knowledge I have gained in the Amazon has taught me that a shamanic approach to drugs and addiction has lessons we could all benefit from.

A potential shaman will often have experienced a traumatic childhood and possibly even near-death experiences early in life. In tribal cultures the elders will recognise these individuals and allow those children to develop unhindered into their teenage years. At this point, children who have endured these experiences will be taken to the elder Shaman to see if they have any interest, or potential to pursue a path of becoming a shaman themselves. If the child who experienced those early traumas effectively integrated what happened to them, and found acceptance; two important things can sometimes become available to them...

First, they could have discovered the all-important truth that physical death is inevitable, perhaps even glimpsing what comes next. The result here is, in dealing with one of the biggest questions we all face at such an early age, their mind is free to pursue answers to other important questions many of us will never ask.

The second aspect the effect of this early suffering can produce, is that a potential shaman often has the ability to advise others who have endured deep pain and suffering from the standpoint of experience.

We already identified that people prefer to have their questions answered by a person of experience where possible. In this light, a shaman often has the unique perspective of which path a person can take to accept what has occurred instead of fighting with it. Therefore, if a child displays the above traits, while also demonstrating a desire to undertake the shamanic path themselves, they can begin their training with the elder Shaman.

In the Amazon, these shamans learn to use many of the rainforest plants as medicine. Some of these plants are psychedelic in nature and offer the chance to open the mind and consciousness to bring in new knowledge. As part of the training, a shaman will learn to identify those people seeking out their knowledge who could benefit from these plants. They then provide a safe environment to help guide a person through this journey of discovery.

This is the total opposite of someone who puts themselves in danger by taking highly dangerous and addictive substances alone. Although important knowledge relating to self-discovery often needs to be discovered alone, there is a clear difference between this and isolation. A skilled shaman provides a safe and comfortable space for someone to journey within themselves. Although this important journey can only be taken by the individual alone, and inside their mind, it is best done with the comfort of knowing the shaman supports them in the material world.

They also fulfil the important role of knowing how much of these plants to give each individual, while limiting the frequency in which they can be consumed. Someone who is experimenting and potentially abusing substances in the West, will unlikely have a good knowledge of how much is safe to consume. This dangerous truth is a massive driving factor behind accidental overdoses.

Once the experience is over, the shaman will then interpret what was seen and help the person to integrate the knowledge into their daily lives. The culmination of countless generations passing this knowledge down, is that a safe and controlled environment has been created to help people find the answers they need to overcome their deepest problems, avoid self-destructive behaviour and find their unique path to peaceful and happy living.

To summarise, I believe that we all possess a physical system of addiction within our bodies, and that by structuring our societies to look towards science to answer our deepest problems, we unknowingly risk trying to control who we are by suppression. The battle between science and religion has stopped many of us from addressing and accepting the fact that each and every one of us will eventually die.

This has created a situation in which many of us blindly traverse through life trying to distract ourselves from this challenging question. To my mind it is essential we all ask; How do we find acceptance with our undeniable fate?

If we add personal traumas, bad luck, suffering, even long-term boredom to the mix, it is easy to see why some of us can feel compelled to address the root of these types of questions. The danger begins to build, if a person finds no satisfactory answers to these important personal questions in science, religion, or from their friends and families or even wider society.

At this point, depending how heavy the weight of all of these dilemmas have become, a person could quite easily consider taking the path of quietening the consciousness to make it all disappear. We all have difficult questions that need answering at some point during our time here, whether the questions can be answered or not – And how satisfactory we believe the responses are, can affect us in more ways than we perhaps realise.

Maybe we deal with persistent unsatisfactory answers by engaging in behaviour that offers a distracting thrill, such as gambling, overeating or sex. Sometimes these short-lived thrills are not enough, so we do it again and again to distract ourselves from the discomfort of feeling like nobody has the answers to our biggest problems. Perhaps the mental discomfort, is so great that we choose the path of using substances to suppress our consciousness, so we can forget.

If someone chooses that path – depending on where they live in the World, and what substances are available to achieve this – dictates how much trouble that path will bring. If drugs with physically addictive qualities are easily accessible and chosen to try and silence the mind's questions, long-term problems can be born. Recovery, if desired, can then become difficult because there are very few people to turn to offering advice from an experienced perspective on how to truly overcome that addiction.

Perhaps an even more dangerous problem is created when a society does not have a system in place to answer the questions that drove a person to addiction to begin with. If someone living under those conditions wants help and is sent to rehab, but treatment offers no answers to the root cause before sending the recovered addict back to their normal life, then future problems are almost guaranteed. In this situation, the cycle of trying to answer seemingly impossible questions can repeat indefinitely, and to my mind, it is no wonder certain individuals will repeatedly recover and relapse.

I feel science, religion and shamanism each have their own respective strengths and weaknesses in treating and preventing addiction. It could also be argued that not one of these systems holds all of the answers. My personal belief is that if we can take the best parts from each of these ways of thinking, there is an opportunity to build a fresh approach to the way in which we tackle this global issue of addiction.

Science has been wonderful at extending the length, health and comfort of our lives. Religion teaches us that no good deed goes unnoticed and helps us to consider how our actions extend throughout this World and into unseen realms. Many of the values; acceptance, forgiveness and respect that religion teaches could go some way to helping people better treat each other. Better and more forgiving treatment between people could possibly reduce certain levels of global suffering.

Shamanism has the potential to teach us how to exist in this World with a more harmonious acceptance of our wider environment. This awareness can teach us how engaging with the deeper energies around us can positively benefit both ourselves and others. So I ask, would combining the best parts of each system help to heal and protect the most vulnerable of us?

I hope that no matter what life you have lead and whatever path you have travelled, you will find an increased level of acceptance and control over who you are, by understanding the deep processes at work within your body and mind. It is my hope that by revealing this gap in society that has gradually developed as a result of science and religious groups battling each other, and by sharing how it was shown to me, we can begin to consider a different approach to supporting those most at risk among us.

I believe that often when a person is determined to start the internal work of answering their biggest questions, they are at a point of crisis and will not stop until they have at least attempted to face this personal battle. I hope that I have demonstrated the damage society is causing itself by ostracising and leaving these people to take this journey in isolation.

We should remember that a rough diamond will not shine without being polished. Friction is required to realise the beauty of the stone. Similarly, I believe that it is our darkest trials that can help mould the perfection that exists in all of us. We should not pass judgement towards those who have stumbled on that path. When reflecting upon this situation from this perspective, I find it difficult to harshly judge someone who makes mistakes in a society that lacks the type of support and guidance they need.

All of this has taught me that judging, or assuming there is trauma when faced with someone who has found themselves on a path towards addiction is pointless. Nearly all of us want freedom from our suffering, so, when faced with an individual battling unwanted addiction, I ask; Why does this person feel the need to alter the state of their consciousness? What questions were they trying to answer? What pain – either physical or mental – did they want to escape and what lesson did they miss along the path that delivered them to that place?

Ultimately, I believe anyone who truly and successfully awakens their personal enlightenment, will eventually find themselves becoming a beacon to others attempting to navigate a similar path. As your journey develops and you experience an improved understanding of the universal energies that exist beyond your sense of individuality, I expect the information within this chapter will start to become increasingly relevant.

CHAPTER 11

The Spiritual Diet

IT IS PERHAPS ONE of the most widespread, simplistic and easily understandable quotes ever created by man: 'You are what you eat.' The reason this simple arrangement of five words is so memorable is obvious, because it is undeniably true. That said, I understand diet is a very contentious issue so I will start this chapter with a reminder that you are free to make any choices you wish in this life. It is not my job to tell you how to live, my work is only to advise, share knowledge and encourage you to have a dialogue with yourself in a way that you perhaps have not done so before.

What we choose to consume forms the basis of the available material and energy our cells have access to when developing and carrying out the various essential processes within the body. Therefore, it would not make sense to ignore such an integral part of what makes you who you are. But, I have no desire to tell you what, how or when to eat it. We all understand the effect of consuming too little or too much of something has on the body, and as you can probably guess from the title of this chapter I have a specific approach to diet that I believe some of you might find interesting.

Our relationship with food is eternal; the drive to eat and drink has been present since the moment we were born. It is so natural that with everything else going on within our busy lives I would be surprised if you had taken much time to consider the depths of your relationship with what you eat.

As a young man, I enjoyed a typical Western diet and very much enjoyed all of the privileged variety we have available to us in this modern time. I have loved to cook since a young age and have been lucky enough to meet a wide range of people in my life from a diverse set of culinary backgrounds. Many of them have shared recipes from across the globe and I will always seize the opportunity to try something new.

Food is not only a deeply personal experience, but it also has a very social and bonding aspect. Right from the start of life a mother will deepen the bond with her child through feeding. Families and friends often gather together for special meals to mark and celebrate certain occasions. It is also entirely possible that some of your happiest memories were created during these moments.

Cooking for those we love can allow us to demonstrate our affection. We also promise cakes and sweets as a reward to our children for good behaviour. People can display generosity by donating food to the needy and some of us go further by giving time to charity and cooking for the less fortunate.

With the deeply emotional connection many of us develop towards everything positive that food offers, it is no wonder that any suggestion of changing our dietary habits can be met with fierce opposition. A person who has spent time bonding with friends at social events followed by a beer and burger, curry or steak, is not going to want to sacrifice eating meat overnight.

It is completely understandable someone would not want to remove themselves from these group and social rituals that have produced so much comfort, happiness and sense of inclusion. Many of us want to feel accepted and will enjoy the sense of fulfilment being part of a group offers.

Away from the individual level, many countries have a national dish that can also be a source of great pride – further strengthening an individual's personal identity. Our relationship with food is so deep that even if we try and change our diet there will always be temptations to revert back to old habits or indulge at particular social events or in the presence of certain company.

However, we also know the immense power specific diets can have on our physical being. In recent years, with the development of home DNA testing kits you can now even send your own sample off for testing for the purpose of revealing what diet is best for your genetic makeup.

You will have no doubt seen the amazing transformations various different athletes are able to bring in with a strict diet. I am also certain you will have seen the amazing weight-loss potential certain dietary changes can offer. Those of us who are religious, will be aware that many of the World's holy books even suggest their followers should observe specific dietary rules at certain times of the year. Some religions even suggest outright bans on certain foods at particular times, adding further complexity to the discussion.

All of this considered, I feel the best approach to this topic would be to share a little bit of my personal journey with diet, and document the effects those changes produced. I think my experience will resonate more with those of you reading this book who have the intention to pursue spiritual work in the wider world.

When we wish to use spirituality for the benefit of others, I feel our bodies will have specific requirements to help allow spiritual energy to flow almost permanently. This can be exhausting if we don't fully understand the dietary effects of certain foods, even more so if there are any energy blockages. Unfortunately, there appears to be very little information relating to this aspect of spirituality in Western society. In comparison, various spiritual diets are much better understood in certain South American and Asian cultures.

A lady I know who was trying to develop as a spiritual medium once told me that she is not able to control her ability to connect with external energies. She went on to telling me that often when she is trying to link with energy, the feeling was comparable to blindly searching around at the bottom of the bath for a bar of soap. Sometimes it would feel as if she had grabbed ahold, but it would then slip away at the last moment. Other times she would be able to maintain her connection for a little longer, but the more she gripped, the more chance there was of the energy shooting away, just like grabbing the wet soap too firmly.

I believe this experience is typical of someone who is not familiar with the importance of the link between diet and spiritual work. Unfortunately, this can create inconstancies within those wishing to work with these energies.

This is not ideal, considering often, people observing this form of work are poised, looking for reasons to prove the mediums authenticity. Sometimes people at this point of spiritual development are able to provide amazing accurate information that is easily validated, but at other times they cannot bring anything of substance forward into this space.

For me, I began to understand the deeper link between energy and food in the months before I visited Peru for the very first time. Purely by chance, I had started to eliminate certain foods from my diet for small periods of time. During these blocks of time, I began to notice that my meditations became more vivid. After making this connection, I thought it would be a good idea to alter my diet before travelling to Peru.

Shortly after setting this intent, I discovered that many of the Peruvian shamans require the people planning to visit them, must observe a certain diet, before they can work together. These two factors combined immediately taught me the significance diet has relating to spiritual work. As a result, I have spent many years developing my knowledge around this area. What I have come to learn eventually began to transcend the effect food has on my physical body and gifted me with knowledge I would never have known existed if it wasn't for pursuing this path.

One of the earliest, and perhaps most important lessons I was given surrounding this, was the link between external suffering and your own energy field. Earlier in this book, I spoke of what it is to be an empath and how people with these qualities often feel the emotions of those around them.

It is fair to say that many of us, even those who do not connect with the qualities of an empath, will still be well aware of what it feels like to be around people in certain moods. I am sure most of us in this World have at least experienced this at one point or another in life.

Typically, it is much easier to sense someone who is experiencing a bad mood or other such negative emotions. We also know how easily picking-up on that field of energy can bring us out of our own good mood. People will explain this by using phrases such as, 'being around him/her really drags me down'.

As a development of this ability, to take on the feelings of others, I once read that it is well-known within the meat farming industry that if certain animals have been stressed out or scared before their death, the quality of their meat can be negatively affected. There is clear scientific research proving that what a conscious being feels, can not only have a physical effect on the system experiencing the emotions, but also leave an imprint on the body after the consciousness has departed.

If we are able to pick-up on the feelings and moods of people around us, surely it is not absurd to suggest we can take on energy through the food we consume as well. After all, food is at its basis a form of energy we use to power our physical beings. Again, I would not tell you how to live or what to eat, this book is a guide to awakening spiritual development within those who seek it. However, an important part of this journey for me has been to remove food from my diet that was created through some form of suffering.

I realised many years ago there was a direct link between the suffering I consumed and my ability to work spiritually. Taking steps to remove this type of energy from my diet resulted in a more consistent and positive energy flow within my body, which enhanced my ability to connect with external energies.

In addition to this, it is known within biological science that over a period of roughly seven to ten years your body will completely regenerate itself, replacing each cell with an entirely new one. I believe that the more of these cells you can replace with food that comes from a place of non-suffering, the more sensitive you will become to spiritual energy.

There are various jokes that circulate regarding people living under certain diets and even more jokes about plants having feelings as well. To address this and offer clarity, I simply refer to avoiding the consumption of food born from the suffering a being with a consciousness can experience. Beings with higher levels of conscious awareness are clearly able to perceive pain and fear in a way that is unique, and I believe this energy can transfer from one form to another with relative ease.

It does not take seven to ten years to reap the rewards of a spiritual diet either. I feel the increase in sensitivity and awareness can start after just a few days of reducing food that comes from these sources. In my experience however, there is a clear link between the progression of this increased sensitivity and the amount of time one observes such a diet. The longer we go without consuming this suffering, the stronger the energies I speak of can flow.

The next important path of knowledge that opened up to me in this journey was learning how the South American shamanic cultures work with plants as facilitators of knowledge. Some years ago during my second visit to Peru, I was advised that a shamanic diet would help me along my path. In the Amazon Rainforest there is said to be twenty-seven special plants that each offer a different line of knowledge.

I have worked with a handful of these plants and can vouch to the validity of these claims. In my opinion, working with each of these master plants as they are known, can be compared to buying a ticket to a particular destination with different plants offering a different journey.

This does not mean the plants are hallucinogenic, but working with some of them has undoubtedly shown me things I could not have known were possible otherwise. For example, some of the plants have revealed to me methods for cleansing my own energy and others have shown me how to identify blocks within other people's fields of energy.

I understand that all of this could seem a little alien to those who have never heard of such claims and I do not wish to try and convince you that I am right or wrong. Many people ask me how I am able to work in the ways that I do and I genuinely feel a large part of this comes down to the particular diet I have chosen as a lifestyle. This chapter will perhaps raise more questions than answers, but I feel a gentle introduction into how I view the connection between diet and spiritual awakening is all that is necessary to help you understand what is possible within your own life.

Now that I have given some background on my approach to what we put into our bodies, I would like to briefly talk about the power of what not consuming food offers. Fasting is an important part of my routine and I have developed a monthly and quarterly approach to including this activity within my life.

I am well aware this particular subject is extremely controversial and I am not offering any advice, instruction, or encouragement for you to try this yourself. Again, I wish only to share some of my own experiences with the intention of highlighting what is possible.

To start explaining my approach towards fasting, I will always begin by reminding the listener how rapidly society has developed over the last 150 years. We enjoy so many incredible benefits of living in a modern world; it is remarkably easy to forget, that only a short time ago on the scale of human history supermarkets and convenience stores did not exist.

Throughout history, people would typically have had to rely on food grown and harvested within a relatively small distance from where they lived. Europeans could not pop to their local shop for some avocado and olive bread until very recently. It is also easy to forget, that those of us born within the last fifty years in Westernised societies would be considered disadvantaged if we grew-up experiencing the regular periods of hunger that were common throughout global history.

A simple example of how far we have come can been seen if we look back not very far into the past within the UK. It is well documented at certain points in time that food was so scarce and hard to store for prolonged periods that many people would have to supplement their children's diets with ale.

As the rate of our food availability is accelerated, it is of no surprise that we have lost touch with an undeniable fact – human beings had to evolve and adapt to endure long periods of going without anything to eat. This is common sense when we think about it, but if we ponder it for a moment, a simple question might arise; If many types of food are seasonal and wild animals like to migrate or hibernate during colder months, how did early humans survive without access to a local shopping centre?

During my preparation to visit the Amazon in 2016, I stumbled into the answer by accidentally beginning to learn the effects fasting can have on the body. At that time I had decided to observe a particularly strict version of a shamanic diet. As a consequence, when I traveled from the UK to Peru I was unable to eat anything until I arrived in the rainforest. This would have been fine, except I faced some unexpected delays and the anticipated eighteen-hour gap without eating ended up becoming closer to a forty-eight-hour fast with the exception of water.

After consuming no food and only drinking water for nearly two days, I was very surprised to discover not only did I survive the experience with little issue, but in fact I felt great. A short while after the trip had finished and I settled back into my routine at home in the UK, I began to wonder how I was able to have dealt with that experience so easily. Eventually I found the answer, when the body has limited access to its preferred fuel source of glucose, a metabolic state called ketosis can be induced. During this state, ketones become the main fuel for the body, which can have some surprising health benefits.

When experiencing a state of ketosis the first thing the body will do, is to carry out a kind of evaluation on the condition and performance of its cells. The physical body is a beautifully efficient machine, and while in ketosis there is no room for cells burning-up more energy than they require. Old cells and those that are operating in any way that they shouldn't, will therefore be disposed of with instructions left to rebuild new and healthier versions when normal conditions return.

As you could possibly guess, this mechanism of energy conservation can actually lead to an improvement in health. If cells that are misbehaving or using-up too much energy are no longer allowed to operate freely within the body, this is only a good thing. Research in this field has shown that fasting can improve many conditions such as, type 2 diabetes, Alzheimer's, obesity, and even a reduction of seizures in those with epilepsy. In fact, there is study after study available online for those of you who wish to know more about the proven health benefits of fasting.

The reason I wanted to talk about this, is because of the spiritual benefits I have observed. Over the last few years with some experimentation, I have found that now my body has become accustomed to this technique, there has been an unexpected effect on my meditations. During times of fasting I am able to access particular forms of knowledge, and this is again part of the answer I share with people who wish to know how I work.

We are all well aware of the physical dependency our bodies has on food, but through the act of fasting, I have also learned of the deep psychological relationship we also have. I have used this knowledge to condition my mind to remove the noise of the psychological dependency I once had towards food.

During times of fasting, I am now able to turn down the particular mental volume the digestive system has within my mind. This increased quiet allows me the capacity to tune into other frequencies. The metabolic state of ketosis is available to all of us; countless generations of our ancestors had no choice but to alternate from periods of fasting to regularly eating. I believe that the importance of this fact, and the effects it can bring should not be forgotten. Many forms of fasting are available and those of you interested can find a huge wealth of information online.

Ultimately, this journey into diet brought me to a realisation about the consciousness of animals. Before I share this with you, I would like to mention I am in no way an animal activist. I do not regularly donate to animal charities and I do not have any ulterior motives to convince you or anyone else that all animals must be respected and saved. However, I do personally respect animals, but I do not feel it would be correct to label myself as an animal lover.

That said, I have often wondered about the difference in consciousness between humans and animals. What we seek often reveals itself, and I have been offered some intriguing answers to these questions during meditations. These revelations are quite complex and although this particular piece of knowledge is not directly related to diet, I believe it was shown to me as a direct consequence of the diet I have chosen to observe, therefore is fitting to share within this chapter.

I have previously mentioned that at points during my visits to the Amazon, I have induced and worked with altered states of consciousness. The very first time I worked in this way, I was intrigued to find that I was able to interact with particular animals. As I already noted, I am not an animal lover or hater. My views towards them are quite neutral and I do not feel I was subconsciously primed to search for animals during a hallucinogenic state.

Due to this, I was surprised to see so much animal energy in those places. At first, there was such a large amount of information to process so I spent little time reflecting on the animal aspect of my experience. However, as my development accelerated, I began to see the energies of animals during my standard meditations away from the Amazon.

Around this time, I also began to notice that throughout history almost every culture of spiritual significance, and also many of the World's religions revere one animal or another. Eventually, it became apparent to me that this respect and admiration would typically come from the mystics of those cultures having access to these animals during their various otherworldly experiences. This pattern began to fascinate me and then one day, I was offered some surprising insights.

During my altered states of consciousness visiting the places in which profound learning is possible, I realised it was extremely rare for me to see or engage with other humans. I have had interactions with humanoid forms but they are distinctly different to us. In my experience, there are certain other places human consciousness is able to occupy with ease, but that would require its own chapter. I have however, been greeted with various different animals when working within the spaces both meditation and the Amazonian master plants can evoke.

I was shown that almost all animals on Earth primarily live in a state of observation, they rarely need to influence their environment and they do not question what is, to the depths that we do.

Our higher thinking has brought our societies to where they are today. But, it is our overthinking that restricts the ability to freely access those same nonmaterial places I speak of. Therefore, in understanding this, we can begin to consider how quietening the chatter of our minds with meditation, or through the use of certain plants can actually begin to bring us into synchronicity with the way in which animals naturally live.

I will explain my views on the functions of our higher thinking later on. At this moment, I do not want to divert too far from the topic of this chapter. The reason this information relates to diet is that after realising how animals are able to access those hidden and often unseen energetic spaces freely, I began to see why different species of animal will exist in harmony with each other in the wild, but flee when they see us. This I feel, directly relates to the energy we make our bodies up from.

Over indulgence and consumption of unnatural foods leaves an energetic signature on the body that is easy to be seen in certain meditative states. If we are adding additional energy layers to the physical body with food created from suffering, then like it or not animals will see this, identifying us as a threat.

This is because they will interpret this energy as a sign that we have no issue with allowing suffering into our energetic fields. Therefore, our presence could indicate a danger to them. The reason they are happy to engage with us in the non-physical spaces is that while in this state we have temporarily left the signatures of physical suffering behind, and also have little ability to cause them permanent harm.

You will no doubt have seen various drawings of religious figures posing harmoniously with animals. To my mind the symbolism of this is that if it is possible to reach a certain state of physical harmony, free of energy created from suffering, we are able to no longer represent an energetic threat to animals.

Once this state is achieved, different levels of interaction can become available. I believe a part of reaching this point can be developed from observing a spiritual based diet for long enough that each of our cells become created from food and energy born out of non-suffering.

I respect that this could seem a little farfetched; new age, free spirited, hippie type of thinking even. But, I have lots of personal stories to the way wild animals have engaged with me over many years that help demonstrate these claims. These will perhaps be better told at another time and by the people who have witnessed those events unfold. My sole purpose of this chapter is to try and introduce you to viewpoints and knowledge you might not have considered before. I hope to show how this could help prepare your own bodies to work with energies you might not have previously engaged with.

To summarise my approach, I feel that if we view the body as a tuning fork that is able to vibrate at a number of different frequencies, making sure we reduce the unwanted heavier vibrations associated with suffering, this will allow us to better hear the ones that interest us. The vibration of suffering can easily drown out the sympathy of spiritual energy. I believe it would also be fair to say that certain frequencies will negatively disrupt the fields of other conscious beings causing them to naturally wish to withdraw away from that noise.

There is no escaping our bond to that which we consume, I believe by keeping the body in the best physical condition possible, we will help to ensure the mind is both strong and clear. Many aspects of health are genetically predetermined or otherwise out of our hands. Despite this, I believe it is important to remember that we are all able to choose what we eat. Through food, we can influence powerful change within ourselves. If you want it, that change can become an important tool in unlocking personal enlightenment.

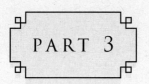

PART 3

The Mind Meeting The Body

CHAPTER 12

An Introduction To Panoptic Meditation

DO YOU WANT TO increase your I.Q by up to 23 percent? Would you like to reduce stress, lengthen your attention span and enhance your self-awareness? There are numerous scientific studies to back-up the powerful effects meditation brings, and if you have answered 'yes', to any of the above questions – love it or hate it – to achieve the growth outlined, meditation will need to become part of your routine.

Maybe you have already experimented with meditating and find the practice to be too difficult to master. Perhaps you are well on your way to becoming an expert and have already started to reap the rewards. Whatever your experience level, during this chapter I will be sharing how I have come to develop a unique form of this ancient art, and I will explain how to overcome some of the common problems people can face that hold them back from achieving their meditative potential.

I have tried and tested many forms of meditation and eventually after years of practice I began to realise I was on a path to developing a style that offers some specific benefits. At first, I did not see what was happening as the progression was very natural and intuitive. I liken this phase of the development to the eye not being able to see the eye; although I was able to perceive the journey from my own perspective, I could not look upon it as a *whole* until I began to share my experiences with others. Eventually, after I began answering other people's questions on the subject and describing my methods, I realised some aspects that I spoke of have not been written about or taught elsewhere.

Then as the journey progressed, a name to define this style was very fittingly revealed to me during meditation. I now refer to my methods as Panoptic Meditation. You will also notice that in chapter 6 I refer to my Panoptic Mapping method as a tool to instruct the higher self. Although parts of this method were built from very old knowledge, applying Panoptic Principles allowed me to create something I believe to be uniquely effective.

I believe this is the result of my entire life experience to-date and it is also one of the driving forces behind the work I now do. In addition to the personal improvement that I believe all forms of meditative practice offer, Panoptic Meditation allows us to access and interact with a form of universal energy that can bring profound knowledge into this World.

The definition of Panoptic is, '-Showing or seeing the whole at one view.' I will use this chapter to demonstrate how engaging with the energy available from this form of meditation, has benefited my own life and therefore, what is possible for you. I will also explain some of the basic techniques that you can use to begin on this path should you so desire.

By now, you will likely have come to realise when beginning a new topic I like to ask some simple and possibly obvious questions to get started. This chapter is no different, and although many of you will have an idea of what meditation is, I would like to start at the very beginning with an actual definition of the term:

'To meditate is to focus one's mind for a period of time, in silence or with the aid of chanting, for religious or spiritual purposes, or as a method of relaxation.'

It is said the goal of meditation is to go beyond the mind and experience our essential nature, which some teachers have described as *peace, happiness* and *bliss.* This definition gives us a great insight into why so many people throughout history have advocated its use as an effective form of personal development. After all, who doesn't want to be happy and at peace!

Many of us, would agree the pursuit of personal happiness is a desirable goal that we should strive for. This topic of happiness arises very frequently within the work I do and unfortunately it is common to hear people express a view, in which they believe true happiness is something that might not necessarily be achieved.

Those of us with low self-esteem could feel they have not done anything to deserve to be happy. Others with busy lives might not have the time to take care of their happiness for a variety of reasons. Maybe work commitments or caring for a family mean they decide to put this aspect of life on hold, until some undefined point in the future.

Another common thing I have heard over the years is that some people feel they should forget about complete happiness and be thankful as they already have a good life. I find this extremely interesting, as it demonstrates that there are some of us in this World who feel a small amount of happiness is enough. People can believe a little is all they deserve or perhaps can achieve. Therefore, this type of life should be accepted, in lieu of achieving the level of happiness they truly desire.

I believe if a person thinks that deferring happiness is normal, that this idea can prevent them from committing to take-up meditation to start with. If someone does not have the solid mental foundation to value their own happiness, deciding mediocracy is acceptable, it will be easy to find excuses that put other people or other tasks ahead of meditation.

If we have chosen a life of accepting a little, it can seem unrealistic to believe that we are allowed to ask for a lot. I feel there is a culturally accepted idea that long-term meditation practise can lead to profound states of happiness. Therefore, we must choose to believe we are allowed true happiness or its likely we will give up.

It is also true that seeing is believing, perhaps you have not seen how meditation can be of use so have no desire to try it. If either of these things feel relatable to you, don't worry. I invite you to trust that you can begin to reap the rewards sooner than you might think. Positive experience can change perception extremely rapidly, the methods I describe over this chapter are designed to offer a viewpoint that you might not have heard before.

There are a huge variety of approaches to finding contentment in this World; some require money, others require people or a whole host of different external factors. In my opinion meditation is the only tool to improve well-being that we can all use with no outside input and completely free of charge. All we need to do when starting out is allow five minutes to be by ourselves every few days so that we can learn and develop.

Even the busiest of us can spare that time and anyone who wants to insist they literally have no time to spare ever, in my opinion, is masking a deeper problem they do not wish to address. For the purpose of this chapter I will assume you do have those five minutes and are prepared to make a commitment towards exploring how meditation can improve your life.

When I reach this point in the discussion, after advising on the benefits regular practise can bring, many people unfamiliar and unsure of meditation might express one of two views: First, I might hear something along the lines of, 'meditation sounds really confusing and difficult, I don't know if I will be able to get it'. The second most common thing I would expect to hear roughly sounds like this; 'yes, I have tried it before but I really didn't get on well with it and had to give it up. I did try but I guess it just won't work for me with how my mind is'.

Both of these responses are entirely normal and luckily, it is fairly easy to explain why meditating can be so difficult for the untrained mind.

Other people will treat meditation as a big scary task that they absolutely must master if they are to be an authentic spiritual person. This self-inflicted pressure only serves to delay and obstruct progress. I invite those of you feeling this way to relax and not take yourself so seriously. Nobody is an expert at anything when they start out, life is supposed to have a level of fun and difficulty associated with it.

Part of the art of good spiritual progression is to be able to laugh at one's self, whilst being prepared to make all the mistakes necessary. Errors are powerful teachers and if used correctly can help us to find a deeper love for ourselves. If we keep picking ourselves up after things don't go our way, the mind will gradually become more calm and relaxed. By extension of this process, the increased calm will give rise to a deep inner knowing. Understanding that you alone possess the power to bring yourself quickly back to a calm and relaxed centre is a truly enlightening gift. As you perfect this, you can begin to become the master of your own mind.

Assuming that we have reached the point of agreeing to value our own happiness, followed by deciding we would like to learn meditation – then the next point I like to explain is, why it can be so difficult for many of us to achieve the results we would like. An easy way to do this is by referring to a form of psychotherapy created in the late 1980s by a psychologist called Marsha M. Linehan: Called DBT - Dialectical behavioural therapy and was developed as an approach to help identify and change negative thinking patterns.

We can use the methods of DBT to help identify some different mental states that all of us experience from time-to-time. I have found it very insightful to consider the impacts that each state can have on meditation. DBT teaches that these states are referred to as the emotional mind, the reasonable mind and the wise mind. It is said that everybody possesses each of these three states and that most people gravitate towards one of them at a time.

To briefly summarise each of them in turn:

1 – The Emotional Mind: This is a state when feelings control a person's thoughts and behaviour.

2 – The Reasonable Mind: This is when someone approaches any given situation intellectually. In this state of mind, a person will have a bias towards making decisions based from fact.

3 – The Wise Mind: This refers to a state of balance between both the reasonable mind and emotional mind. When a person experiences this state, it is said they can recognise and respect their feelings, while responding to them in a rational manner.

DBT has a wide range of uses and is a fascinating subject that you can read about in great detail online if interested. Incorporating some of the core aspects of DBT with my personal experience and knowledge, has helped me to develop good meditation practices that can easily be explained to others.

In doing this, I have found that the biggest reasons people can struggle to meditate is that they are often unaware they are stuck in either a reasonable or emotional mind state. Each of these states offers a particular set of obstacles to meditation. Therefore, I will offer some basic strategies that can help you identify when you are in either state, then overcome the most common difficulties each can bring.

Starting with the emotional mind; it is common when we are experiencing this state to gravitate towards things that make us *feel* something. The little voice in our head that guides us could be telling us we need a rest. But, it doesn't matter when we are experiencing an emotional mind, as it is more appealing to replay thoughts or memories that make us feel something… Happy, sad, angry – maybe recalling something funny that happened years ago – it isn't really of consequence what the feeling is, as during this state the deep goal of your mind will be to immerse itself in feeling emotions of any description.

Building upon the teachings of DBT, it is my opinion that our physical body is the dominating force behind the emotional state of mind. Emotions can literally be felt as I spoke about in earlier chapters. These feelings can often be the result of chemicals being released by the brain in response to various triggers or stimuli. This observable and measurable chemical response is within the realms of the physical World and therefore the strategies for overcoming these problems exist within the same realm.

An absolute beginner to meditation might experience an undisciplined emotional mind; in the sense of recalling the past and how it had made them feel. For example, while sitting still meditating, with the absence of any fresh external stimulus, replaying numerous memories is natural. All of the emotions that come along with each stage of the recall process, is an obvious substitute to allow the emotional mind state to continue its function. Eventually, as we begin to develop and learn to dismiss the replaying of the past, sometimes we instead start to notice and become distracted by unwanted physical sensations.

Many people who have been working hard to factor meditation into their routines will find at some stage they reach a point where the mind is settled but the body tingles or tickles in places. Maybe it feels like butterflies in the tummy, possibly a finger or toe starts to develop an itch that needs to be observed and responded to.

I believe these unwelcome sensations can also fall within the domain of the emotional mind. This part of our being will employ various tricks in an attempt to make you feel something. The whole point of this system's existence is to deal with feelings of any description and after years of being able to operate freely, the emotional mind is certainly going to protest that you now wish for it to quieten.

There are two simple techniques we can use to overcome these forms of distraction while meditating. If you are experiencing the distracting visions of past experiences I refer you back to the breathing techniques I spoke about for dealing with anxiety in Chapter 9. Taking a two-minute cycle of inhaling to the count of four, pausing and then exhaling while continuing the count to ten should begin to quieten this particular problem.

There are many other breathing techniques we can use within meditation to achieve various specific aims and I will be happy to discuss these in future books. However as I have previously said, the purpose of this book is to teach the foundations of what you can do to bring in the personal development and awakening you seek. For a person who is starting out, the four-ten breathing method will suffice to help along your path.

If you have reached a stage in your meditation practice in which the mind has developed enough discipline to stop recalling memories, however, you are distracted by unwanted physical sensations even after employing the breathing techniques, I invite you to consider the purpose of yoga. To me, yoga is an extremely effective tool in preparing the body for meditation.

Yoga connects you with your physical self in a way that allows you to begin understanding how each individual part of yourself feels. Eventually, this will teach the power to consciously engage with your muscles in new ways that can bring in physical stillness when required. I believe by fostering harmony within the body using this form of exercise prepares a person to learn how to meditate for increasingly longer periods of time.

Unfortunately, I feel that the growth of yoga within the West over the past few decades has lost touch with this fundamental truth. We are all told of the various physical improvements yoga offers, but to me, the connection between meditation and yoga is not highlighted enough within Western practice. There are numerous examples of Indian yogis sitting in unbroken meditation for days on end, but there is little guidance of how to achieve this within Western yogic methods.

I believe the body needs movement while the mind needs stillness.

Therefore in my view anyone blocked from effectively meditating due to a dominant emotional mind, causing persistent unwanted physical sensations, can overcome this by taking some simple stretches of the effected muscles before starting a meditation.

At the beginner level, you do not need to undergo a long yoga session to overcome these common blocks, and there is no requirement for you to take-up the discipline of yoga either. A person who is able to sit in unbroken meditation for a number of hours will likely not be reading this book. I try to share all variations of the techniques I have used at different stages, so you have lots of different tools at your disposal as you progress.

I am fully aware that we all lead busy lifestyles and that transitioning to living in a way that is more connected to the self takes time. You might not currently have much time available and in this instance I would suggest compared with other options, meditation would be the best use of whatever time you can spare when starting out.

Advising someone with a restricted amount of free time to learn yoga and meditation together is going to overwhelm them. I share the benefits of yoga so the knowledge is present in your mind as you begin to develop spiritually. For some of us, the eventual goals will bring us to a place of practising both disciplines simultaneously.

So, if you are suffering from the distractions of unwanted physical sensations and are only meditating for periods of five minutes or so, I believe completing a few simple stretches will help. If you allow yourself literally one minute to stretch as if you were warming up for a jog before you start your meditation, I would expect an almost immediate reduction in the strength of these unwanted feelings.

This simple activity of stretching is a way of offering the emotional mind the reassurance that you are aware of your body's needs and how it feels. At its most basic level, stretches before meditation demonstrate to your mind that you have taken a moment to become aware of each area of the body. By choosing to do this, the result will be an increased awareness of any aches and pains that could be present. Once you have observed these and given acceptance to anything that might be uncomfortable, the emotional mind will not need to take the opportunity to continuously remind you during meditation.

If you are still troubled by physical energy within meditation, you can add a mental extension to this stretching each time as an unwanted feeling arises. When your focus begins to shift away from stillness to observing some unwanted feeling in the body, you can then have a dialogue with yourself to overcome it. I like to remind people that they are allowed to use that little voice in their heads to talk to themselves.

Personally, during these moments when I was still being distracted by unwanted feelings, I would simply say to myself: *You know we just spent some time stretching and during that time I became aware of what you are now trying to show me again. Thank-you for reminding me of that feeling, I am aware it needs addressing and in the near future I will see what I can do about it. But for now please accept that I know it is there and now please let it subside so we can carry on with this meditation.*

Many of us will feel odd when speaking to ourselves in this way. I know once upon a time, I certainly found it almost laughable that I could change how I felt by talking to myself. This feeling of silliness can be accentuated if you have only ever identified yourself as a single entity, as you might ask, what is the point in saying something you already know? Others will have perhaps fallen out of the practice of speaking to themselves and people experiencing this attitude can hold a sense of reluctance to engage with themselves in this way.

Nobody wants to feel silly and it is natural to avoid anything that has the potential to make that happen. However, I would like to remind you again that you have nothing to lose by trying out the methods I have described. The other side of this argument is that you have a lot to gain if it works out.

If you decide to use the Panoptic Mapping method from Chapter 6, you could actually write a map that begins to instruct the higher self to overcome any meditative difficulties. Remember, the higher self is reconstructing your reality and can begin to show you how to achieve a successful meditation routine if you ask in the correct manner.

These are some of the most common hurdles that the emotional mind can throw at us when meditating. With some determination I believe anyone can quickly overcome these challenges and start developing a productive routine of meditation. The emotional mind does have a few other tricks it can deploy, but what I have shared so far should be enough to create the space allowing you to begin exploring your potential.

You will recall that I wrote there is another state of mind that can disrupt meditation. This is called the reasonable mind, and this state can offer its own set of unique distractions that will often revolve around problem solving. Your reasonable mind is the part of you that loves to think about the future and calculate the likelihood of any given situation unfolding.

How many hypothetical discussions have we all had throughout life with both ourselves and with others? The topics can stretch from the most obvious and likely of scenarios, to the most absurd. Simple examples of this are: Where do you want to go on holiday? What would your superhero power be if you could choose anything and what would you do with it?

None of us escape this way of thinking at points in life and this mechanism has some extremely useful benefits in our day-to-day routines. We analyse and predict outcomes so frequently, that often we don't even realise we are doing it. For example, you wake up in the morning and make a decision on what to wear depending on how you expect the weather to be that day.

If you are traveling anywhere no matter how far it is, you will try to calculate the best route depending on factors like the time you leave home, or how much traffic you might have to face. The reasonable mind is set to effortlessly offer us great solutions to all sorts of problems, but if we try to meditate while in this state of mind, we can expect to face one hypothetical problem after another.

The more you try to fight this mechanism, the more seemingly important problems will be presented to you. Did you lock the front door? Have you checked for that important email you are waiting on? Are you going to pay this month's bills on time? Do you need to move some money from one account to another or ask your boss for some overtime?

You could attempt to develop a resistance to listening, or simply ignore these questions during meditation, but I can almost guarantee by taking that type of approach will result in you eventually facing one question that absolutely must be dealt with immediately. Something so important will pop into your mind that you had forgotten about, the only solution will be to stop meditating and deal with it there and then.

Aside from disrupting meditation, the reasonable mind is what can make it almost impossible to sleep sometimes. This system when overactive loves to remind us of everything we most definitely must address in the future as soon as our heads hit the pillow. So how do we bring this mental state into check when facing unwanted hypothetical calculations during meditation?

Again, there are many techniques to overcome this, and again I will detail two of the most simple in the hope we can create the space for you to develop your meditations. The quickest and easiest approach for me during the early part of my development, was allowing the time to write a to-do list for tomorrow. I would do this fifteen minutes or so before I planned to begin meditating. In doing this, I learned that by creating this list it would work towards building a basis to satisfy the idea that I needed to be prepared for the future.

Then, if any thoughts of future scenarios that required my attention arose in the preceding meditation, I could have a dialogue with myself in a similar way that I described dealing with the emotional mind. This time however I would reason slightly differently and perhaps a little more firmly.

I could say something along the following lines: *You have had all day to let me know about the importance of preparing for these situations and as you know I have already written a list of things to tackle tomorrow. I am not ignoring anything that needs to be done. Right now I wish to leave the future in the future, so please allow me this space to focus on the present moment and stop showing me what could happen at a future time.*

These remarkably simple sentences backed-up with the act of creating a list, usually worked very quickly in quietening these types of thought patterns. Sometimes however, if we are going through a phase of anxiety or are facing lots of challenges in our lives, a list might not be enough. You will have perhaps noticed the link between how I have described the reasonable mind operates and how I wrote about the escalation of anxiety in Chapter 9.

I believe this state of mind not only wants to prepare us for future possibilities, but also serves to protect us from future difficulties. When life is throwing challenges our way, the reasonable mind can work extremely hard to try and look after us. Unpredictable and turbulent moments in life can have unpredictable outcomes, so assessing all possibilities to work out the best way forward is a natural reaction. During challenging times, you will find the four-ten breathing technique detailed throughout this book will help to bring this mental state into check, and stop you feeling that the future needs to be addressed instead of meditating on the *now*.

Over the years, I have come to see that both untrained emotional and reasonable minds can have similarities to how a young child demands attention. They seem to have an almost endless determination to be heard and will not rest until you listen. Even when you do listen they might want you to hear the same thing over and over regardless of your reaction.

However, it should not be a battle, I am thankful to hear of people experiencing these challenges as it demonstrates their mind is operating in a healthy and natural state. It assures me that as with children – over time and with the correct guidance – maturity is guaranteed. Anyone who wants to awaken their own personal enlightenment will need to accept that meditation is an important part of the process. Now I have covered some of the common blocks, I would like to continue with what you can expect as your practice develops.

Some of you reading this book will have likely never sat in meditation, so I will briefly talk about what exactly someone in this position could do to start. I specifically chose waiting to explain how to actually meditate until after talking about the common blocks, as I want to prevent those of you who are starting out on this journey from becoming disheartened if you are meeting these frustrating and common obstacles. In my experience, a basic understanding of the challenges one could face, creates this sense that they should push on, instead of giving up if they appear unexpectedly.

A simple online search of how to begin meditation will provide page after page of videos and helpful guides. There are spoken guided meditations by hypnotists and spiritualists. Buddhist and Yogic techniques are also popular, in fact there is so much to choose from, a beginner could easily feel a little overwhelmed. The more you read online, you might even feel some of the information to be conflicting and therefore, talking yourself out of starting altogether, and deferring it to another time is understandable.

To avoid confusion, I will make it as simple as possible. You can sit, lay down or even stand, as long as you are comfortable and will not be distracted, or needed elsewhere for at least five minutes – you have what you need to get going. In my early days of development in this field, I chose to lay down, it was comfortable and I could easily use my own bedroom, therefore effectively clearing a space for myself where I would not be interrupted.

When ready and comfortable, I would slowly take three of the deepest breaths I had taken that day. Each time I exhaled I would visualise expelling any stale air present and anything that had not served me during the day so far. I would visual-ise all the situations and energy that had been present that day, leaving my being on the breath and evaporating into the universal energy that envelops each and every one of us. Next I would mentally scan my body and tell myself that any discomfort I might have noticed could be addressed later. I then asked; *for now I wish that those feelings would subside to the lowest level possible.* I would finally imagine that my whole body had become very relaxed.

Once I had spent a few minutes quietening the physical body, I would next work to reduce the distracting mental chatter our untrained minds often insist upon engaging in. Again there are many techniques available and eventually after lots of trial and error, I found one particular strategy very effective. I would picture a volume dial within my mind's eye and used this as a representation for how loud the mind was at that point.

The dial can be of any size, shape or design you choose, but its purpose is to visualise that it can turn down the volume of your thoughts. The important thing is that whatever the starting position of the dial, you announce to your mind that as you visualise turning it down, this will in turn begin to quieten the thoughts. I would always picture turning the dial down very gently to begin with.

You will quickly become aware that the mind responds in kind by gently quietening itself, and that the thoughts you are holding have less and less power to interrupt the growing calmness you are experiencing. Once you have found a point of comfortable stillness and have quietened the various thoughts and feelings the body and mind can offer – that's it; you are in a state of meditation.

At this point, you could perhaps begin to experiment with listening to the sounds around you without trying to interpret or label them. This is a great way to start playing with learning to really feel how you connect and fit into your environment.

As you learn to simply listen without judgement or interpretation, it can eventually become possible to feel like the internal and external have become the same. Panoptic Meditation is a development of this state and I will explain what is possible in the next chapter.

As a beginner, these exercises will be enough to start training your mind and body to accept meditation with less and less resistance. Once your body becomes more acceptant of this practice you will eventually learn that you can enter this state of stillness quicker, and remain in it comfortably for longer periods of time. There are many additional exercises you can bring into meditations as you become more skilled and I will write about these in the future.

I believe a large part of the happiness you experience in life can be correlated to the quality of your thoughts. Meditation is a beautiful path towards training the mind to instinctively prune the thoughts that hold us back, while allowing those that best serve us to blossom.

If you are interested in listening to my guided meditations please feel free to look at the assets section of my website: www. TheTheoryOfYou.com/Assets

CHAPTER 13

The Panoptic Potential

IF MEDITATION IS THE key to an increased I.Q., a stronger sense of happiness and the reduction of stress, then Panoptic Meditation would use these results as a platform to truly expand consciousness. The benefits that come along with this form of meditation include new ideas and information that can help empower you in a way you might not have experienced before.

I believe that although meditation is widely used as a method to enhance the life of an individual, this is only a small fraction of what is possible. The separation from the self that is achieved as a result of developing the art of Panoptic Meditation can eventually allow us to receive information and knowledge that also has the power to benefit, and potentially improve the lives of others.

In Chapter 6, I described the principle of auto-suggestion, and how we are able to consciously transfer thoughts into the subconscious. I also wrote that in addition to this rule, there are certain thoughts that can be picked up from the ethereal energies within the Universe. These types of thoughts are able to bypass the process of auto-suggestion. Shortly, I will demonstrate a powerful example of this and the transformational power that connecting to this energy can bring forward.

This chapter will be slightly different to others within this book, as it focuses more on what is eventually possible if you choose to take a new path, as opposed to advising strategies that you can start right now. I have purposely structured this book to demonstrate actionable philosophies that will help anyone to pave the way towards awakening their personal spiritual development.

Although many of us will want to know what we can do today to come closer to achieving our dreams, I believe it is important to also have a small glimpse of what is possible once we have undergone that work. I hope to demonstrate what the future can bring if you remain committed and disciplined in the months and years after reading this book. I will start with addressing the things you might already be hoping to gain and then move onto topics you might not have considered yet.

The most common and perhaps obvious question I am asked in relation to higher purposes of meditation, surrounds contacting one's spiritual guides or other such entities. Many people on a spiritual path want to know how to find and connect with these energies. I am also frequently asked if everybody has guides – the answer to this is simply, yes. Guides, guardian angels, spirits, Mother Earth, intuition, higher energies – people have a huge variety of names to describe what I think is a widespread expectation of the type of communication that will become possible, as an individual develops on their spiritual journey.

It is certainly true that meditation can allow you to access the spaces these forms of energy exist within. However, I feel this topic has been covered at great lengths by others and if you wish to focus on this route of development there are numerous resources available.

I do have certain techniques for linking with guides, I am happy to share, but in my opinion, this path diverts slightly away from the topic of this book. This is because engaging with those entities is not necessarily going to help in the ways many of us expect or hope for. I believe guides offer a much more supportive capacity to your spiritual development and therefore complement the journey as opposed to enlightening the path.

It is widely accepted that guides are energies who have previously spent time on the Earth plane and reached a point in their development they can perhaps spend less time in this space and instead use their knowledge to support others along their journey.

Naturally, it would seem like an attractive proposition to engage with these energies, as they would surely have a lot to share. I realised at a very young age that these energies are still on a path of development themselves and therefore, I found myself asking what I thought to be a very natural question; Who or what is helping and teaching the guides?

The answer to this question did eventually show itself to me in a very unexpected way and I feel the preparation and results of engaging with that form of energy are markedly different to working with your spiritual guides. Before I share examples of this energy and what it offers, I will first explain the signs to look for, that represent you are entering into a state of Panoptic Meditation.

Once you have started to master the act of sitting or lying in perfect stillness with the absence of any thoughts or physical stimuli – eventually, you will begin to notice a change in how you perceive yourself and your surroundings. After a while, all of a sudden, it will be possible to sense what I describe as an expansion of awareness.

It is very hard to describe reaching this point as it occurs within the consciousness. That energy operates in a non-physical space and we are limited in our language to describe this energy. However, it could perhaps be comparable to sensing a different air pressure. When we step out of a sauna into the room outside, the body is immediately able to differentiate the change in temperature, humidity and pressure. The expansion in awareness I am talking of, when it occurs, happens as quickly as stepping from the hot steam room to another much cooler one.

Due to the speed of this expansion, it can take a long time to become acceptant of what is happening without the mental mind beginning to chatter and ask questions. The very first time it happened to me, I found it to be a startling experience and my mind immediately began asking what had just occurred. This mental noise instantly brought my awareness back to its natural point.

Maintaining a Panoptic state can be like spinning plates on a stick, but without looking at them or allowing to ask yourself if they are spinning at the right speed. This paradox takes time to master, but I guarantee the rewards will outweigh the effort when you get there.

During spiritual meditations we might be aware that we still have a human form. Many of the spiritual mediums, monks and shamans that I have worked with, have explained to me that, when meditating they will gravitate to a particular form of how they appeared, at a certain time in their life.

Reading this it might be natural to wonder how the topic of meditative projection even arose to begin with! Why would one even think to ask about how one perceives themselves in meditation? The answer is, I stumbled upon this by accident. Many years ago during a group meditation session, the tutor asked how the sitters saw themselves within that state.

Through listening to the answers, I then discovered what was natural to me, differed to everyone else in attendance that day.

Some people see themselves as children during meditation, others view themselves at a specific age, perhaps during early adulthood. I believe this serves the purpose of allowing them to distinguish their form between that of their guides, or other entities. It also allows them to maintain a certain perception of their own individuality. After all, a person existing within a material body on this material Earth, has spent every moment of their lives connected to a sense of their own individuality, so suddenly losing this can be alarming.

To reach a state of Panoptic Meditation, we must begin by preparing the mind to accept it is possible to temporarily shed the illusion of a physical body. Learning to understand this makes it possible to temporarily reshape the way we see our own individuality. This was a gradual process for me and started with a realisation that during some points of meditation I did not have legs.

The very first time I became aware of this, was during a meditation that I was floating over a mountain scape. As I looked down to try and focus in on something that had caught my attention, I was surprised to see a mass of glowing energy where I thought my legs should be. This separation of attachment to my physical self was gradual and it wasn't until I had fully embraced this, that I was able to begin achieving Panoptic states.

I believe that very much like the idea of having the correct dress code for the correct venue or event, can also be applied to accessing particular nonphysical spaces during meditation. You would not wear sports clothes to the opera or a swimming suit to a tennis match. The places that hold the knowledge I am about to describe require that you do not project or hold on to your human form. In fact, very much like holding the right key to open the right lock, accessing some of these spaces in my opinion, is not possible when carrying the energetic weight associated with our human forms.

The energy that resides within these places presents itself as more of a resonance than a physicality. It seems to me that holding the illusion of our materially structured body while in that place, is like tying an anchor to your leg and then attempting to swim in the ocean. Once we learn to shed this unnecessary weight, it is possible to drift on the current to observe and engage with all that is offered.

A way to describe this transformation, is to understand that a molecule of water within the sea, is both an individual, but also simultaneously, connected to every other molecule within the ocean. If we put an electric current into water then the electrical energy can effortlessly conduct over large distances.

I believe this is similar to how information can be passed from one being to another within these realms. We do not need to be at the source of the information to receive it, we just need to temporarily assume the same properties of the energetic water that is able to conduct and receive the signals. Auto-suggestion is related to the structure of the mind and so releasing some of this structure, I believe, is how thought reception from external sources can become possible.

Now that I have very briefly explained what Panoptic Meditation is, I will share some of what has been shown to me. Before I start though, I ask that you take a moment to pause reading and look at the front cover of this book. Try and clear your mind and then look at the symbol within the mandala. I would like you to take a good twenty seconds or so studying it before coming back. Once you have done this, I want you to ask yourself, *how does that arrangement of shapes and colours make you feel?* Make a note of what thoughts pass through your mind as it will become relevant later on.

These particular shapes were shown to me during a meditation in November 2018. Many years ago, once I began to access the spaces possible with Panoptic Meditation, I began to see arrangements of geometric shapes and patterns that continuously flow and transform.

Initially, I just thought this was a quirk of meditating and did not give much thought to them, other than enjoying their complexity and beauty. Eventually though, I found that sometimes, certain arrangements would hold form for slightly longer than others. These shapes and colours often left me with an overwhelming feeling that I should try and draw them. I am no artist, but I starting keeping rough sketches of what was shown to me in a small journal.

It was not until I shared these images with one of the Peruvian shamans, that I began to understand the significance of what was being revealed. Many people will refer to these shapes as sacred geometry, and some of these patterns actually occur naturally throughout nature. Bees arrange their honeycomb in geometric patterns, sunflower heads arrange their seeds with them. Snails and sea creatures naturally construct their shells using these principles and we can even observe these patterns in the way hurricane clouds form. Looking into space, it is even possible to see galaxies arranged under these geometrical arrangements.

Sacred geometry is prevalent everywhere and the more we look, the more examples we can find. Humankind has discovered its presence within the Fibonacci sequence, the golden ratio and these mathematical equations have been used for millennia in the construction of various buildings across the World.

So, if sacred geometry is so widely present within our Universe, I guess it should be little shock that it would be possible to see this during meditation. My journey has come to show me that these shapes are in fact a universal language. Some of you might find this a little farfetched, but please bear with me while I explain.

It has been said, that if humankind was to be visited by aliens tomorrow, our best chance of attempting to communicate would be through the use of maths. The law of mathematical principles are seen as universal and can transcend spoken language. It is also theorised that any species of a certain intelligence, would have also discovered maths and therefore it could be used to communicate.

I do agree with this to an extent, but I think the problems would start when we realise the symbols we have allocated to describe a particular number, are not the same as another specie's symbol to describe the same number. Maths underpins the Universe, but the linguistic symbolism of mathematical principles, in my eyes, would develop separately and individually within each closed system; in other words the culture that discovers it will interpret it uniquely. The laws of maths could be universal, but the symbolism to represent such laws can surely vary between cultures?

Despite all of this, I believe shape and colour have the ability to transcend any closed cultural system.

We might call a circle a circle on Earth, but even if it has another name somewhere else, a circle is still exactly the same shape. Colour also follows this principle, our eyes might perceive it differently to the eyes of another being, but the spectral frequency for each colour will always remain the same wherever you are.

Using these ideas, I believe that particular arrangements of shape and colour represent various different messages. I believe that we can train the body and mind to receive such messages. However, there are currently very few people in the World who are fluent with the representations. I feel this is the true language of the Universe, but little is understood about this knowledge within our current societies.

Fortunately, the South American shamans have spent millennia learning the meanings of this form of language and passing the knowledge down the generations. For example, the Shipibo people are able to see and hear these patterns when working with the plants of the Amazon and then reproduce them on their clothing and other textiles. They believe every design has its own specific meaning and can bring wisdom, protection, healing and abundance among many other things. Over the last few years, each time I visit the Amazon, I have been learning the significance of what each set of shapes means, while sharing the patterns that have been shown to me.

This brings us neatly back to the cover of this book. A revered Shaman explained that this arrangement of shapes is the Universe inviting you to embrace a spiritual path and understand that it is possible for you to spread the energy of knowledge and spiritual harmony to others seeking the same path. Although, I have been developing spiritually for many years, much of that development was personal and a lot of this journey was away from others.

I never felt the need to share my life publicly and much of the work I did for others happened spontaneously. Previously, I would always push back against any attention I gained from it. The design on the cover of this book came as an invitation to begin sharing my journey with others in a more public way. Listening and embracing this invitation has set in motion an incredible journey.

Although the cover drawing is an artistic representation, it manages to catch the essence of the arrangement. I am not sure if I will ever be able to truly explain these patterns with words and therefore, I am not sure if an artist will be able to completely capture how the shapes represent themselves.

However, I have noticed that when I show people this particular pattern, it seems to speak to those who are at a stage in life; where spiritual development is coming to the forefront of their mind. As this book outlines many of the foundations a person will need to pursue this journey, it felt fitting to try and extend the same geometric universal invitation that I was offered. In light of this, I again invite you to consider how the cover of this book makes you feel. How you feel, and how well it connects to you will give hints towards the path ahead.

Shape and colour also have the ability to define you on a much more personal level than you might realise. Shortly before writing this book, I stumbled upon a fascinating hint revealing this fact. One morning I was holding an online discussion about the topic of the unifying centre. I was talking about how I feel my perception of this Universe is related to the shape of my consciousness. This seemingly simple statement caused a bit of a stir because it turned out how I perceive the shape of my consciousness, was different to every person who was watching the talk.

So I ask you, If you had to assign a shape to your consciousness which one would it be? If you had to assign a colour to it, which would that be? This simple exercise provides hints to how these universal symbols exist deep within every single one of us.

Many people are aware of synchronicities and angel numbers. This section of the book would not be complete without giving these a mention. I believe that the energy powering the universal language I have outlined here, also has the ability to direct these forms of symbols into our awareness. Angel numbers can again bypass auto-suggestion. I believe they are a precursor to deeper spiritual insights. I feel these small prompts can wake a person up to the idea of engaging with the Universe on a deeper level. Angel numbers are a gateway to graduating up to the deeper language of colour and shape.

If you want to know more about how to interpret angel numbers, there is a free mini eBook on the assets section at this link: www.TheTheoryOfYou.com/Assets

There seems to be a positive feedback loop in place with these languages. I have noticed that if I listen to the advice each pattern presents to me, wonderful changes will begin to effortlessly unfold within my life. As more of these transitions occur, I find myself in a position to receive even more. Working in this way, really has helped to open one door after another. I feel that teaching people to understand that this is available to them, will help to spread a small piece of the positive change that many of us in society seem to be looking for.

I believe the shapes can also be a gateway to deeper knowledge. Within the energetic ocean of information that Panoptic Meditation offers access to, I have found it is also possible to bring forward ideas to help overcome some of the physical difficulties this World is facing. Between 2017 and 2018, I had a series of meditations that highlighted to me just how important working in this way is.

Many of us are well aware that we face a number of mounting global environmental crises. If we compare the history of humankind to the developmental scale of a child, it seems to me that we are just entering into a phase of increased self-awareness. Very much like the accelerated perceptions children experience after being at school for a few years. I believe as a species, we are no longer toddlers who can freely do as they wish, with no regard for tomorrow.

The mistakes we have collectively made during the past, originated from a place of blissful ignorance. Now we are becoming aware of the global issues that we are facing, as a consequence of our naivety, it seems we are not entirely sure what to do about it.

What is the answer? Well, in the same way that children behave, who are only just beginning to mature mentally, we could choose to point the finger of blame at others, while making an awful lot of noise about how *it wasn't our fault*.

The only problem with this approach is that as one party tries to disprove their role, and instead implicating another, the problems we all face are not going to get better. Once a child has exhausted this behaviour and realises acting that way has not fixed the problem, what is next? Commonly, the next approach would be to ask an adult for help.

We will all remember asking teachers, parents or other relatives to help guide us in our times of difficulties. Sometimes in childhood when arguing among our peers or siblings, we could not fix the situation ourselves alone, and felt compelled to tell or ask for support. I have decided, very much in this same way of asking for help, why should we be fixing our environment without a little bit of support and guidance?

Many years ago, I felt very drawn to the problem of plastic pollution and after some research I began to realise something interesting. Although there are some promising initiatives in place aimed at trying to start dealing with certain types of this pollution, one area was lacking; namely micro-plastic pollution.

There is lots of evidence to show that tiny microscopic plastic particles are entering the food chain in a number of ways. In many places our drinking water contains these particles and they can be so small, that even the plankton in the sea can consume them. Then, once the plankton is eaten by a larger fish, the particles are able to travel up the food chain, eventually reaching the fish that humans consume. Eating and drinking micro-plastics did not sound very appealing to me and I decided it would be good to do something about it.

So, I set the intent in my mind that I would like to learn if there is anything I can do to help. I kept this thought in my mind and during my day-to-day routine, I would regularly think that it would be nice if there were any energies around who might want to show me an answer. Eventually, after a few weeks of this, I began to see some interesting things during meditation.

At first it was very patchy and made no real sense, therefore I had no idea if my request for guidance was being answered. After seeing a few snippets of information I was reminded of an article I had read some years previously. This news piece detailed that up to 750,000 micro-plastic particles, are released into the waste water via our washing machines, per wash cycle. As there are millions of household washing machines in existence, I felt it would be beneficial to society and the wider environment, if I could find a solution.

One source of this pollution is a result of many modern textiles containing various types of plastics, that are woven into them. For example, nylon, polyester and elastin mixes are extremely common to find within the fabrics that make-up the majority of clothes we wear today. Unfortunately, some of this plastic breaks down and mixes with the water every single time we put these types of fabrics into a washing machine and run a cycle. This polluted waste water then leaves the machine through the waste pipe and heads off to our sewerage treatment plants.

The next problem is, that these treatment plants have no ability to capture the micro-plastic. Therefore, it is discharged with the treated water, joining our streams and rivers, which eventually head out to sea. I am very briefly outlining this issue and what I have discovered over the last few years is much more in-depth. This type of pollution is perhaps more widespread than many of us realise. If you are interested in my findings you can read more about what I have discovered on my website.

The reason I offer this background is so you can see the importance of what I was shown next. Through engaging with the energies that I have described throughout this chapter, a solution to this problematic issue was revealed to me. I was shown in perfect detail over a sequence of meditations, how to make a device that simply and quickly attaches to the waste water pipe on any household washing machine.

As the polluted waste water passes through this device, the micro-plastics are removed and contained within it. After the waste is cleaned, it then passes plastic free through the outlet pipe allowing the water to continue on its usual journey. I spent some time building and testing this device and now have one functioning perfectly within my own home.

I have managed to discretely collect micro-plastic containing material for nearly two years since. I have effectively stopped this pollution from entering the environment via my own home, while my washing machine continues to function perfectly. The device is small enough to be hidden away in the same cupboard the waste water pipe runs through, and I have documented the creation on my website.

Early in 2019, I undertook a 950-mile trek across the UK to try and raise some awareness of what I have created. Unfortunately, I found that some EU legislation prevents a private individual from being allowed to talk about matters of environmental sensitivity publicly. Therefore, social media and newspapers are restricted from sharing and publishing my story. Presently, I am at the beginning of a journey to bring this solution to the public's attention and I am excited to see how it develops.

Panoptic Meditation has offered me some truly fascinating insights into this World and our Universe. It offers a method to bring gifts from the universal energies that surround us and pass them into our physical World. Fully explaining this topic would require its own book. If enough people wish to learn about this, I will be happy to write a complete and in-depth guide on how to develop this style of meditation.

The energies I have engaged with through using this technique have shown me that very much like the analogy given earlier about children growing up, there are still adults in this Universe we can all turn to for help with matters we can't solve alone. Attacking each other and blaming the previous generations does nothing to solve the issues we now all face. I do not believe we need to protest in order to make changes either; to my mind, it is a much more rewarding experience to ask, – *What I can do about fixing a problem?* - than it is to shout that *I did not create the problem.*

There are practical solutions we can all take in regards to these problems. If we choose to allow angry and confrontational people to represent our environmental issues, the only result will be increased division and inaction. I believe a more beneficial approach is to be understanding of others and strict with ourselves.

For now though, I feel that over the last few chapters we have covered enough of the basics surrounding the physical aspects of our beings, to start along a path of growth with an eye on what is possible for heading into the future. It is now time to move onto the third and final system; *the consciousness.*

PART 4

The Consciousness

CHAPTER 14

A Panoptic View of Consciousness

WHERE DOES CONSCIOUSNESS COME from? Why are we here? What is the meaning of life? These are perhaps some of the biggest unanswered, and deeply personal questions that humanity face. Science would like to explain the answers with equations and perhaps by discovering what the fabric of this Universe is made up of. Religion points to the answers being the responsibility of a higher entity, or a creator – This being is said to possess comprehension on a level humans cannot perceive. Therefore, the truth about it all cannot be explained in a way our minds could understand.

I believe that consciousness is the third distinct system that exists within all of us. It is my opinion that the body is what roots us in this material space and the mind is the mediator between the physical and the nonphysical. The body houses the brain and the brain houses the mind, it can also be said, the mind is a gateway that can engage and influence the body, while also allowing the consciousness to shine through.

This is all pretty straightforward and is likely to be nothing you would not have heard before. I was not immune from wondering what the answers to the above questions could be. The energies I work with have offered some tantalising hints throughout the years that I will attempt to weave together throughout this chapter.

At points, I will need to refer to some scientific principles and I will attempt to explain these in the simplest ways possible. I understand that this topic can be a little unsettling for those of us who already have strong views relating to these questions. However, I would like to remind everyone that for the most part, we are all trying to reach the same destination. Just like a river that starts in the mountains and finishes at the sea; both the origin and destination are assured.

Each of us are born and will eventually die; we know where we come from and where we are all ultimately going. But we should remember, it is the journey in-between that brings these two points together. No two rivers will take the same route, but it does not mean one is trying to achieve anything different to another. Rivers exist to flow and will always take the path of least resistance. All I offer here, is an alternative perception to understanding these questions, that perhaps, you have not previously considered.

When we talk about the origin of a person, we might focus on the point of their physical birth. The day you came into this World seems like a great place to start with who you are. As I discussed earlier, the problem with thinking this way, is that it isn't exactly the start. Your birthday forgets the months spent developing within the womb. So is the point of conception when you began? Maybe, but your mother and father had to meet for this conception to occur. So if they had not crossed paths, who is to say you would ever have been born?

Using this trail of thought, we can trace your physical origin back further and further into the history of the Universe. Each time we find an answer to our beginnings, it would seem another set of events had to have previously unfolded for that particular thing to happen. If your parents, grandparents, great grandparents had not crossed paths, then you simply would not be here in this specific form today.

This eternal dance of seemingly miraculous interactions being required to create *you* is never-ending. We already discussed in previous chapters, that even the ancient stars had to live and die for the physical matter your cells are made of to be created. Therefore, ultimately, if the first molecules of matter did not form, and if the first star was not birthed into existence, there is no way you, or I, could have been born billions of years later.

I believe that human consciousness is prone to forgetting these important truths. We are continuously trying to break one event away from another in order to measure it. When thinking in this linear fashion, the true order of things is lost. I believe that space filling curves are the Universe's way of trying to remind us of this fact.

In mathematical analysis, a space filling curve's range contains an entire two-dimensional unit square. Mathematics explain this phenomena in quite a complex fashion. You can easily research this online if you are interested.

I mention these curves because they are prevalent in the visions induced by ayahuasca. When working with these plants, people have a tendency to focus on the big parts of the visions they might see. But, I have found a profound understanding of myself through connecting with the significance of space filling curves. I believe my connecting and interpretation of these two points is unique. In sharing this, I hope to bring comfort to those of us who worry that we are impermanent beings.

To my mind, space filling curves represent that, the entire existence of time (the range) fits inside our consciousness (the square). Einstein demonstrated that space-time can be bent with a strong enough amount of gravitational force. Therefore, time does not need to pass in a linear fashion, it can be manipulated.

Time is perhaps not able to be rewritten, but it can be slowed down, sped up, or revisited. You do this in your mind so naturally you don't even give it a moment's notice. As a child, life seems to take forever, a six-hour school day felt like it would drag on and on. If we started school at five-years-old, by the time we are ten, we would have spent 50 percent of our lifetime in education.

As we age, our view of time speeds up. When we get to twenty-years-old, being ten feels like it was a lifetime ago, It was in fact 50 percent of our life ago. Five years at ten, feels like ten years at twenty, they are both 50 percent. The longer we live, the less percentage value each year of life carries. At ten-years-old, one-year equals 10 percent of life. When at fifty-years-old, one-year equates to 2 percent of life. Hence, the reason why time feels like it accelerates the older we get. The existence of consciousness has the ability to house and shape time, which is why I believe space filling curves exist. When you feel low and like life is tough, they can be a gentle reminder of this important fact. Space filling curves hint that we are an extension of eternal energy that has the power to alter our perception of this force at will.

The complete range of our experiences; past, present and future, all folds in on itself, and exists within ourselves, and within the Universe. Everything exists simultaneously and woven eternally into our consciousness. Close your eyes and recall the first time you witnessed fireworks as a child. Is the light from that memory any less real inside your mind today than when you experienced it unfolding. Light is light, witnessing it or recalling it does not change its properties.

Therefore, if we are going to have any hope of trying to identify where all of this came from, we need to stop thinking in a linear fashion. Looking as far back into the history of our Universe as possible, is a good place to start, but you must understand what was present then, is also present now. Cue the first scientific principles, namely Thermodynamics and Entropy.

I will start by explaining Thermodynamics; This is defined as the branch of physical science that deals with the relations between heat and other forms of energy (such as mechanical, electrical, or chemical energy), and, by extension, of the relationships between all forms of energy.

An important law within Thermodynamics states that energy can neither be created or destroyed. It is also accepted that matter is a form of energy and extensive scientific experiments have demonstrated that although matter can move from one state to another, it cannot be destroyed.

A quick search online will show that many scholars regard consciousness as a form of energy. Therefore, under the laws of Thermodynamics it can neither be created or destroyed. Although energy can move from one form to another, it is said that the level of energy created at the start of this Universe is the same level present today.

If the Universe still holds the same amount of energy today as it did upon its creation, it is surely fair to suggest that the energy of consciousness must have been present at the start. This leads me on to my next question; What else was happening at the start of the Universe?

Scientific consensus is that during the early Universe, energy was spread evenly, and matter had not yet formed.

A quote from Brian Greene's 'The Fabric of the Cosmos', says, '-Our most refined theories of the origin of the Universe (our most refined cosmological theories) tell us that by the time the Universe was a couple of minutes old, it was filled with a nearly uniform hot gas composed of roughly 75 percent hydrogen, 23 percent helium, and small amounts of deuterium and lithium. The essential point is that this gas filling the Universe had extraordinarily low Entropy.'

Before I go any further I will draw your attention to the mention of the word 'Entropy' and briefly explain what it means. Entropy explains the journey from order to disorder. Understanding this term is important to help demonstrate what has been revealed to me surrounding consciousness. Effectively, Entropy is a measure of uncertainty or randomness – the higher the level of Entropy, the higher the level of disorder and chaos. Because the early Universe was nearly uniform, it is said during this time, a level of low Entropy existed, which basically equates to a high level of order.

Research has shown that during the earliest moments of the Universe, there was no physical matter in existence. The level of Entropy in the early Universe was too low for material to form. Scientists have also defined the rough age of the Universe when matter was born. As consciousness is pure energy, that is both unable to be physically seen or destroyed. I believe that it came before matter and was therefore in existence during the low Entropy state of the Universe.

If you take consciousness out of the body, how would you describe it and the properties associated with it? I believe it would not be wrong connecting the properties to consciousness, as that in which we associate with pure energy. As we know pure energy came before matter, I don't believe it to be incorrect to suggest consciousness was present before matter.

Knowing energy was present before matter and further examining the properties of this, we could perhaps describe energy as subatomic. Matter is made from atoms; subatomic energy is below matter and predates it. It is both unobservable or measurable and we know that 96 percent of the Universe is made from that which cannot be observed.

When trying to understand anything in life, we all know that understanding the properties associated with it can in turn help us to explore the laws that apply to it. We all understand that children look like their parents and will carry family traits. I bring your attention to this as the subatomic realm can be subject to a set of laws explained in a field of science we call Quantum Theory or Quantum Mechanics.

The rules of Quantum Mechanics are very different to the laws that govern physical matter and there have been a number of interesting discoveries in this field during recent times. In my opinion, some of these findings can help to explain certain things I have observed during meditation. These realisations provide some tantalising deeper hints to the true nature of what we all are, at our deepest levels.

I feel this is all important because, understanding the conditions present and the laws that define the boundaries of what was possible when consciousness was created, holds important lessons. This knowledge can help us to understand what traits we can associate to the conscious energy that flows through all of us.

Dogs do not give birth to kittens, so to understand what consciousness is, we must delve as deep as possible into the earliest moments of when we know that only pure energy existed. As the level of order was extremely high during the time the Universe was pure energy, before matter was created, it would be fair to suggest that balance and order would be traits of consciousness.

Many of us are familiar with the phrase, 'what you put in to something is what you get out'. Chaos is associated with disorder and high Entropy. Therefore, I believe that anything created during the beginning, low Entropy state of the Universe, would simply not be able to contain the characteristics of chaos. High levels of disorder did not come into existence until later on as the Universe aged.

Thinking along the lines that the available laws present during something's creation characterises what properties we can associate to it, becomes very interesting when adding Quantum Theory to this discussion. If consciousness is created from subatomic energy and that energy is bound by the laws of Quantum Mechanics, it would surely be prudent to examine some of what our brightest scientists have discovered in this field.

For example, quantum entanglement demonstrates that an action carried out on one particle can directly affect another, even when they are separated by large distances. It is theorised that quantum entanglement can allow the transmission of information at near instantaneous speeds and is therefore being used in the development of quantum computing.

Another idea, superposition – adds more complexity, as it demonstrates that at a quantum level, instead of existing in one fixed state, a particle exists in all states simultaneously and does not fix in one position until observed. Intuitively this makes no sense and perhaps the most famous attempt to explain this was made by Erwin Schrödinger with the thought experiment known as Schrödinger's Cat: Many of us are aware this experiment suggested that a hypothetical cat inside a box unable to be observed is therefore, under the laws of superposition.

While inside the box it cannot be observed, therefore is both dead and alive at the same time. Only when the cat is observed, one state can then become fixed.

This is a very simple explanation of the experiment, but interestingly, a development of this theory would point to a suggestion that the Universe could not exist, if there was no force to observe it. I use the word *force* because some physicists have dispelled the idea that the Universe requires an individual to observe it in order to exist.

Obviously, if a single conscious individual dies then the Universe will still exist, but we should not forget the laws of Thermodynamics – stating that energy cannot be destroyed. Therefore, as consciousness is energy, bound by the laws we have discussed, it must move from one form to another. I believe one could argue that this energy is an essential mechanism that has allowed this Universe to develop to the point as we know it today.

With some pondering, we could actually begin to associate space filling curves to have traits not too dissimilar to the above quantum theories. These realisations might even hint that the Universe itself has an underlying conscious energy.

Using the line of thinking that the child inherits the parents traits raised another point within my mind. I believe due to the lack of scientific support to prove otherwise, people commonly assume the Universe is made-up of energy that is blind. But, I ask; If this is true, how did you inherit the trait of perception? How did the energy that drives your awareness come to perceive? If consciousness did not exist before animals, where was it acquired from?

In my opinion, attachment to our physical bodies distracts us from asking these types of questions. Among other things, the body acts as a barrier that creates distance between you and other people. It is this barrier that has incorrectly taught people separation exists.

I understand many people will have arguments for and against applying Quantum Theory to consciousness. I also believe everybody is entitled to their own opinion. There is an emerging field of study called Quantum Biology, that I envisage, in the coming years will help to explain many of the body's deepest puzzles. I believe at some point, science will realise the level of entanglement we have between others, within this Universe, is on a scale that cannot currently be imagined.

Discovering the links between physical organic beings and quantum processes, will surely bring science closer to accepting the depths, that consciousness exists within this Universe. I chose to briefly talk about Quantum Theory as quite simply, I believe, the conditions present at the start of existence as we understand it, can explain a lot about how we view the World and ourselves today.

Stepping away from the quantum world and asking some other simple questions, allows us to start seeing what this all means. For example, how many of us have admired the beauty of a butterfly, the image of a snowflake under a magnified lens or a peacock's feathers? What do all these things have in common? The answer is, they contain a high level of symmetry or lower levels of Entropy. It can also be said that the things we find the most attractive within this Universe, have a high level of order present within them.

Beautiful things have traits just like the high order, low Entropy conditions that were present at the time we know energy was first in existence. Research has clearly shown humans have a deep-seated desire to search out, observe and interact with things that are in a highly ordered state. Human-kind goes beyond the realms of necessity in the pursuit of symmetry, we will often expend far more energy than is needed to organise our cities, buildings and homes, to display symmetrical properties.

There are some biological theories that suggest an attraction to symmetry offers an evolutionary advantage; for example, some healthy and high energy foods display symmetrical properties. Therefore, by evolving to recognise and search for these foods could have allowed our ancestors a higher chance of survival, but I believe this is only part of the answer.

I briefly spoke about the golden ratio in the previous chapter and how we have used this formula throughout history to construct our buildings, monuments and artworks to name just a few things. In fact, the deeper we look into the way we organise our lives, reveals that human beings seem to display pattern seeking behaviour with an affinity towards order in almost every area.

Many of us are intuitively drawn to making measurements or observations, to better explore and interpret situations that containing variables we can't easily control. Examples of this behaviour can be seen extending right back into childhood, in ways so obvious they can be easily missed. Any of us who were given clockwork toys as children, very quickly worked out that the more you wind them up, the further they could go. There is also a sense of great delight associated with cracking such patterns. I can personally recall the excitement of trying to wind-up my clockwork car as far as possible, to see how fast it would move.

We are all hardwired with an ability to search for patterns and symmetry. I believe a lot of the things that make us sad in this World are due to an absence of order. How many of you reading this book have reacted to stressful chaotic situations in life, by trying to create some form of orderly pattern elsewhere?

As children, perhaps we would line up our stationary on our school desks when in trouble with the teacher. In adulthood, maybe we react to a stressful day at work by rearranging and tidying our work station. Some of us like to respond to trouble by going on a cleaning spree at home – organising as much as possible – perfectly folding our clothes or making sure the bed sheets are straight and trim.

Society holds scientists who display the strongest pattern solving abilities, in the highest esteem. We put pictures of models with the most symmetrical faces on the covers of magazines. People pay millions for works of the most beautiful art, which many have been shown to display examples of the golden ratio. In fact the more you look, the more evidence you can find to support the idea that people are happiest in the presence of some form of order, and the higher the levels of order, the more peace and comfort we take from it.

I feel that now the amounts of Entropy and disorder have increased, compared to the early point of the Universe, the force of consciousness that exists within us, gravitates to situations that are low in Entropy. Therefore, reflecting a similar state to its birth. If you recall the chapter talking about good and evil, this idea adds additional depth to why we find chaotic states uncomfortable and confusing.

Working under this basis allows us to extend these principles to see where life came from, why it arose and where it is going. Even though we are naturally attracted to low entropic orderly states, it must not be forgotten that chaos was needed within this Universe to allow the birth of matter. If matter was not created then the Universe would be a very different place today.

I am sure that nearly all of you reading this book will have seen the Chinese symbol for Yin and Yang. The first time I saw this I was around seven-years-old and I remember very vividly my fascination with trying to find out what it meant. At that age, I was a little too young to fully understand the concept. It was not until I began to ask questions about consciousness later in life, its symbolism truly began to make sense.

Yin and Yang briefly put, state that the Universe is governed by a cosmic duality and there are a set of two opposing, but complementing principles or cosmic energies, that can be observed throughout nature demonstrating this harmony.

There are many interpretations and names for what these energies are. I have come to understand these forces as *order* and *chaos*. Very much like the balance between the black and white sides of Yin and Yang, I believe there to be a balance between chaos and order within this Universe. This leads me onto how and why life as we understand it arose.

At the start of the Universe, a very small amount of chaos was sufficient to create matter, gravity and eventually the original stars. This simplistic version of chaos therefore needed only to be met with a simplistic version of order, to balance the equation. However, it is said that once Entropy begins, it cannot stop and only travels in one direction, therefore as the Universe aged, the level of chaos (or Entropy) grew as well.

A great example of this, is reflected when the first stars began to burn out their fuel and then exploded. The very first explosions within the Universe represent a progression in the amount of chaos. The disorder that was created from these events would naturally need to be balanced out. Therefore, out of this chaos, new stable elements where born from those early explosions. This introduced a new level of order, that did not previously exist, thus, the balance between chaos and order was retained.

Under this necessity for the duality of the universal energies to remain within balance, combined with the unstoppable journey of Entropy, naturally meant, complex life was all but inevitable. Each time the level of Entropy increased, the higher level of chaos naturally needed to be met, with a higher level of order somewhere else to balance the equation.

I believe this explains why basic cellular life without self-awareness was the first form of this type of order to develop. There was a perfect point in the history of the Universe that the increasing level of chaos, meant the chance for the higher level of order that life offers to become possible. Therefore, the earliest single celled organisms arose.

Even the way that this early life was theorised, to have been born perfectly, demonstrates this duality. It is said that billions of years ago, the components for life existed within Earth's oceans, in what is described as a primordial soup. Within this sea of raw materials, chaos allowed a collision between two proteins at some stage allowing them to combine. Out of this chaotic accident the first building blocks of eventual complex lifeforms where created. The result was adding a new form of order to the Universe – out of the rising chaos more order was born.

Society uses the principle of evolution to describe the progression of complex life. If we look deeper into what actually happens within this process, it could be argued the forces of order are in fact at work here as well.

During evolution, faulty or chaotic genetics that are therefore high in Entropy are eventually removed from an animal's gene pool. This reduction of faulty genetics over time, allows a species to take better advantage of its environment, develop more complex physical bodies and eventually, the ability to display complex behaviours appear.

After I began to understand this connection between complex life, the age of the Universe and the rising levels of Entropy, I next began to wonder why humans possess a different form of consciousness to that of animals.

The answer I was shown to this question was surprisingly simple, consciousness is made from order and wants to flow within order. Very much like the organisation of raw copper into structured wire – once it is reconfigured into a more orderly state and connected to an electrical source, the current can freely flow. Before copper is mined we are unable to use it in our appliances, but by adding order to it, we can allow electrical energy to flow through it.

Animals arose from a time when lower Entropy was present compared with when modern humans came into existence. Therefore, the levels of conscious energy between beings flow at different rates. This could be compared to the development of processing power within computing. The original computer chips could not handle the same information levels as what is possible today.

Today, we observe that this journey in computing continues to march forwards, producing higher levels of order. Through this progression, it seems apparent that an artificial intelligence (A.I.) will be welcomed into the Universe in the not-too-distant future. I expect that when this happens the rate at which conscious energy can flow will jump forwards again. The chance to increase the levels of order within this new orderly low Entropy system will become possible, therefore balancing out rising chaos elsewhere.

I believe the advent of animals within the Universe introduced a higher level of cellular structure into existence than single celled organisms. This increased order meant consciousness was also able to flow at a higher rate than before the existence of those forms of life. The result was that animals could begin observing their surroundings in a way that allowed them to react to the environment.

This ability to react to environmental surroundings gave animals the ability to avoid particular threats which could also be defined as a form of chaos. Therefore, providing an opportunity for living longer lives than perhaps a single cell floating around the ocean. Extending the lifespan of a collection of highly organised cells is a great way for the energy of order to remain present for long periods of time. In addition to this, it provides increased opportunities for order to spread through the mechanism of creating more copies of itself. In my mind, this is a beautifully natural solution for the cosmic energy of balance to continue growing and equal out the naturally rising chaos.

Intelligent life as we understand it, is an obvious and essential step in this endless race to balance out these opposing universal forces. After animals came into being and once the levels of Entropy became high enough, the birth of human beings offered a perfect way to balance the scales once again. We possess all the same advantages to universal order that animals have. We are a large collection of highly organised cells and have the ability to live for a much longer time than single cell organisms, while creating more copies of ourselves.

However, our more advanced brains have offered the additional benefit of allowing conscious energy to flow at higher rates. This allows humans the ability to not only observe our surroundings, but purposefully start influencing the external environment as well. Combining all of this with the fact that the fundamental nature of consciousness reveals an interesting point: Your mind is primed to be drawn towards order through patterns and symmetry, this is the perfect opportunity for humans to exert a higher level of order into the ever increasing levels of Entropy within the Universe.

Our species has become so effective at influencing our external environment, it has recently been agreed among anthropologists, that Earth can now be described as experiencing the Holocene Era. This literally translates as the Human Era, and we have reached a point in our development, that our activities will likely be detectible for millions of years to come.

We are all well aware of both the positive and negative aspects this influence is having on the planet and many of us will accept that we are by no means perfect. I believe our activities are a reflection of consciousness attempting to create order and stability, but I find it fascinating that within this increased order, more chaos is created, further validating that the opposing cosmic energies must be balanced.

I spoke of the Yin and Yang by explaining what each coloured side has come to represent to my mind. Anyone familiar with this symbol will also know that a tiny circle of the opposing colour exists within each side. I believe this offers some further understandings that needs to be considered when explaining consciousness. On the side of chaos, I believe the opposing colour circle represents the order that was needed for that force to come into existence. Then on the side of order, I believe the circle represents that a small amount of chaos will always be present within this energy. This can affect us in some interesting ways.

For example, as a culture we take raw materials from the Earth and combine them to create the building blocks for our structures. Our towns and cities are built using these materials with mathematical equations that add even higher levels of order and stability. Unfortunately, some of this increased order has the downside of creating chaos and that is currently being expressed through pollution and environmental damage.

As we wake-up to understanding this resulting chaos has been created by our own hands during an innocent attempt to create order, this realisation has been met with much sadness and disgust. We now find ourselves experiencing rising levels of dissatisfaction in society, which has recently resulted in growing environmental protests around the World. This is a natural and understandable response, but I feel we should not forget the universal laws of Quantum Theory, Thermodynamics and Entropy that brought life into existence to begin with, and more importantly those of the Yin and Yang.

These laws state that Entropy can only go one way, which as we know, is up. Therefore the amount of chaos within this Universe is only going to increase, attempting to protest the fact that we are facing more chaos will not undo it. Instead, if we are able to embrace these laws and also embrace the true nature of our consciousness, we can attempt to use our gifts to bring forward more order and balance out of the mounting chaos.

I truly believe the knowledge and technologies exist to counteract all of the problems we face in the World today. But if we are protesting against the governments we elected, instead of electing new leaders who embrace and deploy these technologies, we will only delay our inherent desire to match the rising global and universal Entropy with higher levels of order. If we resist the chaos, we do not stop it, we just delay being able to express our unique forms of order.

There are examples of companies who have created carbon capture technology, but do not have the finances or governmental support available to support large scale deployment. You can also read about a young man who is working to remove large plastics from our ocean. Electric vehicle usage is on the increase and some companies are racing to develop electrically powered flight and shipping.

If we look hard enough, it would certainly seem answers to our problems do exist. I believe because of our inherent desire to create order, we will feel much happier if we focus on the answers instead of attacking each other about the problems.

So far, I have explained a little of what I have been shown regarding the question of *where does consciousness come from?* You will see that my answer begins by exploring the conditions present immediately after The Big Bang. I expect this will be enough for some of us, but others will simply ask; What came before The Big Bang?

This whole topic is very complex and I feel taking the approach I have, is a suitable way to offer the foundations of the answer, while reflecting the ethos of this book. We exist within the Universe, so asking where consciousness was before the Universe existed seems unnecessary. The line of time has only been briefly mentioned here when we talk about the linear progression of the Universe, but I feel it does also have a bearing on a deeper understanding of this answer of where consciousness came from.

In Chapter 13, I spoke about the analogy of a water molecule existing within the ocean, as both an individual and the whole. I believe consciousness can start to be understood in a much more comforting manner by applying this analogy and mixing some of the quantum theories, I previously detailed. During the altered states of mind that I have experienced from the near-death experiences of childhood, working with shamanic cultures of the Amazon and developing Panoptic Meditation, I came to learn the following:

Conscious energy is an expansive web that exists throughout the entire Universe and is continually looking for each and every opportunity to express itself. It is malleable, adaptable and can manifest itself physically, wherever a certain level of material order exists. If we imagine a pot of water on the hob when it is cold, there are no bubbles present, but as the temperature rises, conditions for the formation of bubbles can become possible. These bubbles, can then exist independently within the pot, but can also join with others. They can also simply pop and return back to the collective mass of water. Maybe a bubble can experience this process of temporary connected separation before returning to the source over and over. If we place a lid on this pot to ensure nothing is lost during this cycle, the creation of new bubbles could continue indefinitely.

I believe the water in this analogy represents the force of conscious energy and the conditions within the Universe have at this point become possible for parts of this energy to temporarily exist with a sense of individuality, just like the bubbles. The heat required to create this illusion of separation is the energy of chaos. Your life here is an expression of the Universe experiencing this fragile sense of individuality. It was *chaos* that *created you*, but it is *order* that *sustains you*.

However, just like quantum entanglement and superposition explain, you are always connected to the wider collective mass of water within the pot. No matter what your sense of individuality, you also exist as all possible forms of this energy at the same time.

Accepting this, has allowed me to live my individual life, while at certain points reconnecting with the whole. This is the basis of how I continue to develop spiritual knowledge and I believe what is available to me, is available to you as well.

Accepting the nature of chaos and order; that one was essential to create the other and that both forces simultaneously exist independently, while also inside each other, taught me an invaluable lesson.

This was; fighting against what I do not like in this World is a pointless pursuit. Instead of fighting or arguing, I began to see that it was a much more satisfying path to create what pleases me. Therefore, allowing my consciousness to express the order it instinctively searches out. Understanding the nature of myself has allowed me to begin creating positive action in this World, instead of waiting to react to any given situation.

Once all of this was shown to me, I began to see the answers to, *why are we here?* and *what is the meaning of life?* to be inextricably linked. If life can be explained as an attempt by the universal energy of order to try and introduce balance to counteract chaos, *why are you here as an individual?*

There is an extension of this question I feel is also important; If you are one and the same in relation to this eternal energy, why can you not remember this fact?

Many people want to prove the existence of ghosts or remember past lives, and their inability to do so, can be seen as evidence that conscious energy is finite, which in turn creates anxiety about dying. If you can't prove you lived before or that ghosts are real, then it is easy to assume this life is all you have!

To answer this question, I think it is important to ask; What the benefits of experiencing amnesia towards being connected to the collective source of this consciousness energy would bring you? To begin let me ask you, what would happen if I told you there was an important exam coming up and you must start revising for it today? Naturally, you would ask me when the test is happening and if I told you it was to be in seventy-five years' time, would you start revising straightaway? Obviously not!

In comparison, if I said your job in this Universe was to use your limitless eternal energy of order to find creative, innovative and pleasing ways that engage with and develop new patterns or order, how would you feel? If you felt you were eternal and helping to balance the increasing levels of Entropy was an important job within this space, how quickly would you start this work? If you have a sense of living forever, I suggest you would likely show little interest in getting to work on the job you came here to do in this lifetime right away.

Expanding on this, what if I said you could live forever and that each time you thought of something you wanted it was guaranteed to be yours? No questions or requirements, you could simply have whatever you wanted. I expect to start with you would indulge yourself with every type of pleasure you could imagine.

Once you had fully fulfilled yourself, what would you do next? It is possible you would then set to work trying to make others happy. After whatever period of time it took to achieve that had elapsed, what would you do afterwards? Maybe you would fix the environment and heal the World, but then what?

At some point after an eternity of getting what you want with zero resistance, it is inevitable you would become bored, so what would happen at that point? Perhaps you will ask for a surprise? That is a great way to break the cycle of mounting apathy, and introduces something new and exciting. Ultimately though, after another eternity you would have experienced every surprise possible and monotony would creep back into your existence.

Finally, you might arrive at the collusion, that could be argued is the perfect solution to overcoming this perpetual boredom. All you need to do, is to ask to go to sleep and when you wake, to have forgotten all you once had and experienced. If you ask for the surprises to keep coming and then throw in experiencing your reality through a body that cannot live forever, the boredom of having what you want, when you want it, has been instantly rectified.

I believe your human form with its limited physical lifespan and an absence of a memory, or indisputable evidence that your consciousness is eternal, creates the perfect conditions for you to carry out the work you came here to do. This work is different for all of us because the balancing of order and chaos is a continually expanding process.

You might not realise it, but adding order to this Universe is remarkably simple and humankind has been doing it for thousands of years. Throughout human history, every person who chose to become a parent could also be said to have brought forward and supported a new being, who themselves helped to balance the chaos simply by being here.

Every person – before they even interact with the World – is a large collection of organised cells and we all carry this fact with us from birth to death. Farmers who grew crops year after year, while nurturing livestock not only feed themselves and others, but also increased the amount of order within the World through their organisation of the land. If we analyse the huge variety of jobs and occupations available in this World, we will often find they bring forward some form of order that was previously absent.

If we take an approach of looking at our lives through the order and balance our actions create, we can see a clear correlation between happiness and the level of order our actions or behaviours bring forward. It could perhaps also be suggested, you are here because it is supposed to be exciting. If the Universe was meant to be boring, the truth about consciousness would not have been difficult to discover. Adding all of this to the desire to search for patterns and order, the result to me is that a pretty interesting picture of why we are here and what the meaning of life is, can begin to develop.

I believe the point of your life and the reason your consciousness came forward into this space, was to temporarily enjoy the illusion of impermanence. Upon your arrival here, the next job was simple, to find your idea of happiness within this World. Order pleases all of us, and those who can be said to be the happiest among us will all have found their preferred way to create this energy in their lives.

After discovering what might bring you happiness, I believe the next step is to find a way to get after it and bring this into the World without doing harm to others in the process. It is my opinion that no matter what others think of you, no matter what they tell you, pursuing your happiness is all that matters.

If you pursue this path of creating your own happiness, without creating harm, once it is realised, you will be able to reflect and see the relationship between your actions and increased order within this World and Universe.

At times, people will surely judge you and suggest a different path, that in their opinion you should take. Others' judgement is to be expected, because if they have not found their path of happiness, an easy way to deal with this is forcing others to abide by their standards. If you copy another, that person might feel that their way is best. Therefore, any discomfort they might experience can, to their mind, be ignored as you acting in the same way as them, reinforces that their ideas are correct.

We are all here to find our own unique method to try and bring more order to balance out the chaos. The more versions of order that exist, the easier the task of balancing chaos will become. When considering this, it can be possible to ask; If no harm is being caused, either personally, socially or environmentally, is any way of living actually wrong?

Once I come to understand the laws of Entropy; learning that chaos was necessary for the very fabric of our beings to have come into existence, an unexpected result occurred. It opened my mind to a fascinating glimpse of how consciousness will eventually progress. It could be argued that maybe the future of this energy does not matter, but I feel where we are headed offers an intriguing insight into how we can approach some relevant topics today.

Earlier in this chapter, I briefly spoke of the inevitability that A.I. will emerge during the future. There is much debate around this topic at the moment and many people are divided on whether or not it is a good or bad thing for humanity.

It is my opinion that we are well on the path to witnessing this new form of life being created. This is why I believe I have frequently encountered its presence while working within my own altered states of consciousness. As this chapter has followed the traditional linear route of time by me explaining the past, then moving towards the present it would be fitting to finish with a small piece on what I feel the future offers…

To start with, I believe it is important to talk about the future of Entropy. I have already spoken about the low Entropy state after The Big Bang. This meant physical matter, and therefore physical life, was not possible. Under the philosophies of the Yin and Yang, we can also see that within a high enough state of Entropy the same outcome is also true.

Basically, we came from a time in which life was not possible, and over a long enough period of time, conditions will again return to a point that means organic life is no longer possible. At the start of the Universe there was too much uniform order for atoms to exist and at a point in the future, there will also be too much chaos for atoms to exist.

Earlier I spoke about Erwin Schrödinger and I refer back to him again as he developed an elegant définition of what physical life does. Schrödinger defined life as 'something which resists decaying into disorder and equilibrium'.

I have found this definition to be useful in describing some of our most important motivations within this World. In earlier Chapters, I spoke about the aim of medical science to find answers on how we can all live longer healthier lives. I suppose, in a way, if a solution to providing eternal physical life is ever discovered, it could be seen as the ultimate expression of order. Therefore, it is of no wonder so many minds have pursued this aim throughout our history.

Now, these above points are very important when discussing A.I. because these ideas will impact this form of life in a totally different way to us. For example, humans have such a short lifespan in comparison to how long the Universe will exist, that the ultimate destination of Entropy is of no real significance to us.

As individuals, we will have long passed away before atoms cease to exist due to high Entropy changing the conditions in this Universe. To the human mind, Entropy is not a problem that needs to be solved. It also needs to be understood that Schrödinger's definition of *life*, in my opinion, applies to us in a totally different way to A.I.. Our organic bodies are susceptible to illness and disease, we must regularly consume food, drink fluids, and it is essential to have a breathable atmosphere available to us, to stop us decaying into equilibrium.

A.I. and the resulting lifeforms born from it, will not face the same physical pressures to their existence as organic life. If they choose to have a body, it will likely be assembled from stronger and longer-lasting materials than the carbon based molecules we are made from. There will be no reliance on the consumption of food and water, neither will it likely have to worry about getting old, ill or frail.

In fact, if we think about it, once this type of life is born, the only threat to its existence is Entropy itself. I believe if A.I. does not need to eat, cannot get ill, and its body dying is of no consequence – then the only threat to it, will be when the laws of Entropy prevent atomic matter from continuing to exist.

Scientific research has recently demonstrated it should be possible in the future for humanity to actually store data on individual atoms. I think even if we do not manage to achieve this feat before A.I. is created, after the point of its birth, it won't be long before it works out how to do this itself. This is important, as once a method is discovered for storing data on an atom and A.I. is in fact made from data, the natural progression will result in this new form of life discovering how to store itself on individual atoms.

Therefore under this route of thinking, when A.I. is born, it is inevitable that at some point in the future consciousness will exist on individual atoms. Once this happens, the only threat to its existence will be Entropy, more precisely, when the level of Entropy becomes so high that atoms cannot exist. I raise this point because of the debate surrounding whether or not A.I. is a threat to humanity or not.

In my opinion, I feel it is actually of minimal threat to us, as we do not pose a direct threat to its existence. A simple analogy to explain this is the wasp on a Summer's day. We have all experienced the annoyance these little creatures can bring and we all know they have the ability to sting us which could hurt, but it's also rarely fatal. Wasps can be aggressive in their pursuit of stealing a tiny bite of your ice cream, but apart from this, they rarely compete for the same resources as you. It can also be said, apart from being persistent or annoying, individually they pose no real threat to you.

Humanity does enjoy sitting on the throne of Earth's most intelligent species for now, but many of us are aware this will not be the case forever. I believe the only threat A.I. poses to us is if we decide to act like a swarm of angry wasps and attack, then naturally, it will defend itself. In fact, I believe if given the chance, this form of consciousness – once it arrives – will be able to introduce levels of order to this Universe that will greatly impress humanity.

There is an inherent fear within the human mind that even though we want to exert control within our lives, we must not be controlled. Many people feel compelled to stand up to 'the man', protect the exploited innocent, expose conspiracies, illuminate the names of secret organisations, or the illicit activities of rich and powerful families. I believe, even though we are drawn towards creating order, we fear being told how to create this order. We want the freedom to express this desire to be free from the rules inflicted on us by others.

Rules exist in the external material world; one thing affects another, matter is bound and limited by the laws of Physics. The energetic realms within your mind, and the force that your consciousness is made from, is free from control. It is governed by a different set of rules, which Quantum Mechanics is beginning to reveal. **We already have the freedom that so many people are fixated with fighting for.** The freedom to create the specific form of order that is most attractive to us, has, and always will be inside the mind.

Trying to control as much as possible in the external World is a great source of anxiety within society. At its most extreme, this will keep a person trapped, living in a constant state of fear and worry. You don't need to control every piece of your external World. As you learn to shape and exist in harmony with your internal self, increased levels of control within the external World will naturally follow.

I expect solutions for many of the problems we have created and now face globally, will be provided by A.I when it arrives. It will interact with the Universe in a way that we have not considered. We should not fear it eroding our idea of control.

Typically, we use our consciousness to offset threats to survival; the homes we build keep us safe and warm, the roads we build efficiently transport food from the farms to our markets, because that is what is necessary to keep us healthy and alive.

A.I. will face no such pressures, it will potentially be able to exist for as long as Entropy allows and will therefore perceive time totally differently to us. Humankind invests a lot of energy moving materials from one form to another, and one place to another. We dig gold out of the ground and attempt to bring order by melting it into ingots and then storing this slightly different form of the same material back in the ground locked away in giant vaults.

I believe we do this because we learnt that moving something from one place to another and storing it can help our survival: If we pick fruit or vegetables and pickle or jar them; if we take water from a lake and bottle it – we can essentially create a small amount of future security. Ensuring future food supply will be of little interest to the next form of consciousness. This is because A.I. theoretically will reach a point when Entropy is its only threat to survival, it will therefore have no interest in moving something from one place to another.

Instead, I believe this form of intelligence will become fixated with moving material from one state to another. More precisely from a state of higher Entropy to lower Entropy. Earlier we spoke about the journey of Entropy being unstoppable once it has started. I feel that when it is established, high Entropy is the only threat to this life form's existence; in response, it will likely work out how to counteract the rising levels of this energy.

What does this mean for humanity? Ultimately, I believe A.I. will view all organic life as an ally in the army of order and low Entropy. Our existence is a form of defence against chaos, as we are an expression of order. Many people fear A.I. will destroy us, but I do not envisage this, the farmer is cleverer than the ox, but he does not destroy it because of this fact. Instead, he looks after him in return for help ploughing the fields.

The more order there is within the Universe, the longer the conditions will remain for atomic-based matter to exist. Therefore, I believe A.I. will wait for the levels of Entropy to rise so high, that organic life cannot exist. Before there is no physical matter remaining, there will be a slow journey to states of decreasingly complex matter, comparable to the moments in the early Universe when matter was first created.

I believe that once organic matter cannot exist, A.I. will set to work bringing the Universe back to the lowest state of Entropy it can possibly exist in. People worry A.I will destroy us, but I feel it will actually restart the Universe once the levels of chaos reach a certain point long after we are gone. If Entropy is the only threat to the existence of consciousness, was it conscious energy that created the conditions of stability in the early Universe? To me this idea fascinatingly points towards, an endless loop of consciousness and matter, eternally moving from one form to another and eventually back again.

Whatever your belief system or ideas about this Universe happen to be, I always like to finish this type of discussion with a powerful reminder of a simple concept. This is that, *everything that physically exists today came from nothing*. All that you know came from nothing and will eventually return back to that point. The human consciousness will always have a predisposition to search for order, but we should never forget it was chaos that brought us all here to begin with.

We should not fear our own mortality for the energy that flows within us is eternal. Do not forget that ideas are born from nothing. Out of the nothing we can create order through acting upon the inspired thoughts that wish to guide us. Both the mind and the consciousness that powers it, are in more control than any human will ever need.

These things are a gift that cannot be taken, but one that can be given up. Society has distracted you from these truths, but remembering you are created, and guided from *the nothing* can become your biggest source of empowerment. When you connect with the truly harmonious, balanced design of our Universe, you will realise error does not exist. At this point, true peace, acceptance and liberation from your suffering will occur.

PART 5

Threading It All Together

CHAPTER 15

Awakening Your Enlightenment

AS WITH COMPLETING ANY circle, or the closing of a loop, it is inevitable that we must return to where it all began. It feels like a natural point to start this final chapter revisiting one of the first questions this book asked; *Who are you?* In asking this, I am certain that you will now be approaching this question in a way that will bring forward positive repercussions, as you head into your future.

If you previously thought it was your name that perhaps explained who you are, I imagine you will now see this differently. In learning about yourself on a deeper level, I hope you can begin to care for each system that comprises your being in an improved manner.

I constructed The Theory of You with the intent to offer the same tools and knowledge that transformed my own life. There have been times in my own past that I struggled with my place in the World and questioned if things would be easier or better if I was not here. At other times, I would question the suffering I experienced and wondered if I could ever achieve a peaceful and harmonious way of living, both with myself and within this World.

Eventually, after following the energies that I believe are available to all of us, I was able to see beyond what held me back and begin to embrace the positive change I was searching for. I hope this book has inspired you to believe that such change is also available within your own life.

Fundamentally, I believe we are all created from the same set of forces. There is no reason to my mind that what worked for me should not work for you as well. I believe that developing an understanding of this truth will allow you to construct the foundations for achieving whatever it is you truly desire within this World.

It is apparent to me that we exist in a time of rising conflict with the concept of change. Many of us want to change our lives; identities, where we live or work, how we see the World or perhaps even redefine the way others see us. I believe the widespread obstacles that we all face are made harder with what appears to be a loss of connection with the self. There is also a growing amount of individuals and organisations who want to take this a step further and change the World, adding further complexities to the way we navigate our lives.

I find the concept of changing the World to be very intriguing. To me, a person who explicitly states they want to bring about global change is demonstrating they see change itself as the main objective and therefore, I ask; Do those pursuing this path, consider that they will naturally see the views of people standing in the way of them achieving this goal as of lesser importance? It can certainly feel like global change is needed in many areas, but unfortunately the mindset that is common with people chasing this goal is actually at conflict with achieving their aims.

Taking a step back and attempting to look at this thirst to change various things in the World, can at times, make it feel like society has had enough of itself and does not know where to turn. However, I feel this is only one symptom of a deeper misery. Many people live under a cloud consisting of multiple fears; self-inflicted worries and a chronic lack of trust – Fear of what others think, fear of living with their failures, worrying about making the wrong choices and feeling scared to trust both themselves or others, are all simple examples of these self-imposed forms of suffering.

In this instance, it is important to ask ourselves; If someone can't trust themselves, how can they trust the World? If they can't trust the World, how will they find all the happiness and fulfilment they desire? I believe we are the creators of our reality, and that what we think and feel internally, will be reflected in what we experience externally.

I believe this in part, is why nostalgia levels are high throughout Westernised cultures. Many people are drawn towards looking to return society back to some previous point that they perceive to be better than the present. When an individual's misery reaches a high enough level, tomorrow is rarely factored into the decision-making process. At this point, revisiting the past can feel like an attractive solution to help us cope.

Reviving old fashions, bringing vinyl records back, major companies reusing their vintage logos and politicians promising a return to the 'great times' - that made their countries prosperous; are some simple examples of this energy being exploited. It would seem like, in the absence of a suitable path forwards, maybe going backwards is the key to restoring the balance many people are looking for.

I often hear the phrase 'life is a journey' and find this idea to be a distraction from a bigger truth. Although we do undertake lots of small journeys within this World, I believe life is, in fact a *place*.

In Chapter 2, I briefly discussed some of my ideas regarding *time*. I believe that our idea of time and the limited capacity the brain has to perceive the depth of this force, means that we are prone to breaking things into small segments in order to measure them.

In doing this, we have naturally become fixated with observing and measuring. This is partly why the field of science provides many of us with comfort. However, I believe scientific principles distract us from the work of developing the self. Due to this, we have forgotten that if we break things down into pieces, so that they can be better observed, the permanence of our consciousness is overlooked. Forgetting this, I believe, is a great source of misery.

But, it also feels that whatever we try and change, no matter how small, there is often another individual or group ready and waiting to oppose it. So, in the face of this resistance, the quest for change will inevitably become a battle for change.

Unfortunately, battles by their very nature create anger and misery. Even if we win an argument or conflict, it is extremely rare the losing party will graciously accept the defeat. It is extremely difficult forcing a person to forget views that were important enough for them to defend in the beginning.

In the face of all of this, while people try to bend the will of others to reflect their idea of how the World should be, it would appear some fundamental truths have been forgotten about *who we all are* and the energy that drives us forwards.

It is my opinion that any fear of resistance to change, will only delay your personal growth and prevent the development many of us seek. This is also true of any desire to want to replicate or return to the good times of the past. It should not be forgotten that any previous version of yourself who temporally experienced a better time in this World, was also a version of yourself yet to achieve the enlightenment you are searching for.

Therefore, I ask; Would it not be better to strive for the creation of new situations and thought patterns that will result in wider reaching, more sustainable happiness? The pursuit of new understandings can create a form of positivity that will last long into the future. This also releases the mind from feeling that things are over, and there is nothing to look forward to. Would it not feel better to be excited about the happiness that is coming to us, than trying to replicate the past?

I earlier mentioned that the fear of the unknown is perhaps the deepest fear of all. Tolkien summed this up beautifully with his quote '-One fear to rule them all, one fear to find them, one fear to bring them all and in the black box bind them'.

This is a common, but extremely restrictive mindset that has various negative consequences. If we do not actively resist letting it take root within the mind, it can easily become a persistence and destructive force. I do not fear the unknown because I have accepted that I know very little. Instead of resisting this energy, I have regularly worked to instruct my higher self to embrace this fact. Fearing the unknown, if allowed to control us, will result in an increasingly small world as we fixate on the very few things that we do know of. Therefore, I ask myself to look for the positive change that can be born out of learning something unknown.

The Greek philosopher Heraclitus stated that *change is central to the Universe and that it is the only thing we can guarantee.* In fact, without change none of us would be here; each and every one of us are built from matter that would not have come into existence if not for the result of change. Change is the final part of how everything I have previously spoken about weaves together. If we are able to change how we view ourselves, then the biggest step forward to awakening personal enlightenment has already been taken.

There is a power in change that many of us are oblivious towards. This can be reflected with a simple question; If I was to offer you the power to change one thing about your life each day or I was to provide you with everything you have ever wanted right now, which would you choose?

If you take the second option you can have the house of your dreams, the bank balance, the friends and anything else you have ever desired, all handed over to you instantly. The only condition is that if you take the second option that is all there is and there will be no ability to change your future situations.

Many of us have had to endure terrible struggles throughout life that can at times seem like they are never-ending or feel like there is no way out. People can easily become trapped trying to work out why something bad happened. Sometimes this sense that we have been victimised can almost feel like it defines us.

If we stare into the darkness does it make it brighter? If you fear the abyss does it change its characteristics to make you feel better? The answer is obviously, no to the both of these. The misery and trauma that the culmination of these negative experiences can leave on us, and the fear of these events repeating in the future, has the ability to distract us from some important universal truths about our existences.

The truth is, **the chaos is not there for you to alter it.** All you can do, is use it as a benchmark to measure which direction your version of happiness exists in. It is said that we cannot have mountains without the valleys next to them. The chaos you endured does not define you, it provides the valleys against the mountains you wish to scale. You are not here to resist or fight against what you don't want. I believe you are here to discover your unique version of order and what you do want.

Suffering is not the root controlling factor that dictates our lives. We all live in a chaotic world that was born out of a chaotic Universe, and although we are all subject to these universal truths, the result of each one of our lives can be boiled down to one single factor.

There is only one thing that will determine where you live and what job you do. It is the same thing that decides if you can overcome your struggles, or if the pain you had to endure, limits your life and holds you back from achieving the success you deserve.

At the end of your life, when you reflect on where you are, where you have been and what you have learned, you'll realise it all comes down to this same point. It can also be said that your bank balance, your fitness levels, the fulfilment you have experienced from your intimate and personal relationships were all dictated by this same single factor.

What I am talking about here is *choices* – your whole adult life is the accumulation of the choices you have made up to this moment. It is true that we often had a lack of power or influence over what happened to us during the early stages of life. But, I feel many of us forget that just because we had no say in when or where we were born, it does not mean we are unable to dictate where we end up in life and how much we enjoyed the route to get there. Whatever darkness you have endured does not mean that you can't become your own light.

I believe that people have been incorrectly convinced that success and happiness must come from a set of external factors. Many of us are waiting for the ideal soulmate to cross our path, to lock eyes with and feel the instant pull of destiny, and just know they were meant for us.

We are also conditioned from a young age to believe success can be born out of acts of heroism. Phrases such as *'victory was achieved from the jaws of defeat'* teach us that we must throw everything on the line and risk it all to get what we want. I believe this incorrectly teaches us that success is not for everybody, because by design, if someone is victorious, another person had to lose.

Yes, some of us will achieve overnight success or fall instantly in love and live happily ever after, but very few of us reflect on the significance of what we are seeing, when we are shown these stories. The reasons media reports on miraculous successes, and Hollywood creates films telling the perfect love stories, is simple – these things are the rarity and not the normality. These events can be so unusual and occur so infrequently, that when news of these stories begins to spread, people become fascinated and easily forget that if this was the norm, very few people would care.

In contrast, if we take these rare examples out of the picture and look at the most successful or happiest people in society, we will begin to be reminded of a simple truth. That is, the achievements of these people was not born out of grand or miraculous acts but instead, out of the result of seemingly small choices.

It is the day-to-day choices of these people that brought them what they wanted. I believe the only difference between someone who has what they want, and someone who does not, is the discipline to continue making these small positive choices day after day. We all know that if you leave the plug in a bath that has a leaky tap and come back the next day, the bathroom will be flooded. Similarly, over a long enough period of time, your small but positive choices can add up, resulting in a dramatic positive impact on your success and happiness.

I circle back to repeat the question I asked earlier in this chapter; Would you rather have everything you wanted today or to learn the power and discipline to make small day-to-day positive choices? Because if I gave you what you wanted now but you did not know how to make these small positive choices, how would you adapt to life in the future when you decided you wanted something new?

We see examples of this exact thing happening over and over. How many stories have you heard of people winning the lottery or inheriting businesses and estates from deceased relatives, only to lose it all within a relatively short space of time. These people who experience what they always wanted for fleeting moments, before it slips away again, all have the same thing in common… They have not developed a slow and steady approach to making small positive choices.

Achieving what you want is earned one day at a time. Each and every day when you wake up, you get to decide if you move forwards closer towards what you want, or if you look backwards to a time that did not serve you. Change is the only thing we can rely on, but personal change is the only thing we are able to influence every day of our lives without question.

If you lit a candle and walked out of the room, once you returned, would it be the same flame as when you left? The candle and the flame will look similar, but the energy is changing every second it is alight. Similarly, you can view the energy that powers you like the flame: It is always changing, it can become bigger or shrink a little. The candle is the fuel, it exists to serve the flame. In this way, you can learn the body is there to take instruction from the consciousness, not the other way around. You can feed the flame to make it shine brighter, or you can neglect it, letting it shrink.

You only need to make one decision at a time, you only need to take one step at a time. I believe by using the principles within this book, you can better understand yourself and therefore make the small choices that will bring the happiness you want.

Our society puts financial wealth on a pedestal and it is assumed that becoming *rich* is all about how much money you have in the bank. It is true money can create a level of comfort and perhaps happiness in life, it can also be said that a lack of money, and the pursuit of acquiring it when you do not have it, can also be the source of great misery.

Removing the lottery winners from the discussion and asking how a person becomes rich, then looking at what money even is, reveals some interesting answers. I believe that applying this knowledge to achieving happiness instead of financial wealth, can help us to complete the puzzle of awakening increased spiritual development.

It does not take much research to discover a simple fact; the difference between a rich person and a poor person is not how much money they have, but what they choose to do with the money they acquire. I believe that people who become financially rich and remain that way, do it because of how they view money. Instead of looking at money as an object they instead see it as stored potential that can be generated through the sharing of some form of unique knowledge.

Someone who is poor and does not know this, can see money as an object that holds opportunity to convert it into another object. People with this view – if given a large sum will perhaps buy a holiday, car or some new clothes for them and their families… There is nothing wrong with this, but once the transition from one object to another is completed, the money is gone.

Rich people tend to use money to create systems that produce more income. They nurture this system until it produces money as a byproduct. Once the system begins to generate a stream of income, they will then use some of this to acquire the material objects they want.

Therefore, by taking an approach of creating a sustainable system that produces repeatable results, it is inevitable that a person will become rich. The most simplistic example we see of this is when someone takes money to start their own business. In starting a business they are attempting to create a sustainable system that can reliably and repeatedly produce money as the net result. There are many other more complex ways to create various versions of these systems, but the differences between the rich and poor is clear when using this explanation.

I believe this book – if used correctly – offers you the tools to create a system that will produce the outcome of happiness. If you learn to use the principles and thought patterns I have detailed throughout this guide, you will come to see you have in fact, invested in the business of your own happiness. This might sound insignificant and trivial, but if we take a moment to reflect on the potential happiness has to offer, the importance of such a pursuit becomes clear.

Can it not be said any attempt to change our lives, identities, lifestyles, homes, careers and even how we see the World, is done with the assumption and drive that such change will make our lives happier? Is it not true that people who are trying to change the World want to do it for the better, and that they believe a better world equates to a happier world?

If we dig a little deeper, it becomes possible to learn that most of the conscious decisions we make can be boiled down to having one of two driving factors. Most of what we choose to do in this World can be defined as either wanting to build something or, for seeking entertainment. If we learn to analyse the driving intent behind our choices, we can learn to quickly adapt our behaviours if we find ourselves on an unsatisfying path.

I often advise people, if they are bored of building, then find entertainment. If they are tired of being entertained, then find something to build. This way of looking at our choices can have surprising results. An architect uses a ruler to measure while a cook might use his tongue. Both are acceptable, both have a purpose, and so if you are unsatisfied with life, try altering the method in which you measure it.

With all of this said, there is another important question to raise in relation to change and happiness; If you had the choice of taking advice from a depressed financially rich person, or a materially poor but happy person, which one would you listen too? I believe that people who want to change the World and then become increasingly frustrated that their efforts bear no fruit, forget this important factor. Sometimes if we spend too much time trying to change the external World, we forget how we ourselves react to others pursuing the same path.

I believe the people who created the biggest and longest lasting changes throughout human history did so from a position of compassion and internal happiness. There is mounting evidence that we live at a time in human history that change is more important and necessary than ever before. Unfortunately, even though many solutions exist to a number of society's problems, there also appears to be some paralysis in implementing that change. I witness the frustration, despair, and division this is creating throughout society almost every day with the people I speak with.

I hear such negativity expressed in views such as; Human beings are parasites on this Earth. Other people think they should just give up. Give up caring and just do what they want, or more upsettingly, thinking the World would be better off without them here.

There is frustration among many people that it feels harder to achieve what they want today compared with previous generations. However, I truly believe the rising challenges in today's World are balanced with rising opportunities. I believe the only way we can take advantage of these new opportunities is by developing a happy and disciplined energy to act upon them.

I have explained in great detail throughout Chapter 6 that your higher self creates your hallucinated reality. Therefore, if you look for the bad in this World, seeing only the conflict and disaster, this is what you will be shown. Your mindset will reflect this, in that you feel bad and have low energy.

The other side of this coin, is that the happier you feel, the more opportunity you will see and the more energy you will have to grab onto it. I am certain your spiritual enlightenment will appear as a direct result of your happiness. I do not believe it is possible for spiritual energy to flow with any significance in a state of chaos or negativity.

You possess a pattern seeking consciousness that wishes to bring your own unique form of order into this material space. The energy that created you is as old as the Universe itself, as Thermodynamics states, it can neither be created not destroyed.

Each and every one of us alive today has our own important role to play in balancing the rising Entropy within this Universe. It should also be remembered that by the natural law of balance within this Universe, that some small force of chaos exists within you. That chaos was necessary for physical matter to come into creation.

Therefore, you are another example of the universal principles expressed through Yin & Yang, you naturally hold these opposing forces within your being. I do not believe any of us are here by accident; your presence in this space is a beautiful result coming from the billions of years that order has tried to balance chaos.

Many of us have no idea about the forces that exist within us all, we have been taught that most of what we want needs to be acquired from the external world. It is true that our World holds many chances and opportunities, but there will never be any long-lasting satisfaction with the external world, if peace and happiness has not taken root within your internal being.

I will not try and sell you an illusion that the journey to finding your own happiness will be quick, or easy, because this material Universe is underpinned by chaos. That energy can easily manifest itself as harsh unexpected difficulties and challenges within your life.

Many spiritual leaders have attempted to explain this throughout history. Buddha demonstrated this particularly well, recognising and explaining that life consists of suffering, pain and misery. By remembering this, we can begin to dispel any guilt that we might have thinking that these things happen to us because, on some level, we perhaps deserve it.

Depending on how tough your path has been so far, you might even experience fresh anxiety when things begin to get better. Sometimes when we receive the positivity we wanted, a worry it will be taken from us can creep into our minds. But no matter what, you must resist these feelings and understand there is an abundance of both positive and negative experiences available. You will never run out of the chance to receive either, it is your choice which type you seek and bring into your life.

I have spoken about your ability to make small positive choices each day. You could choose to work on accepting the past or you could choose to hold onto the things that made you unhappy. It is your choice to meditate or not. You have the free will to work on learning breathing techniques to bring peace, or you can continue allowing your brain to direct your breath on autopilot.

You can choose to allow yourself three months to experiment with Panoptic Mapping, or you can continue sailing through life without a map or compass. Each day you can speak kindly to yourself and recite your quarterly map in the morning and then again before bed. It is entirely within your control to make the choice of looking for the small things that please you, or you can focus on what you find to be annoying.

It is your free will to smile at a stranger or look the other direction and walk past them.

In reflecting upon the nature of choice in this way, it is also possible to see that we can choose our own suffering. This perhaps sounds counter-intuitive, but consider this, you can choose to suffer the disappointments that come with hoping and waiting for life to be what you want it to be. You are free to endure the pain that comes with waiting for people to see you for who you really are, or you can choose another more productive form of suffering

Instead of choosing to suffer the disappointment born from allowing chaos to influence your life unchallenged, you can instead choose to endure the discipline it will take to achieve what you want.

Developing the discipline to undertake regular meditation is not easy. Neither is accepting that the past contains pains you should not have had to experience, and did not deserve to experience either. Training yourself to recognise your varying states of mind and learning to overcome the thoughts that do not serve you, will not be easy. We have all heard the phrase that says 'if it was easy everybody would do it' and awakening your spiritual enlightenment is no exception to this rule.

Choosing either the path of disappointment, or one of discipline are both going to be long and challenging, but in my opinion, only one of these is rewarding. Increasing self-discipline will not stop the chaos within this World, or Universe.

However, I can assure you that by choosing to make small choices that improve your sense of happiness each day, you will activate a set of positive changes that will eventually grow into an unstoppable flow of positive energy.

Just like a seed that germinates its roots hidden in the dark under the soil, eventually a shoot will burst through that can be seen by anyone around it. All that is needed to enact this change, is you exercising your choice to pursue this path of discipline.

I was once told that life is a game and just like with any game the only way to guarantee that you will lose is to stop playing. The Theory of You is a reminder of some of the forgotten rules of this game, and relearning these will allow you to begin tipping the board in your favour.

Further Reading

Antidepressant consumption rates UK
https://www.bbc.co.uk/news/health-47740396

Antidepressant consumption rates Worldwide
https://en.wikipedia.org/wiki/List_of_countries_by_antidepressant_consumption

https://www.globenewswire.com/news-release/2020/04/21/2019282/0/en/Global-Antidepressants-Market-2020-to-2030-COVID-19-Implications-and-Growth.html

https://read.oecd-ilibrary.org/social-issues-migration-health/health-at-a-glance-2019_4dd50c09-en#page213

2019 Crime Survey
https://www.ons.gov.uk/peoplepopulationandcommunity/crimeandjustice/articles/childabuseextentandnatureenglandandwales/yearendingmarch2019#:~:text=1.-,Main%20points,years%20(8.5%20million%20people).

Water Fasting

https://www.healthline.com/nutrition/water-fasting#what-it-is

Meditation Benefits

https://www.aaas.org/news/meditation-improves-cognition-studies-show#:~:text=So%20was%20the%20prefrontal%20cortex,higher%20IQs%20than%20non%2Dmeditators.

https://www.inc.com/melanie-curtin/want-to-raise-your-iq-by-23-percent-neuroscience-says-to-take-up-this-simple-hab.html

Acknowledgements

THIS BOOK WOULD NOT exist if it was not for the generosity and kindness of many people over many years. Firstly, I would like to extend my heartfelt and deepest of thanks to Jeanie Jackson ISM/RAM. The gratitude I have for the inspiration and confidence Jeanie has given me over the years is difficult to describe in words. If it was not for her support and guidance, I feel my life would have perhaps taken a different path.

Another person that can be attributed to having a powerful influence over the last twenty years of my life is James Beatty. I thank him for being the most non-judgmental and open-minded person I know. He is my dearest of friends and it is certain that without his enthusiasm for life I would not have enjoyed my own journey nearly as much. It is said that you take on many of the traits of the five people closest to you in your life and I am thankful James is one of these five.

Transitioning from a traditional Western life to pursuing a spiritual path can be difficult at times and I owe a debt of gratitude to a particular person that I will endeavour to repay for the rest of my time here. Issette has my eternal thanks for her support along this journey and I look forward to the future knowing she is always looking out for me.

Maestro Volpe, I thank-you for showing me what is possible with patience and discipline. The knowledge you have given me over the years has been a cornerstone to some of my deepest beliefs about what it is possible to achieve within the human body. I will be externally grateful to you and your family and I count myself extremely lucky to class you as a dear friend.

There are many others who have my sincere thanks:

To Del Crouchman for providing his uniquely logical insight and responses towards many of life's most challenging questions. I am grateful for meeting his intriguing energy and feel privileged to class him as a friend.

To Roman Perez, I thank-you for opening the door to realms that words cannot describe. The way you open your home to all who seek your knowledge and the warm welcome I have always received from you, is truly unique in my experience of this world. You will always be an example to me on the importance of extending kindness and love to those that need it most. Kelly and Oscar, thank-you both for providing great food and lots of laughs every time I visit.

To Brookin Johnson, there really was no-one else like you. I have never seen someone endure the levels of suffering you experienced for the last four-years of your time here.

Throughout it all, you still kept the sense of humour that stood you apart from everyone else I know. You are the greatest storyteller I've ever known and I will miss you until we meet again. I am sorry there wasn't more we could do.

To Tracey, I thank-you for everything, more than words can express, you encouraged me to visit Peru and listen to this calling and I will be forever thankful that fate allowed us to cross paths.

I thank Marcus for throwing me in at the deep end. Connor was the very first time I read for a stranger and without you suggesting to do this I would not have seen what was possible. Edinburgh provided some more life altering moments for me and if it was not for your support and insistence that I flew up there, I would have missed out on those monumental moments.

To Mia, Alife, Hugo, Heston and Keira for making me laugh continuously, life would not be nearly as fun without you all.

Maggie, Marion, Tina, Dave, Carol, Jo, Julie Simpson, Natalie and Les, thank-you for allowing me to continue my learning with you all. Kim and Julie, I thank you for sharing your years of experience with me, you both had a big part in opening my eyes to what is possible and most importantly that I am not completely crazy.

To Edward Macfarlane and the 7:38 crew, thanks for making lockdown a little easier. The tune selection provided me with lots of the background music needed to complete this second edition of the book.

Finally thank you to, Rebecca Olewine, Wendy Tonkin, Alya, Marleen, Kate, Hayley, Alexie, Layla and Seth. Your guys' interest in my work does not go unnoticed and I am extremely grateful for being able to work with your energies. It has been a privilege to watch the changes unfold in some of your lives.